How to Drive

How to Drive

REAL-WORLD INSTRUCTION AND ADVICE FROM HOLLYWOOD'S TOP DRIVER

Ben Collins

CHRONICLE BOOKS

SAN FRANCISCO

First published in the United States of America in 2016 by
Chronicle Books LLC.
First published in Great Britain in 2014 by Macmillan, an imprint
of Pan Macmillan, a division of Macmillan Publishers Limited.

Library of Congress Cataloging-in-Publication Data available.
ISBN: 978-1-4521-4529-7
Manufactured in China

Design by Sam Potts and Neil Egan
Typesetting by Howie Severson
Cover design by Neil Egan and Ben Kither
Cover photo © Alex D. James

10 9 8 7 6 5 4 3 2 1
Chronicle Books LLC
680 Second Street
San Francisco, California 94107
www.chroniclebooks.com

CONTENTS

0.1 *PREFACE: HOW NOT TO DRIVE*

1998. A twisting country lane in the middle of nowhere, traveling at 80 mph.

The sound of fourteen tons of metal colliding is almost deafening when you're right next to it. Imagine one hundred heavy doors slamming in unison and you're not even close. It's loud enough to summon people from farmhouses half a mile away to search for plane wreckage; but, inside the crash . . . you hardly hear a thing.

That's because your brain is moving—and as it thumps the inside of your skull it disrupts the electrical activity powering things like sight and hearing.

My Toyota Supra handled like it was on rails. It sat on enormous wide tires and had a whale-tail spoiler with enough downforce to leave a dent in the floor. At the time I was a Formula One hopeful and one of the fastest men in Formula Three— even F1 World Champion Sir Jackie Stewart said so, and boy did I know it.

I was *so* clever and knew my local roads *so* well that I had a braking plan for every conceivable scenario. One flowing section in particular had a bottleneck into a one-lane road with no passing space. I calculated my velocity precisely to be able to make it all the way through it and out the other side before an approaching car filled the gap, or if there was a car coming through I would throw the anchors and screech to a halt to buy enough time for it to emerge.

According to a recent insurance survey there are certain types of music that make you put your foot down and generally drive like a complete moron. The Black Eyed Peas topped this deadly driving chart with "Hey Mama," a banging tune no doubt, but at the time I had the Beastie Boys busting decibels.

I pumped the stereo up a notch and tipped into the familiar dusty right-hander toward the mouth of the funnel at full speed. Over the course of the next second, the vanishing point ran into a scene that I hadn't budgeted for.

Inside the crash . . . you hardly hear a thing.

Thick mud was spread lavishly across the road. Alarm bells were ringing, but the mud was quickly replaced by a more pressing issue. A very large, slow-moving truck was lumbering through the bottleneck, too slowly to clear it at my rate of closure.

Time slowed down, but the car didn't.

I braked. Wide tires and downforce were powerless on the greasy mud, and my front tires locked instantly. The trajectory involved a double whammy of hedge and a lethal side impact with the truck. *Think fast.*

Just 0.25 seconds later I released the useless brakes, hoping to recover enough steering to swing across the front of the truck and punch through the gateway into a field.

Nope.

The mouth-like radiator grill and the word *VOLVO* filled the windshield.

Then it was that big moment. There were no more choices, only consequences. I could have been an accountant. I could have been a yoga teacher. But there I was with no more tricks up my sleeve. It was time to take the hit, and I had no airbag.

I closed my eyes as the hood of the Supra exploded into the truck's bumper and deformed until it met with the Volvo's front axle, which didn't bend much. The Supra's engine and gearbox traveled two feet my way as the physics of displacement and momentum did their thing. Stopping a twelve-ton truck, fully laden with turf, dead in its tracks put a force of deceleration through my body in excess of sixty times the force of gravity. I did not feel well.

The head-on impact and abrupt stop rearranged all sorts of things inside the Supra, including my kidneys, which ruptured and bled for several days. Pens, loose change, and a half-eaten sandwich all relocated themselves to the dashboard.

Temperament has always been a problem for me, and although I've learned to control it I know that there are demons lurking. The track offers me a positive outlet for unleashing that side of my personality in very controlled bursts. But there are certain things I can't combine with driving, and loud music is one of them.

Time slowed down, but the car didn't.

0.2 *INTRODUCTION: HOW TO DRIVE*

Driving is one of the most pleasurable things that most people do on a daily basis.

It is also the most dangerous. And it doesn't matter whether you drive on the right or the left, using an automatic gearbox or a stick—the fundamental principles and physics of driving are the same everywhere.

The world population of motor vehicles exceeded one billion a couple of years ago. Car crashes kill 50 percent more people than malaria, and the World Health Organization predicts that road deaths will rise 52 percent by 2030, overtaking HIV/AIDS as a global killer within the decade. In America the death toll is around 33,000 lives lost *every* year, which is twice as high as the bloodiest years of combat operations during the Vietnam War.

Whichever country you're from, you want to go from being a learner to a driver as fast as possible. Having tackled a tough multiple-choice questionnaire, reversed around a curve, and successfully navigated a supermarket parking lot, you throw away your learner's permit, and take a ton of speeding metal out onto the open road. Millions of drivers will receive their licenses this year with less than eighteen hours' driving experience under their belts.

A Starbucks barista receives twenty-four hours of training before being handed the keys to an espresso machine.

The robotic syllabus of the driving test itself remains painfully inadequate—not so much in what it contains as how much is left out: controlling a skid, driving on a freeway, tackling a curve, driving at night, and passing, to name but a few. And of those who pass, less than 1 percent receive further training.

Governments, road safety groups, even the Green lobby want to wrap us in cotton wool and then pull it over our eyes. They would have us believe that speeding, among other things, is the biggest danger facing modern drivers, but 700,000

Millions of drivers will receive their licenses this year with less than eighteen hours' driving experience under their belt.

In America the death toll is around 33,000 lives lost every year, which is twice as high as the bloodiest years of combat operations during the Vietnam War.

police road accident reports gathered over the last five years tell a different story. The real killer is simply poor driving.

Exceeding the speed limit contributes to less than 14 percent of fatal accidents, but driver error is a significant factor in more than 65 percent. Poor turns, dodgy maneuvers, and failing to negotiate slippery roads contribute to many times more road deaths than manufacturer defects. Losing control of the car is the primary cause of driving fatalities, and failing to look properly causes the most accidents.

In the past, insurance companies only concerned themselves with information you can find on the electoral roll—such as your age, address, and gender—to determine your risk profile. Recently they started looking into driver telemetry to see if there was a link between *how you drive* and accident probability. There was. Drivers who jerk the steering or stomp the brakes and throttle like they're putting out a fire are high-risk. Smooth drivers don't crash, because driving smoothly requires you to control the machine properly and look further ahead.

How to Drive provides these missing chapters in your driving education. During the course of this book, I plan to share the skills developed and employed over my twenty-year career at the cutting edge of motorsport, from Le Mans racing to NASCAR, to driving the Batmobile and dodging bullets with James Bond, as well as eight years' duty as The Stig for *Top Gear*.

The skills I describe were honed on racetracks by the greatest drivers in the world. As we'll come to see, their philosophy of speed is really one of economy of motion, and with that comes greater fuel efficiency, safety, and control. So this book is about driving better, not faster. Whether you've been behind the wheel for the better part of thirty years or you passed your learner's permit test ten seconds ago, this is the stuff your instructor missed, your dad forgot, and your friends pretend to know . . . but don't.

The journey begins with understanding why we drive the way we do—and how we can do better. Stage two involves getting your hands dirty as we open up the machinery that will transport you to heaven and back. And despite what Google thinks, the ultimate operating system riding on board this marvel of engineering is you—not the damned computer.

Then we hit the open road, and I'll show you how to drive more smoothly than a jazz band surfing a soap dish down a butter mountain. You'll be so sexy through the curves that your passengers will need a cold shower after every journey.

To avoid any slip-ups along the way, you'll learn to see the road through a racing driver's eyes—looking so far ahead that you'll know what your great-grandchildren will be having for breakfast in 2216. Clear your head, light a stick of incense, and ease into the Zen of Driving.

Once fate is firmly in the back pocket, we'll venture into the parts of life we can't always master but can learn to control: driving on ice, handling skids, dealing with emergencies, and still managing to enjoy the ride.

We finish with some soul food: stunt driving.

The Department of Motor Vehicles' Playbook this isn't, but in the following chapters you'll learn to read the road for the sea of asphalt, take control of the car with confidence, and develop a driving style to be proud of.

Driving is about becoming the master of your fate, and, believe me, there's no better or more worthwhile journey.

I'll show you how to drive more smoothly than a jazz band surfing a soap dish down a butter mountain.

01

A VERY SHORT HISTORY OF DRIVING

1.1 ROADS AREN'T STRAIGHTFORWARD

The rules of the road inevitably shape the way we travel. Man and cart made their way along the left-hand side of Ancient Roman pathways, and this was no accident.

I blame Napoleon.

The vast majority of humans are right-handed and right-eye dominant; by hanging left, they could most easily identify and wield a weapon against any oncoming threat.

The Romans were a clever bunch; they built straight roads across their burgeoning empire, from the Appian Way in Italy to the trunk roads that still connect Great Britain. With reins in their left hand and a whip in their right, Roman riders were as ergonomically sound as modern-day right-seated drivers whose dominant right hand never leaves the steering wheel. The entire world followed this logic—until the French got involved. I blame Napoleon.

The Frogs began hauling goods in bulk using teams of horses whose master was seated on the rearmost horse to the left, for no good reason other than to be different. In order to jostle their cumbersome wagons past oncoming traffic, they had no choice but to drive past each other on the right to observe the clearance. Napoleon, who was left-handed and naturally biased, was so impressed that he imposed the system everywhere he went. Wellington's armies prevented this madness spreading to Britain and her colonies, but the rot was setting in.

America began using French packhorses and adopted the keep-right rule, no doubt relishing the opportunity to assert independence from the British colonial system. The Canadians eventually followed suit in 1923 to stave off carnage at their border. Hitler enforced driving on the right across the parts of Europe that Napoleon had unaccountably missed, and China took the plunge in 1946 to accommodate imported US gas-guzzlers.

So today, two-thirds of the world's population drives on the wrong side of the road, using the weaker left eye to check the left side mirror and pass other cars, all because of a little Frenchman and a disagreement over some tea in Boston. Britain, India, Australia, and Japan remain notable exceptions to the global decline in common sense.

Research in 1969 by J. J. Leeming showed that countries driving on the left have a lower collision rate than countries driving on the right. Cyclists and horse riders typically mount from the left-hand side, placing them safely on the curb when vehicles are traveling on the left. And if you still don't believe me, then check out the military: All aircraft carriers, from American and British to Chinese, have their control towers on the right-hand side, so that pilots can approach for landing and takeoff from the left, with their dominant eye watching out for the only building they might accidentally crash into for a hundred miles.

So today, two-thirds of the world's population drives on the wrong side of the road.

A Nation of Drivers

America has always been in a hurry, and road safety hasn't necessarily kept up. The year 2008 marked a significant reduction in road casualties, by a quarter, but this had nothing to do with a silent revolution behind the wheel. The economy tanked, so we drove fewer miles and therefore had fewer accidents. But even this new crash rate is three times higher per capita than in Europe, and it's not just because Americans drive more. The end of the road has much to do with its origin.

The first American trails were natural channels in the landscape created by people and by roaming animals searching for grazing pastures using the path of least resistance, and by other natural features such as rivers or creeks. When colonists arrived, they used these trails to herd livestock and trade tobacco.

Early trailblazers cutting through impassable terrain classified a road as anything that was cleared of boulders and fallen trees. The US Postal Department and the military led the charge, clearing essential connections between distant outposts to deliver mail and blow up French invaders.

One fighting man, President George Washington, observed in 1785:

> The credit, the saving, and convenience of this country all require that our great roads leading from one public place to another should be straightened and established by law. . . . To me these things seem indispensably necessary.

As the road network expanded, so did the rush of settlers racing West by horse and handcart to stake a claim, pan for gold, and build a new world. The biggest killer in the frontier was neither natives nor robbers but disease, largely from bad water. Liquor provided a safe alternative, and travelers were well serviced by the network of taverns and backdoor brewhouses that sprang up to greet them.

Cyclists, whose tailbones were most directly exposed to errant potholes and tree stumps along these muddy routes, instigated the Good Roads movement in 1880 that began paving the way for the automobile. By 1900, eight thousand cars shared the roads with fourteen million horses.

The first metal monsters were viewed with suspicion. Tennessee required a week's notice from anyone planning to drive there, and in San Diego you faced thirty days in jail for breaking the 8-mph speed limit. Henry Ford's production line quickly turned these oddities from the preserve of the rich into the affordable dream of every American citizen, selling fifteen million Model T's by 1927.

Frustrated by rough dirt roads and a need for speed, a man named Carl Fisher unveiled the world's fastest racing speedway at Indianapolis. His vision went beyond mere racing. Fisher conspired with like-minded businesses to seed-fund the Lincoln Highway, a smooth ribbon of concrete that stretched coast-to-coast from New York to San Francisco.

In 1903 only a fraction of rural roads had any surfacing. By 1935, over a third of roads were "improved," and Ford produced just the car to make use of them: the V-8. Eight throbbing pistons propelled occupants up to 80 mph and, according to Clyde Barrow, of Bonnie and Clyde fame, it was a "dandy car . . . For sustained speed and freedom from trouble the Ford has got every other car skinned."

Bootleggers running illicit moonshine were on that bandwagon with some enthusiasm. To evade detection by the army of federal revenue agents sweeping the Appalachian Mountains in search of their precious cargos and stills, the moonshine runners tuned these standard stock V-8s into something juicier. They bored out and stroked their engines to increase capacity, and beefed up the suspension to cope with the weight of "white lightning" crowding the rear axle. That left just one vital ingredient to keep one step ahead of the law: the driver.

Screaming through tree-lined valleys by night with the cops on your tail and dust filling the sky was not for the fainthearted, and many a runner met his fate in a crumpled pile of metal by the roadside. Those that made it became the stuff of legend. So much so that a feud broke out over who was the best driver. There had to be a reckoning.

Some say the first race was held around a quarter-mile dirt oval in a cow pasture in the town of Stockbridge, Georgia. The race was urgent, physical, even desperate. The drivers slammed and crunched their hot rods into one another, and the small crowd went wild for it. In 1938 a smart man called Bill France set up a similar racecourse on Daytona Beach and charged the crowd 50-cents admission. NASCAR, second only to NFL in popularity, was born.

World War II turned the automotive industry into a war machine with the likes of Studebaker, Ford, and GM producing tanks, bombers, and military transports. On switching back to civilian mode, the US quickly became the world's leading automobile manufacturer.

Baby boomers bought in, and car sales quadrupled. The postwar euphoria led to a love affair with and renaissance for automobile design that inspired the finest works of art on four wheels. Substance gave way to style—space-age tail fins, rocket-shaped trunks, torpedo tubes for headlamps, and enough glinting chrome to signal to aliens in deep space that dinner was ready.

President Eisenhower admired the groomed superhighways of Germany's Autobahn network during the war, noting the speed with which retreating Nazis moved along it with his boot up their asses. Ike decided to bring superhighways to America, and fast. The National System of Interstate and Defense Highways rolled out in 1956, primarily to enable rapid strategic deployment of military assets across the United States for defense purposes. It also provided American cities with an emergency valve for major evacuations during hurricanes or, more worryingly, nuclear attack by the Soviets.

It was the "biggest public works program since the Pharaohs piled up the Pyramids" (Time magazine), consuming billions of tons of steel and cement to create 54,663 bridges, 104 tunnels, and 47,182 miles of road. Like any major public works, it went over budget, got delayed, and suffered the myriad headaches of marrying the new Interstate Freeway System with a creaking network of older highways. Interstates plowed through existing neighborhoods or curled around those that resisted, as many did. Rivers were diverted and mountains climbed or cleaved.

As Eisenhower noted, "Its impact on the American economy was beyond calculation." Trucks laden with consumer goods filled the highways, prompting the truism "If you bought it, a truck brought it." Remote communities were connected, local businesses turned national, and suburban living flourished. Shopping malls relocated outside of city centers, easing traffic congestion on one hand, extending commuting distances on the other. The entire nation became mobilized, and in so doing moved the art of courtship from the front porch to the backseat.

There's no doubt that the interstate represents a monumental success story for the nation. When added to the rest of the National Highway System's arterial roads, freeways cover 200,000 miles. They are by far the safest roads in America, though not always safe. Highways range from six lanes down to two, with steep grades over mountain passes and as many bold curves as long straightaways. Freeways regularly divide to both right and left, leaving drivers to contend with lane hoppers coming at them from both sides. Signage overload abounds, and despite the efforts of the brave and the few who use their turn signals, it's basically yield or die.

The materials coating the surface of freeways vary wildly—from grippy asphalt to the worn-out and polished kind, or the more robust concrete that is prone to icing in winter. And America does tempestuous weather as no other, adding a further variable in traction.

By the swinging '60s there were 90 million cars on the road. Today there are over 254 million cars in America, collectively logging 11 billion miles a year. A full 91 percent of personal travel takes place by car, and Americans average longer commutes to work than the rest of the world. Despite the extent of multilane highways, they are positively dwarfed in scale by the older road network. Four *million* miles of it!

The rural road, like any sexy beast, is captivating and deadly in equal measure. This is where we cover the most ground, and over half of road fatalities occur here. These country roads hustle out of the metropolis, fly across the savannahs, dive into canyons, snake around jaw-dropping ridges, and generally track the steps of those frontiersmen who slept under the stars wondering what lay around the curve. The cars we drive have evolved so much since then, but old habits die hard.

Seventy percent of the people killed in car crashes last year were not wearing seatbelts. Had I skipped this simple procedure, my life story would have ended on page 7. One-third of those killed are impaired by alcohol, and of that third, more than half are twice over the legal limit—meaning completely, barking-at-the-moon hammered. This sad little paragraph is probably responsible for the majority of road deaths in America, and the solution is so stupefyingly simple that it requires no further discussion.

On that sobering note, let's buckle up and take a ride.

1.2 BURNING RUBBER

"Modern tires have become such normal objects of the roadside that the marvel of their existence ceases to excite wonder. Yet it is something of a miracle that a column of compressed air can be bound round a wheel, endowing it with a life and luxuriousness absolutely unknown to a former generation, whose carriage wheels were shod with iron, and whose use of horse power was strictly limited to the equine meaning of that phrase."

—*The Dunlop Book: The Motorist's Guide, Counsellor and Friend*, 1920

The first self-propelled "automobile" was probably the steam-powered three-wheeler built in 1769 by a Frenchman named Nicolas-Joseph Cugnot. Nic demonstrated the shortcomings of three wheels by crashing into a wall on his first display . . . at 2 mph. I did so too when I barrel-rolled a Robin Reliant at our Dunsfold test track on *Top Gear* in 2010.

Early vehicles were cumbersome and tricky to control; stopping them on their skinny wagon wheels was an act of faith. Thanks to a little divine intervention in 1839, a bankrupt American inventor by the name of Charles Goodyear was displaying a ball of sulfur-treated gum he had concocted, when it flew out of his hands onto a stove, which scorched its surface and created the world's first weatherproof rubber compound. The air-filled tire was subsequently invented in 1846 by Robert Thomson, a self-taught genius who also invented a machine for drying his mother's laundry. Another Scotsman—John Dunlop—brought tires into the mainstream by building his first factory in 1889.

The "pneumatic" tire behaved more like a living organism than the rigid, clunking load-bearers of the previous age. The cushioned ride spared passengers the displeasure of having their rumps tenderized on every journey. The capacity of inflated rubber to absorb energy from multiple directions was the key to its success. It would transform motoring. Even the cream of tire anecdotes still won't get you invited to dinner parties, but on the racing circuit it's all we talk about. Tire dynamics is what sticks the car to the road, not the metal bit sitting on top of them. Above all else, the chassis and suspension settings of a race car are tuned to maximize the performance of the tires. Some cars are better communicators than others, but every sensation the driver feels, every experience you will ever have on the road, travels along the hotline that connects the tire to your backside.

The Michelin company mascot earned his name, Bibendum (Latin for "Let's drink"), in 1903 by literally swallowing the debris littering the course to win the Paris Road Race. Their durability over nails and broken glass was such that Michelin runners occupied eight of the top ten finishing positions, taking the fight to the drawbridge of Fort Dunlop.

The recipe for creating a good tire is even more complex than the culinary delights promoted in the *Michelin Guide*. Research and development departments push the physical boundaries by constantly testing new materials to add to the two hundred existing ingredients.

The tread pattern we find ourselves studying as we stand in line for our latest servicing is the bit that works on a wet road. At 50 mph it displaces around eight gallons of water per second—enough to fill fifteen bathtubs every minute.

The black rubber stuff comes in a variety of compounds that determine how sticky the tire is. But grip is nothing without the strength of the underlying construction: a vulcanized blend of steel cords, polyester, and Kevlar tailored to the size, stiffness, and performance demanded by each particular vehicle.

There have been a few hiccups along the way. American car manufacturers at first dismissed the innovation of steel-belted radials after World War II. They preferred jelly for suspension. Radials eventually won out because they were so much more fuel-efficient. The tire, quite simply, was more important than the car.

Every experience you will ever have on the road travels along the hotline that connects the tire to your backside.

1.3 ROAD RAGE

Back in 1865 the Red Flag Act still restricted national speeds to a dizzying 4 mph and required that each vehicle had at all times a man walking in front of it, brandishing the said ensign (until it was finally put to one side in 1878).

The world's first road fatality came in 1896 when Mrs. Bridget Driscoll stepped into the path of a Roger-Benz "horseless carriage" and stood "bewildered" by the machine as it zigzagged toward her at a "tremendous pace" (no more than 8 mph). Frozen with fear, she was run over and later died in what was judged to be an accidental death.

Cars were feared because they were different—but there was nothing new about the way people drove them. In 1720, traffic fatalities from "furiously driven" carts and coaches were claimed to be the leading cause of death in London. In the New York of 1867, horses were killing an average of four pedestrians a week—roughly the same number as are killed by cars today, with denser traffic and a significantly larger population.

In 1817 Lord Byron wrote thus to Thomas Moore:

Last week I had a row on the road . . . with a fellow in a carriage, who was impudent to my horse. . . . I wheeled round, rode up to the window, and asked him what he meant. He grinned, and said some foolery, which produced him an immediate slap in the face, to his utter discomfiture. Much blasphemy ensued, and some menace, which I stopped by dismounting and opening the carriage door, and intimating an intention of mending the road with his immediate remains, if he did not hold his tongue. He held it.

A Texas City grand jury recently heard the case of a truck driver tailgating a young woman and waving his arms at her, prompting her father, who was observing

"Much blasphemy ensued, and some menace, which I stopped by dismounting and opening the carriage door."

the fracas from another car, to give chase in his Mercedes. "There was evidentially some swerving between the two vehicles, and the two exchanged words and were cussing at each other," explained Captain Goetschius of the Texas City Police. The men pulled over and faced down. The Merc driver pulled out his pistol, but the trucker was faster on the draw. He floored Merc Man by planting a bowl of oatmeal in his face—proof, if any was needed, of the perils of regression when in possession of the keys to something shiny. And the benefit of a healthy diet.

We become as stubborn as mules inside our tin cans, even when confronted with the threat of losing more than our license. On the edge of an otherwise serene village in the heart of England's countryside, one enraged woman rammed another from behind with her tiny Vauxhall Nova. She was so angry that she sat there gunning the engine until the front wheels shredded through to the steel cords. The resulting sparks ignited her engine's fluids and the whole vehicle lit up with her inside it. She threatened would-be rescuers with a clenched fist, preferring to perish in the flames.

The machines we use these days have been through a time warp, but the human psyche hasn't always kept up. It's a jungle out there.

MOTOR RACING

In Victorian times health and safety was regarded with a disdainful curl of the lip, so there was little serious driving regulation. "Motor racing" took place on long stretches of dusty country road and so gripped the pioneers and engineers of the age that technology, once triggered, advanced rapidly. By 1900 the world speed record (set by an electric car, no less) topped 65 mph.

In 1903, two million enthusiasts lined the route from Paris to Madrid as 274 cars of all shapes and sizes battled for supremacy. British racing ace Charlie Jarrott set the scene:

> Long avenues of trees, top-heavy with foliage and gaunt in their very nakedness of trunk; a long, never-ending white ribbon, stretching away to the horizon; the holding of a bullet directed to that spot on the sky-line where earth and heaven met; fleeting glimpses of towns and dense masses of people—mad people, insane and reckless, holding themselves in front of the bullet to be ploughed and cut and maimed to extinction, evading the inevitable at the last

moment in frantic haste; overpowering relief, as each mass was passed and each chance of catastrophe escaped; and beyond all, the horrible feeling of being hunted.

The first day saw eight fatalities and twenty injured—perhaps unsurprising in an environment where drivers achieved *average* speeds of 65 mph on narrow lanes packed with spectators. The French authorities shut the contest down before it left Bordeaux. Road racing was abandoned, and the pioneers moved to closed circuits at places like Indianapolis, Le Mans, and Brooklands.

The grueling, high-speed epics that followed would eventually spawn every piece of technology on the modern car, from disk brakes to power steering. And what's more, it created a set of driving principles that continues to be developed inside the cauldron of competition in Formula One and NASCAR, and across the spectrum of the sport. These principles involve looking ahead, as well as within—a mental game that requires you to tie up emotional loose ends that might lead to mistakes or influence your ability to make calculated decisions. It is a cold and methodical approach to addressing a fast-developing situation.

The grueling, high-speed epics that followed would eventually spawn every piece of technology on the modern car.

1.4 THE DRIVING TEST

The transition from horse to horseless carriage took the authorities by surprise.

Being good at the test does not equal being a good driver.

The first driving exams in America were set up by high schools, arguably the best model, before state legislatures intervened in order to regulate traffic with a licensing scheme for vehicles and their operators, starting with Chicago in 1899. The red tape started flowing in Europe with authorities looking to everyone from steam boiler associations to car salesmen for guidance and training in how to drive. A test finally materialized in Britain as late as 1934.

The coveted scraps of paper providing motorists their ticket to ride still amount to dubious currency when you take them overseas, with the Germans refusing to recognize driving licenses granted in California or Georgia. Only the residents of these great states could know why.

The modern driving test allegedly teaches safe driving for life, but the newly passed are four times more likely to crash than the rest of us. And most of us believe we would fail the test if we had to retake it. In other words: Being good at the test does not equal being a good driver.

The skills we learn to pass the test come from the highest possible authorities—the government and the police. So we might expect to find some answers about our evolution here. The Brits love doing things by the book, and they revere one driving credential above all others: the "advanced driving license." It is based on the Police System of Car Control and presided over by instructors who hold Police Advanced Driving Certificates. The Police System has been described as the Holy Grail of driving: Followers of the system believe that questioning its teachings is tantamount to heresy. But it is not just obsolete—it can be dangerous. In Britain the first words a student hears from his police instructor on the open road are: "Golf-Lima-Foxtrot," or "Go Like F***."

Lord Trenchard (1873–1956) was a visionary with a taste for speed. Having lost a lung and been paralyzed from the waist down after being shot during the Boer War, he took up bobsledding during his recuperation in Switzerland. When the impact of a hefty crash on the Cresta Run miraculously cured him, he returned to active duty and was appointed police commissioner in 1931.

Meanwhile, people with no formal training and no idea how to operate heavy machinery were discovering new ways to kill themselves—and others—on the roads. The average police driver had a crunch every eight thousand miles. The new commissioner decided to do something about it.

He picked up the telephone to a man who had been busy writing the history of motoring with his right foot. A Grand Prix winner in the early days of the sport, Sir Malcolm Campbell would take the world speed record to beyond 300 mph by 1935 at the Bonneville Salt Flats in Utah. Having evaluated the fleet, Campbell concluded that the lack of training and experience was the root cause of their attrition rate.

Trenchard recruited the "Stig" of his time, Lord Cottenham—aka racing driver and MI5 secret agent Mark Pepys—to oversee the creation of a police driving course. Cottenham set out the Ten Commandments of Motoring in his book *Steering Wheel Papers*, a manual on maintaining control of the cumbersome vehicles of the day. He taught the police:

▸ to pull the desperately large, heavy wheel with one hand and push it with the other (power steering had not yet been invented);

▸ to apply their 10 horsepower gently and continuously through the curve so as not to upset their delicate suspension and hard, skinny tires; and

▸ to use the brakes independently of changing down gears so that both feet were free to "double de-clutch" (pumping the clutch several times to swing the gears while right-footing the accelerator to match the revs).

A Ford Fiesta has ten times the power of a 1930s cop car.

The results spoke for themselves. His training saw the police accident rate improve to one in 27,000 miles. Cottenham's work was done. He left his post with the police after just three years, but his gospel of Police Roadcraft was canonized in 1935 and passed through the generations *unchanged*. Roadcraft's system of car control continues to form the backbone of police driver training and is at the root of the physical skills required to pass the driving test. The fundamentals of car control, however, have changed a bit since the 1930s . . .

Some eighty years on, even a Ford Fiesta has ten times the power of a 1930s cop car; it could leave Sir Malcolm's Grand Prix racer dead at the traffic lights and hit curves on tires with twice as much grip. Synchromesh gearboxes don't require double de-clutching. Power steering points the vehicle in whichever direction you want it to go, and braking distances are up to 40 percent shorter than in yesteryear.

And Cottenham wouldn't have expected his 1930s methods to remain unchanged any more than an Air Force pilot would expect a P-51 Mustang manual to help him fly an F-15 fighter jet. Yet with the creaking gospel of the DMV handbook in one hand and the gear shift in the other, we duly line up to receive the wisdom of these authorities like disciples at the temple. Somewhere during the grinding of gear ratios, burning clutch plates, and jarring emergency braking, we stop thinking about what we are doing and sometimes even sacrifice good sense on the altar of *just passing the damn test.*

Cottenham wouldn't have expected his 1930s methods to remain unchanged any more than an Air Force pilot would expect a P-51 Mustang manual to help him fly an F-15 fighter jet.

1.5 KING OF THE ROAD

Not long after obtaining my driver's license, after just three lessons, I enrolled at a Motorsport Academy hosted at the Silverstone Grand Prix Circuit to apply for a competition license.

I had to learn the different flags and display proficiency in late braking, tackling a corner at speed, and controlling the twitching rocket that was a Peugeot 306 around the Grand Prix circuit. Before I knew it, I was flying around the track less than an inch off the ground in a single-seater that was the closest thing to a Formula One car, and to heaven, that I had ever experienced.

That took me all of a single day, fuelling my conviction that I was a pretty damn good driver.

My dad decided to take out an insurance policy by having me attend a specialized skid-control course at the Silverstone racetrack. The course took place using a normal car fitted to a frame that lifted the front or rear tires off the asphalt to induce a skid. And skid we did. I learned to pulse the brake pedal to unlock a stopped wheel, throw the steering into opposite lock to catch the car as it fishtailed, and perfect the recovery of a 360-degree spin at 70 mph by spotting the desired direction and fixing on it like a ballerina.

Armed with knowledge spanning not just how to execute a three-point turn but also how to nail a chicane and stop the world from turning, I was primed to become an insurance statistic.

I set off on a long trip with a mate to test a single-seater race car at some far-flung airfield. I returned at the end of the session to discover that my buddy, who was never renowned for his common sense, had locked my keys in the trunk. So began the kind of journey of self-discovery they don't teach in classrooms.

I had to hotwire the ignition, and the delay meant I was running late to get to Brands Hatch for a season-opening Formula First Championship race. With a gut full of nerves and my friend jabbering in my ear, I ventured onto the freeway for the first time just as it started to rain.

My front tires were on the bald side, owing to the extra air pressure I had cleverly pumped into them for the five minutes of extra grip this afforded on a dry road . . . until the tread wore away. With the rain lashing at the windshield and some fascinating London radio stations to choose from, I failed to notice the traffic slowing in front.

They stopped.

I didn't.

Crunch: a five-car concertina.

I arrived at Brands late, with what remained of my Honda on the back of a flatbed truck. Fortunately I was already wearing my racing suit, since my normal clothes were still locked inside the trunk with my keys. I qualified on the front row. Then it started to pelt down with rain, and through further ignorance I opted for brand-new, and therefore greasy, tires for the race.

Having survived the first lap, I took the lead. Then I braked so late for the Paddock Hill bend that I could see the incredulous look on the flag marshal's face as I shot past him. For the second time in twenty-four hours I locked up my front wheels, and no amount of pulse braking could prevent me firing off the track at 80 mph to an ignominious finish in the gravel trap.

Gutted.

Understanding how my choices had set this disastrous chain of events in motion took me longer than it should have. In the words of my race team manager, I needed to "break the cycle before you kick the bucket."

If only I had paid more attention to that bucket. I destroyed a further three race cars that season, to be awarded the championship's inglorious Bent Wishbone trophy for the hardest hit of the season.

But it finally sank in: I'd been ambushed by sheer ignorance of the real world at the very moment my mind and body were most eager to explore every nuance of it. The desire to tinker with machinery, push personal boundaries, and ignore the advice of crusty old men with too much time on their hands is a trap that most of us have fallen into somewhere along the line.

The process that began, very slowly, was a painful one. I desperately needed to understand *why* I was failing on so many levels. Over time, I ruthlessly set about picking apart the patterns that led to my mistakes and began conditioning my responses.

To this day I'm still learning, and because there's so much to discover I'll never claim to be an expert. But that's what makes driving such an art.

I was primed to become an insurance statistic.

02

THE BASICS

2.1 ARE YOU SITTING COMFORTABLY?

Once you get used to whatever car you're driving, it becomes an extension of your body, of your mind even.

When you're completely in tune with it, you lose awareness of rudimentary controls like the pedals. All that is left is your perception as you float through a colorful universe where the present meets the future.

To achieve Zen, the car should fit like a glove. Conversely, a bad seating position can turn a car into a torture chamber on a long journey. Chiropractors rub their hands with glee at the sight of drivers resting their noses on the tops of their steering wheels, or with their feet so far from the pedals that only telepathy can link them to the road. Optimizing your driving position is the first step toward optimizing your drive.

Optimizing your driving position is the first step toward optimizing your drive.

1. Driving Position

FEET, NOT LEGS

It's your feet that operate the pedals, not your legs. If I'd known this at the age of four, I'd have averted my first major crash. Having achieved terminal velocity aboard a riding lawn mower in a neighboring farmer's field, I realized that I was hurtling toward the chicken pens. Emergency braking alone stood between me and a giant omelet. But my foot could barely reach the pedal. Ditching the machine into some pig wire was the only option—and not one I'd wholeheartedly recommend.

It goes without saying that choice of footwear—whether stilettos or oversized hobnail boots—can present a similar challenge.

Manufacturers spend millions of dollars on ergonomics, and modern vehicles mold the instruments around you. It's worth spending a few minutes to tailor them to your particular needs; you'll be more comfortable, and drive better.

Adjust the seat to position yourself as low down in the car as possible. The lower you are, the closer to the center of gravity you become, and the more you will feel part of the machine. Just make sure you have a clear view above the steering wheel.

If your legs are straight when you press the brake pedal, you won't be able to use it fully. Maximum braking requires a strong continuous force on the pedal, which simply isn't possible without a 15-to-30-degree bend at the knee. With your heels on the deck you should be able to easily move your foot, not your whole leg, between the pedals.

Most cars have a footrest down in the footwell to keep your left foot out of the way. This enables you to brace yourself in a curve by pushing on your left leg when you need to.

ARMS

You should be able to relax into the back of the seat and find that your arms are still bent when you hold the steering wheel. Driving with straight arms uses only a fraction of their strength, and you won't be able to turn the wheel properly. Sit too close to the wheel and you will (a) look ridiculous and (b) break your nose on it someday. Ideally, your hands should be level with your shoulders in the quarter-to-three position on the wheel face. Then relax. And if you can't relax, start over until you can.

SEAT BELTS

Two-thirds of passengers killed in the US weren't wearing seat belts. The lap belt in particular prevents your core mass from turning into a projectile and your thick skull from annihilating everyone in the car like a cannonball.

A friend of mine called Tony Harris, a soldier who lost half his leg courtesy of the Taliban, was competing in the world's most grueling rally: Dakar. His team of exhausted former soldiers was commuting between stages on a placid stretch of highway connecting the dusty planes between Peru and Chile when a taxi driver coming the other way decided it would be a great idea to pass right in front of them and drive headlong into their vehicle. The lads could have been forgiven for not wearing their belts and catching some shut-eye after all they had been through. But they did wear them, so they all survived, while the unbelted occupants of the taxi did not.

From a driving perspective the belts offer a convenient way of staying in the chair, especially if you have to swerve to avoid something. In any form of racing, the belts are

If your butt is rolling around the seat like a Jennifer Lopez video, you've got no chance.

crucial for feeling what the car is doing through the divining rod that is your backside. If your butt is rolling around the seat like a Jennifer Lopez video, you've got no chance.

HOT TIPS

▸ The headrest isn't actually a "rest," and if you remove it, or it's not lined up with your melon, you're more likely to break your neck if you have a crash.

▸ Wear comfortable clothing that doesn't restrict your movements, especially your arms.

▸ Keep sunglasses at the ready to handle low-lying sun and glare off a wet road. At all costs, avoid polarized sunglasses. I don't know who invented them or why, but they ruin your ability to judge perspective and are totally unsuitable for driving.

MIRROR, SIGNAL, MANEUVER . . . AND REVERSING

I'm very particular about my mirrors because these are my third eye. I tweak the right side mirror down a fraction toward the curb for parking, and aim the left side mirror for a longer view down the side of the car for monitoring traffic. I'm not alone in this.

Jean-Claude Van Damme, legendary martial artist, also respects the angle of dangle. To my knowledge he is the only man to have performed splits on the side mirrors of a pair of reversing Volvo trucks without dismembering his undercarriage.

I unleashed my inner Van Damme a few years ago for a Volvo S60 commercial on a similarly wind-streaked airfield. Scott, the director, was an old pal from *Top Gear*, now living the Hollywood dream and looking the part with his Yankees baseball cap and aviator sunglasses. He casually understated the order of events as "the usual driving stuff."

I was handed the keys to a prototype vehicle worth $3 million and invited to reverse it at high speed through a slalom of solid metal posts and up a set of ramps onto a moving car carrier with six inches to spare between the tires and the inner edges of the ramps. The transporter had no sides. If I overcooked it, $3 million was going overboard. Scott wanted to start filming in ten minutes.

If I overcooked it, $3 million was going overboard.

Unleashing my inner Van Damme, California 2010.

I confessed early on that this wasn't something I had done before, and it might be a good idea to do some practice using rubber cones.

I lined up the cones, looked over my shoulder through the rear windshield, and went for it at 40 mph. The first weave went OK, then the cones disappeared out of sight as soon as the car turned the other way. With the car effectively rear-wheel-steering, going from left to right was totally unstable, and before long there was a cone massacre.

The only way to accurately reverse that worked for me was using the side mirrors. I adjusted them a little lower down so that I could see more ground than air, and I practiced using smaller, more precise steering movements to avoid getting caught out by the tendency for the car to over-rotate. It was seamless.

With the slalom under control we turned our attention to the car carrier. The good news was that my initial approach would be driving forward. Then they wanted a 180-degree hand-brake turn to spin the car backward; then I would select reverse and drive up the ramps. Easier said than done, since Volvo, like many carmakers, had done away with hand brakes in favor of a parking button that worked only when stationary.

When nobody was looking, we unplugged the antilock braking system's chip that would otherwise override what was to come and dialed in the move. The truck was rolling at 40 mph, so I drove toward it at 65 mph to allow for the speed that would scrub off during my pirouette. Then came the hard part.

With the car carrier ramps dead ahead, I jinked to the right, accelerated hard, then jinked left, and thumped the brake pedal. As this was a front-wheel-drive car, the acceleration countered the braking effect on the front wheels, allowing the brakes to act solely on the rears as a hand brake would. The rears locked, and around she went.

I kept my hand in one position throughout the turn so that I could whip the wheel straight as soon as I finished spinning. Then I engaged reverse, checked my position in the broader view of the rearview mirror, and floored it. The left side mirror was naturally my favorite for the close-quarter reverse, and I used it to line up my rear tire with a support strut I noticed beneath the on-ramp. I knew that if I hit that mark, I had metal rather than air underneath my other tires. And, as I'd picked out that mark in advance of reversing, it turned a complicated job into a walk in the park.

As soon as the car shot up the ramp, the side mirrors lost their perspective, so I switched back to the rearview mirror to maintain a straight course, alternating with the odd glance to the sides once I leveled out, then back to the rearview mirror until I closed up to the back of the towing rig. And relaxed.

When nobody was looking, we unplugged the anti-lock braking system's chip.

2.2 *THE BEAST*

You're about to connect your consciousness with a miracle of engineering that will, as far I'm concerned, transport you to the center of the universe.

The stretching of rubber, connecting of shafts and flanges, and all the torque of thrusting is enough to get pulses racing, but let's look at the functions of the equipment before we push analogies too far.

Turn the key and fire the engine: *Suck, squeeze, bang, blow.* The pistons deep inside the engine bay circulate like the legs of a cyclist pumping the pedals. As the piston falls within its chamber it *sucks* in a mixture of air and fuel, then *squeezes* it so hard that the fiery cocktail is compressed to a tenth of its original volume. The heat of this molecular crush alone is enough to ignite diesel. With gasoline, a spark is introduced, creating an explosion that *bangs* the piston into its next cycle, and exhaust gases are *blown* out along the way.

When the engine is free of the drivetrain, it idles at around 22 piston revolutions every second, or 1,320 revs per minute, without breaking a sweat. Pressing the accelerator introduces more fuel and power to the system, so the pistons revolve faster. They report their rate of progress with a rising note and rumble, and via the needle within the oft-ignored tachometer next to the speedometer.

Somewhere between idle and the point where the needle ventures into the red on the tachometer, the engine develops its peak turning force, or torque. You wish that sweet spot would last forever, as all that rotational power begs to be harnessed in some way. The clutch has the means to do it by enslaving the engine to the gearbox, which in turn connects to the wheels that sit on the road.

The engine spins constantly, whereas the gearbox and the car's wheels do not. The clutch manages the speed differential between the engine and gearbox by holding the gear in one hand and harnessing the engine's spinning flywheel with a high-friction pressure plate in the other.

A spark is introduced, creating an explosion.

When you climb aboard, think of the flywheel as a spinning merry-go-round and your feet as the clutch plate. When your feet land on the ride, your speeds suddenly match, and round you go.

As you release the clutch pedal with a gear engaged, the clutch plate rubs on the flywheel and begins turning until their speeds match. As the clutch plate turns it delivers drive to the gear and through to the wheels. Forward motion commences. When the clutch is fully released, the car's road speed matches the engine speed for that gear.

The gearbox contains a gear for each different range of road speed from zero all the way up to the car's maximum, enabling the engine to unleash its finest torque again and again as we accelerate from one gear to the next.

Imagine the gears as athletes running a relay race with different physiques and specialist skills.

Imagine the gears as athletes running a relay race, each with different physiques and specialist skills. First gear has short, powerful legs like a weight lifter, delivering maximum force to the wheels to get a ton of metal moving from a standing start. But as the car begins to speed up, our short, fat, hairy man in Lycra reaches his top speed and runs out of steam. We need to pass the baton to a new gear with longer legs for faster running, and so on, until we reach top gear with the likes of Usain Bolt.

Handing the baton back to a slower runner when the vehicle is still sprinting at high speed forces short legs to spin much faster than they were designed to. The engine screams, and the tachometer sees red.

When the gear exceeds its speed range in this way and is enslaved to the engine by a cruel master releasing the clutch, it creates an engine speed so fast that the pistons try to relieve themselves by exploding out of their housing. So you use the gears that marry engine revolutions with road speed to avoid a meltdown.

All the pounding metal and churning fluid within the engine and gearbox creates internal resistance by friction. The faster the engine is turning, the greater the resistance. When you hit the road there are other frictional forces acting on the beast as the tires meet the road and the car's shell encounters resistance from the air. These natural forces want to slow the car, so by lifting off the accelerator pedal and cutting power to the engine, you decelerate. Now it's time to adopt this pedal's real name: the throttle. Because the throttle can be used to accelerate as well as decelerate by choking the engine.

Last, but by no means least, is the brake pedal with its near-infinite range of pressure adjustment. This is the primary device for slowing the car. A mere brush compresses the fluid underfoot. It instantly winds its way through a series of pipes to squeeze four sets of clamps onto their respective disks, themselves attached to the rotating wheels. Friction on the disks drags speed from the car and transmits weight to the front tires.

It sounds like a lot to take in at first, but the engineering quickly synchronizes with biology to make the process as thoughtless as breathing. Being clumsy with any element of the control process is no bad thing; the only mistake would be not to admit it.

For me it was the clutch. I was so insensitive to its powers that passengers were handed neck braces, but a winter racing series forced me to change: 100-mph curves became ice rinks where *every* passage of the clutch pedal would break traction unless it was accompanied by acute patience and feel. I developed my left foot accordingly, and in years to come this would prove vital with *Top Gear*.

LIGHT TOUCH

Operating a vehicle for the first time is rather like being in an egg-and-spoon race while riding a unicycle. There are bumps and shudders aplenty, a few expletives, and grazed knees. Multitasking with hands, feet, and brain in concert with the way the car is responding is no picnic. Most drivers settle for a mediocre performance, and it stays that way for the rest of their lives.

I was forced to relearn the basics when I drove a Skoda with a helicopter balanced on the roof for *Top Gear*. Any sudden movements would have resulted in a beheading. When I accelerated, it tilted up the rotors as the weight of the car moved rearward; so if I'd tramped the gas pedal the chopper would have fallen off the back. If I slowed too quickly or fumbled a downshift it would send weight forward; the rotors would dip and threaten to transform the chopper into a lively hood ornament.

A rooftop helicopter is an expensive training device, but what you can do is plant an imaginary glass of water on the dashboard and drive in such a way

I was forced to relearn the basics when I drove a Skoda with a helicopter balanced on the roof.

that you don't spill a single drop. If you can avoid getting wet, you will benefit in three ways:

> - You will be much less likely to be involved in a crash.
> - You will save up to 25 percent on your gas bill.
> - You will be a better driver, on the road and on the racetrack.

BALANCE

The entire business of operating a car revolves around the transfer of weight. You're basically sitting in the middle of a seesaw, with the engine at one end and the passengers and whatever's in the trunk at the other.

The seesaw starts out level.

It moves only when you do something, like standing on the brakes, at which point it tips forward and loads its weight onto the front tires, giving them grip for stopping or turning into a corner. The plank goes level mid-corner and then tips back to load the rear wheels when you press the accelerator. This front-and-back transfer of weight creates what is called *vertical load*.

The plank also leans from one side to the other in the curve, weighing down the outside wheels to create steering grip and turning thrust. That's *lateral load*.

The important thing to get your head around is that when the weight of the car moves and bears down on a given tire, that tire generates grip. The rubber takes a fraction of a second to respond, which is why it pays to ask politely. If you suddenly hit the accelerator, it can spin the wheels; but if you moderate the initial touch and then go hard, the tire has time to accept it.

When the weight of the car moves and bears down on a given tire, that tire generates grip.

Philippe Petit, hands spread equally apart, walks a wire between New York's Twin Towers shortly after their construction in 1974. With every step, he makes tiny adjustments of pressure from his toes to his heels and from side to side to maintain his balance. He remains totally calm. His hands and body are relaxed, bringing enormous accuracy and sensitivity to each step. And he looks ahead, never down.

Likewise, when you turn the steering wheel, the weight leans across the vehicle. The rate at which it leans depends on how much *force* you put into the steering—i.e., how much grip *you* put into the front tires in the first place, coupled with how quickly *you* turn. Yes—*you* create the grip. And once you know how, you can command the weight to be exactly where you want it, when you want it, for perfect handling throughout the curve.

Balancing a car involves shifting its weight around the tires at the right time. Each movement flows harmoniously into the next. When driving a car, go for maximum sensitivity. The more you feel at one with the machine, the better you will drive it. When you place your foot on the accelerator or the brakes, feel the pressure through the tips of your toes rather than via the force in your thigh. Control your strength so that you are conscious of the movement in your toes and the ball of your foot as it reaches your ankle. It allows for a far more delicate touch, with power in reserve if you need it.

Similarly, holding the steering wheel with the tips of your fingers provides more sensory feedback. If you clasp it like a vise, your inputs become heavy-handed and decrease the car's stability, reducing your ability to create grip and increasing the likelihood of a skid.

With your hands equidistant from each other, cradling the wheel in the quarter-to-three position, you create a perfect sense of balance. Balance in the palm of your hands makes the physical inputs measured and soft, like you're lifting a cup of tea

Like you're lifting a cup of tea rather than smacking Mike Tyson on the kisser.

rather than smacking Mike Tyson on the kisser. It matters because the corresponding weight transfers in the machine amplify your inputs.

The worst kind of weight transfer occurs when the driver creates a violent pendulum effect. This is usually the result of a sudden switch in direction that puts momentum into a weight transfer, causing the suspension to whip one way and then another, like a charging elephant swishing its buttocks. The sudden overload can cause a loss of traction and rapid departure from the road.

2. Balance

Static

Braking

Accelerating

Ben leading the field in the FIA World Endurance Championship in 2014, aboard the Ferrari 458 Italia GTE. So much weight has shifted across to the outer side of the car that the inner front tire lifts off the ground.

Cornering Thrust

Dynamic Handling

Every car is unique, which is why we end up feeling so at home in the daily steed.

The traits we learn to love or hate are conveniently known as *dynamic handling characteristics*, which really means how the car throws its weight around. The biggest weight sitting in the car, unless you've spent your life in McDonald's, is the engine, so we tend to notice the effects of weight most during acceleration.

Loosely speaking, all cars fall within the following categories:

FRONT-WHEEL DRIVE— FRONT-ENGINE

This is the garden variety favored by manufacturers because it's cheaper to build. Front-wheel drive means that the engine is delivering rotational power only to the front axle; the back tires are merely freewheeling behind. With the engine weight over the front wheels, the driver senses more inertia through the steering when taking a curve. The front-loading over the driven wheels is an advantage in snow and ice.

The disadvantage is that the front tires have two jobs to do in both accelerating and steering the car, which ultimately compromises their adhesion.

The resulting loss in steering ability is obvious to the driver (as the hands no longer agree with the vehicle's direction), and equally simple to remedy by reducing speed. The result is that they are perceptibly easier to drive than their rear-wheel-drive cousins.

FOUR-WHEEL DRIVE (AKA ALL-WHEEL DRIVE)

These are nearly always front-engine cars, with the exception of the Bugatti Veyron. Weight is slightly more evenly split front to rear, but 4x4s generally handle like a front-wheel-drive/front-engine. They have superior traction in slippery conditions, but they weigh more and use more fuel.

REAR-WHEEL DRIVE— FRONT-ENGINE

The weight is balanced more evenly with the engine in the front and the driven elements spread toward the rear. These models tend to respond eagerly to steering inputs due to their engine weighing down the front tires, but they can bite or feel nervous when the rear loses traction during acceleration.

-WHEEL DRIVE—
ENGINE

car is designed for optimum performance
weight oriented around the center and to the

rear of where the driver sits, providing a height
sense of the polar inertia as the car rotates i
curve. This is the best . . . but there's not much
for golf clubs or groceries.

3. Engine Types

Front-Engine
Front-Wheel Drive

Front-Engine
Rear-Wheel Drive

Front-Engine
4 x 4

Rear-Engine
Rear-Wheel Drive

2.3 SMOOTH OPERATOR

Three-time world champion racing driver Sir Jackie Stewart is one of the coolest cats ever, whether sporting fireproof Nomex or an immaculately tailored blazer and tartan slacks.

"The smoothest way, the quietest way, the slowest way around Monte Carlo is the fastest way."

You know he's taken time to think ahead. As a result, very little takes him by surprise, on the road or in life. When he coached me as a young driver in his race team (Stewart Racing), I quickly realized that he set the bar very high, and saw us novices coming a mile off.

Balancing a car throughout the transitions of a curve is all about being smooth. Here's what Sir Jackie had to say about it: "The smoothest way, the quietest way, the slowest way around Monte Carlo is the fastest way." He won three F1 world championships and countless races by driving "as slowly as possible."

The strange irony about going "fast" on a racing circuit is that your technique is slow and measured. Of the hundred or so celebrities I coached around the *Top Gear* circuit, I never told anyone to steer faster, or to hurry their feet across the pedals. Good driving is smooth driving; everything is under control, and nothing catches you unawares.

Contrary to popular belief, the faster the car is going, the slower your inputs have to become in order to keep the weight of the machine stable. You nurture the precious patch of rubber sticking you to the black stuff. It's as true on the road as it is on the track. Fluid inputs through the steering wheel and pedals permeate the machine and dictate its road-holding capability. Your perception of the road improves, and you become more accurate.

Jackie exhorted us to drive flat out around the racetrack, watching as we lurched and growled our way to the finish line, always at the edge of what the car could take. Whenever he spotted anything remotely untidy with our performance, he would begin his sermon thus: "Don't upset the balance, laddie."

To achieve this, you had to drive super smooth, which meant you couldn't afford any last-minute corrections for failing to plan ahead. You climbed gently onto the brakes and squeezed, eased the steering toward the corner, and then gradually picked up the gas.

Jackie's way taught us discipline and came with several bonuses. It saved the tires, and it saved fuel. And, over the course of a race, that made us faster.

PULLING AWAY

Teach us to pull away, Ben? Have you mistaken the reader for a complete moron?

I promise I haven't. But every mountain starts with a single grain of sand—and you didn't complain when Julia Child taught you how to boil an egg.

On a flat road you can pull away in first gear without even pressing the accelerator pedal, and it's a great way to train your left foot. With the engine just ticking over, you slowly release the clutch and feel the plates bite as the car begins to creep forward. By keeping your heel on the carpet and the ball of your left foot on the pedal, your calf muscle can create a powerful, slow, and deliberate hinge.

If you're in more of a hurry or on a hill, then you add some revs to bolster the process, but don't overdo it or you'll be treated to the acrid waft of burning clutch plate.

Bond does not favor this method.

HOT TIPS	▸ Gently tense your calf muscles and ease up the ball of your foot, or curl your big toe slowly upward, until you reach the biting point. With only a light weight on the clutch pedal, forward motion will commence. And after you've released it completely, the car will travel at its natural pace for that gear.
	▸ Slowing your clutch foot demonstrates the kind of self-control that might, just might, convince a potential date that you really are James Bond or Lara Croft in your spare time. And adding a little extra gas thereafter just makes the whole thing sing.

COMMON MISTAKES	▸ Lifting your whole leg: This makes the whole process lumpier than a plastic surgeon's waiting room. Keep your heel on the deck.
	▸ Rushing the clutch up and past the biting point, then stalling: Remember, slow and steady wins the race.
	▸ Snapping the foot off the last few millimeters of clutch and lurching forward or stalling: Bond does not favor this method.

Ah, but there's more. Your driving instructor taught you to apply the hand brake and release it as you pull away. That doesn't cut it for me because (a) it's a pain for anything less than a super steep hill-start and (b) I like to have all four tires in my vise rather than the one or two rear tires that the hand brake latches onto. So I use "heel-and-toe."

Whoa—an advanced racing technique this early on?

I'll give you chapter and verse on heel-and-toe as a braking technique later. Suffice it to say here that your right foot can cover both the brake and throttle pedals at the same time in most road cars. You use the ball of your foot to hold the car still on the foot brake and swivel your ankle to put some pressure on the throttle and raise the revs if you need to. It's quicker and easier for pulling away.

4. Heel-and-Toe

SMOOTH ACCELERATION

Fixed heel pivot point.

Once mobile, the idea is to be as smooth with the throttle as possible. The Holy Grail is for your foot to progressively build up to the maximum pressure required for the piece of road you're traveling along before decelerating for the next event. Throttle, once applied, should not need to be released in the middle of the curve, otherwise it implies that you accelerated too soon and have to correct the mistake. You can apply that rule to every aspect of driving because you should always be able to set your speed appropriately.

What that really means is that you don't poke and prod the pedal in a series of clunky encounters. A practical demonstration that you can recreate in the safety of your driveway is to attach a piece of string from your big toe to the six o'clock position on the steering wheel. When the wheel is straight, the string is tight at full throttle, but as you turn the wheel in either direction it pulls your foot off the gas and vice versa. It teaches you only to accelerate as the corner opens out and to unwind the steering on departure.

Another feature of acceleration is its relation to speed. The slower you are driving, the faster the car will accelerate and therefore the slower you apply the loud pedal. The faster you're going, the slower it will accelerate and therefore the faster you can apply power.

At low speed this relationship is relevant for maintaining traction and smoothness. At higher speeds, your lack of acceleration affects passing. As we shall see, this curve affects more than just speeding up; it also affects braking.

Don't poke and prod the pedal in a series of clunky encounters.

2.4 *SHIFTING GEARS*

The perfect gear shift should be neither felt nor heard.

Look, I'm sure that you can physically shift gears, and most of you will be driving an automatic anyway. What I'm proposing is the ninja method, smoother than a cashmere codpiece, and bulletproof for driving any car, anywhere, anytime.

The perfect gear shift is no less satisfying than a perfectly fried egg, and just as regularly scrambled. Running roughshod through the gears sends shock waves through the transmission to the wheels, where it creates unregulated weight transfers and can even cause the tires to skid.

For pure locomotion—or if you're about to get T-boned—you can shift any way you like. But I'm hoping to teach you to turn off your lunacy switch and lay down some smooth moves.

What I'm proposing is the ninja method, smoother than a cashmere codpiece.

GEAR SELECTION
Every engine has a sweet spot, where its pulling power, or torque, is maximized. In the dead zone at 1,500 rpm it has little to offer, but at peak revs the engine runs out of breath, so your aim is to keep the revs somewhere in between so that the engine can pull you out of the turn. Ignore the textbooks and don't drive around staring at the rev counter. If you listen carefully to the engine and feel the power underfoot, you can develop a keen sense of your speed.

Always try to select the appropriate gear for the turn before you get to it. Mid-turn shifts are far more likely to get fumbled.

HOW TO HOLD A MANUAL GEAR STICK
Modern engines and transmissions may be pretty macho, but the shrieking protest of cogs and pistons when you accidently grind into the wrong gear leaves a terrible impression.

Palming—applying pressure to one side of the gear stick or the other—minimizes the risk of wrong gearing. Hold the knob as you would a handshake—that's the thumbs-up position—to stay left when changing first to second, or to cross back down for third to second and fifth to fourth.

Invert the hand, so your thumb faces down, to cross the gate from second to third and fourth to fifth. In other words: thumbs-up to pull the gear toward you, thumbs-down to push away.

The gear stick sits in a spring-loaded housing. It will naturally find the center of neutral, the third/fourth axis, so you only need to apply sideways pressure to find lower (to the left) or higher (to the right) gears.

Whenever you get lost, take a breath and pop the thing into neutral, without any side pressure, so that you know where you are. Then take it from there.

Using the spring is also the easiest way to change from second to third. Just push forward into neutral—the stick will flip across to the center of its own accord—then slip it forward.

Having proven your dexterity beyond question, you are ready for the secret ingredient to a cool gear shift: the accelerator.

SHIFTING UP (I.E., GOING FASTER)

The hardest change is from first to second while accelerating. You have the most power under your right foot, and the engine responds aggressively. It gets easier as you go up the gears, but the same technique applies.

You actually have to guide the gear stick through three phases: pulling out of first, crossing neutral, and then taking second.

When you're about to shift gears, release some pressure on the gas pedal first, to reduce the rate of acceleration. Then, as you come off the accelerator, you start to depress the clutch, but for those seeking heaven on a gear stick: *leave a tiny touch of accelerator on*—just enough to keep the revs hovering above idle and cushion the flow.

Float the gear stick from first through neutral and, as you move toward second, don't rush it. Allow half a second to pass as the next gear engages, then gradually release the clutch pedal. It makes all the difference, because this fraction of time allows the new gear to start jogging and synchronize with the engine speed, take the baton from the previous gear, and run away with it. Once the clutch is fully released you can accelerate away as swiftly as you like, without any bumps.

HOT TIPS

▸ Cheat. If you're having trouble you can "short-shift" by changing to second gear early at lower rpms to avoid kissing the dashboard.

COMMON MISTAKES

▸ Holding the knob too tight when taking a curve. Too much sideways pressure and you'll stick it into the wrong hole. (No snickering at the back.)

▸ Impatience with the gear shift. You'll get snagged on the gate. Chill out; less haste means more speed.

▸ Accelerating between shifts. The engine note goes from a groan to a shriek, the clutch sizzles and pedestrians crane their necks and stare. Use only a hint of accelerator.

▸ Releasing the gas altogether when you depress the clutch pedal: The revs drop, then when the clutch is released and you accelerate again, the car jolts forward, or there's a thud as the engine speed suddenly catches up with the road speed, Mr. Bean–style, in the new gear.

▸ Rushing the transition: If you whip your foot off the gas prior to the gear shift, the resulting kangaroo hop will have your passengers kissing the dashboard. After taking a gear, if you then dump the clutch by suddenly taking your foot off the clutch pedal, everyone gets a second bounce off the dash as the engine abruptly reconnects with the gear. You finally pound your audience into their seatbacks by reapplying the loud pedal. It's like Tarzan's first driving lesson. Slow it down; release the accelerator pressure gently at first, but not all the way, ease the clutch, then gently reapply the power.

A little patience as you cross the gate goes a long way toward achieving a smooth ride and will save a lot of explaining to your local mechanic as to why the gearbox contains so much shrapnel. Once you're slick with the basics, your shifting will speed up by itself.

SLOWING DOWN, BRAKING, SHIFTING DOWN THE GEARS

ENGINE BRAKING

Engine braking works just as effectively with automatics, so don't be shy to try. On a good road trip when you're floating around traffic, you should hardly need the foot brake at all. When you lift off the throttle in gear, it cuts propulsion to the engine, but the internals, the pistons, and other widgets continue spinning, and the friction of these moving parts causes drag known as *engine braking*. It's a superb tool for controlled deceleration.

Engine braking by itself will not stop the car anything like pressing the brake pedal, but by looking ahead and reading the traffic flow you can just roll off the gas and let engine braking do the work. When you do have to brake, the idea is to operate the pedal once with a consistent pressure, rather than a sequence of lurches.

Where engine braking really comes into play is for slowing on hills, in slippery conditions, and for stopping in an emergency.

For the wannabe racers out there: None of the above includes dropping a cog at every opportunity to kick bass from the exhaust. But your local garage will welcome you like a lost son when the gearbox collapses at the traffic lights.

REV MATCHING (MANUAL TRANSMISSIONS ONLY!)

If you're driving up a hill, for example, you might need to shift down from fourth to third gear in order to boost your pulling power. With a speed of 65 mph in fourth, the engine might be running at 2,500 rpm, but the corresponding rpm in third at that speed might be 4,000. You already have your right foot on the gas pedal, so all you need to do is leave it there as you depress the clutch. The revs will naturally rise from 2,500 to 4,000 rpm. Slide the gear into third, release the clutch, and then continue accelerating. There shouldn't be a jerk, because you've matched the revs.

Boost your pulling power.

Conversely, if you're driving toward a curve or a downhill section where you don't need to brake, you can control your speed by selecting a lower gear. Depress the clutch, raise the revs with the throttle, engage the gear, then gently release the clutch, and you will feel the drag of the engine holding back your speed.

COMMON FALLACIES ABOUT GEAR SHIFTING

The method prescribed by certain police experts is: "Gears to go, brakes to slow." This system forbids the overlapping of braking and downshifting phases; they don't want you doing both at the same time.

In the old days before the invention of synchromesh gearboxes, finding a gear was like stirring tar. To get the cogs to disengage you had to pump the clutch pedal, then blip the throttle to match the engine speed, and finally operate the clutch again as you selected the gear. Your feet couldn't be everywhere at once, so this necessitated a separation between braking and downshifting. In short, there might have been a good reason for splitting the phases in the 1930s, digging out the next gear with a stick that resembled a crowbar.

But not now.

The separation of braking and downshifting doubles the distance required to slow down, or, as the Police Roadcraft manual neatly explains: "The problem is that if you brake some distance before the turn to avoid an overlap, you can confuse other drivers . . . [who] may be tempted to pass."

Engine braking gives you more stability in a curve and proves critical in restraining the inertia of the gearbox and engine when you descend a steep hill.

SKIPPING GEARS

Going up through the box, I often skip gears to save fuel. A good automatic will do it for you if you tread lightly. *Block changing* is when you drop down from, say, fourth to second in a single leap. If you know ahead of time that second is the gear you ultimately want, then it can be convenient to skip third by leaving your downshift later than if you went through each gear. There's no hard-and-fast rule on this, but I personally prefer to be in the right gear at all times during braking, with control over the engine and the ability to react to any situation. In traffic a squirt of acceleration can often prevent an accident just as much as a hard brake.

DOWNSHIFTING USING THE CLUTCH

Downshifting keeps the engine jogging along as you slow down, and the internal resistance complements the braking effort. Going through all the gears means that you always have the power and stability to maneuver if you need to.

As you slow down with your right foot on the brakes, it falls on your left foot to work the clutch in order to make smooth transitions from the longer gears to the short-legged ones as you switch from fourth down to third and so on. Smooth clutch work allows the engine revolutions to gradually adjust to the road speed in each new gear.

Most people never operate the clutch pedal at the same time as the brake. They automatically take their foot off the brake whenever they release the clutch pedal. My explaining this might seem about as helpful as getting you to consider which way you swing your arms when you walk . . . and watching you fall over.

The trick is to start thinking of your right and left feet independently of each other, so that you can modulate brake pressure with one while easing the clutch in and out with the other. Then you'll be equally ready to drive a Fiat or a Ferrari . . .

You'll be equally ready to drive a Fiat or a Ferrari.

Shifting Gears

COMMON MISTAKES

▸ Modern gearboxes have a *synchromesh*, a synchronizer that helps the internal gear cogs get up to speed with each other. This takes only a fraction of a second, but if you try to slam the gear lever home, it will resist.

▸ Dumping the clutch by releasing the pedal too quickly is another common error. When you do this, the engine suddenly engages, sending a jarring force to the driven wheels.

Simultaneously braking and changing down utilizes engine braking, so your brake pads will last longer. More importantly it keeps the weight consistently on the front tires during the deceleration phase. That's not only smoother, it also creates additional grip in the front tires just when you want it for turning into the curve.

Now that you can place the weight of your beast precisely where you want it, it's time to turn and burn.

BRAKING AND ENTERING

Dunsfold Aerodrome, 8 a.m. A crisp morning, good for engines, especially ones with giant turbochargers force-feeding them air like crack to a junkie. I grew up with the poster of the Ferrari F40 on my wall, right next to the brazen image of Cindy Crawford (both of which were, to my twelve-year-old self, equally attractive).

I was jogging on the spot, not so much to keep warm but to give my legs something to do while I waited for Jeremy Clarkson to finish salivating. He called it "the best car ever," and from where I was hopping he just might have been right.

On closer inspection the car looked like something you might have made from a corn-flakes package. It was boxy, with gaps between the bloodred body panels, and protruding through some Perspex was an engine that must have fallen off the back of a truck on its way to the F-16 factory. It made a hissing sound just like a jet as it forced air out of the way at 201 mph.

Dunsfold was no stranger to that sound. Safely tucked away deep within the wilderness south of Guildford in Surrey, Dunsfold's creaking hangars with their distant echoes of rushing airmen had been host to top-secret aviation projects for fifty years. From the dawn of the Spitfire to the revolutionary Harrier Jump Jet, the broad, expansive runways had seen them all.

In track mode we joined Dunsfold's two parallel straights together to form the familiar figure 8 now immortalized as the *Top Gear* circuit. But for pushing maximum velocity we ran it the way that nature and fast jet pilots intended, using the full length of the landing strip.

It flew past again like a stray tracer bullet scorching across the greenbelt. Even after a *Top Gear* diet of double espresso and bacon sandwiches, our twitchiest cameraman put his neck out, whipping his lens across in hot pursuit.

When it was finally my turn I fell into the bucket seat, my feet thudded into the carpetless floor, and *kunk* went the door. To keep the weight down to an anorexic 2,400 pounds, there were no creature comforts on board. Just a chair, some well-appointed pedals, and a gear lever shaped like a Victorian door handle. The steering wheel felt like it was cast from solid iron and was angled forward, challenging the driver to an arm wrestle. The Ferrari F40 was a brute, all right.

I limbered up with a few passes through the Hammerhead loop to see how the '80s girl handled. In a word, evil.

It flew past again like a stray tracer bullet scorching across the greenbelt.

The heavy steering lightened up, marginally, once I got going but it bucked, pulled, and bit over every bump and burp in the track's surface. I held on firmly with both hands.

The tight chicane approached. When I pressed the brake pedal I realized that someone had replaced it with an anvil and pushed harder for more response. It eventually came. The nose of the seesaw dipped, and I felt the rear lighten. Then came the moment I feared: the downshift.

I dipped the clutch, grasped the black ball atop the long metal gear lever, and ushered it across the tight metal gate toward third. The satisfying brush of metal took longer than expected to find home, by which time the revs had dropped considerably. I needed to keep braking to make the curve, but I also needed to tickle the throttle to raise the revs or face retribution from the motor when it re-engaged . . .

The obvious solution to a race-car driver would be to *heel-and-toe*. The term was coined during the days when signaling meant sticking your arm out of the window, and the brake pedal was located to the *right* of the throttle!

In modern race cars and supercars like the F40, the pedals are aligned closely so that your right foot can easily cover both the brake and the throttle pedals. This allows the driver to apply pressure to the brake pedal with the ball of the foot, while simultaneously "blipping" the throttle by swiveling the side of the sole.

The *blip* is a short, sharp snap of the gas pedal that sends the revs high enough to match the running speed of the shorter gear. Matching the revs cushions the bite of the downshift and prevents a sudden load of engine braking affecting the driven axle. In the case of the rear-wheel-drive Ferrari, its engine braking was strong enough to stop the wheels from turning and send it skidding across the road. I was certainly keen to avoid spinning backward; it would have presented Clarkson with an enduring, unbearable punchline.

Well, my right foot went deep into the brake and past the point where it was able to reach the throttle. Perhaps the owner had set the pedals to suit a lighter braking style, but it came as no surprise. With the majority of cars I lapped on *Top Gear*, I found it impossible to heel-and-toe.

Unless the pedals are perfectly aligned *for you*, the technique does more harm than good when you're braking close to the limit because the slightest imbalance in your foot affects the pressure asserted on the pedal. My solution was simply smooth clutch work. I remembered my ice training and treated the left pedal like a second brake.

I delicately released the clutch, and the thunderous engine of the F40 sprang slowly back to life.

I delicately released the clutch, and the thunderous engine of the F40 sprang slowly back to life, pulling gradually on the hard rear suspension, helping me to slow for the curve. I boldly shoved her into second and repeated the process. With the weight over the fronts and the nose tucked in, I bled off the foot brake and turned the chunky wheel toward the sharp left.

The hard steering communicated everything the tires encountered; she was growing on me, and I switched directions for the longer, bumpier ride onto the next stretch of runway.

The suspension and springs that supported the car like a mattress were fairly compliant as I plodded through the curve in the lower rev range. In fact, at 2,500 rpm I could have mistaken it for a Fiat Punto. Then something shuddered inside its belly as a pair of turbos spooled up behind me. Then the Ferrari's phenomenal torque tapped me on the shoulder and whispered, "You should've brought more guys."

The F40 had only 470 horsepower, so I had driven beefier models in terms of power output. But the turbocharged 2.9-liter V-8 engine in the F40 produced a colossal amount of torque at around 4,500 rpm. Torque is a wonderful feature for tractors that plow fields, with hundreds of gears to harness the gob of pulling power packed within an infinitesimally narrow rev range between, oh, 4,468 and 4,496 rpm.

The torque surging through the car lifted its nose and squashed the rear tires into the ground, taking the tire rubber to its limit. I noticed the steering was no longer taking me where I wanted to go. I knew what was coming next, just not how much.

With the wheel cranked to a perilous degree, the savage turbos suddenly erupted. The car snapped sideways as the power overwhelmed the rear tires. I squeaked involuntarily, the way you do when you bench-press one too many and nearly swallow the bar. I spun the wheel as many times as it would go, like a submariner closing the hatch to prevent the flood, as the F40 embarked on the gnarliest power slide this side of a Prince concert.

Even Iain May, the toughest cameraman ever to wear North Face, took his eye off his camera monocle to cock an eyebrow and check my trajectory as I streaked past in a blaze of glory. About half a mile later, I had the rig back under control and sort of fell in love.

With the F40 the rev needle never left your attention because it was the best way to time the rush of power and live to die another day. It was undoubtedly the best supercar to come out of the '80s, but you really had to grab it by the scruff of the neck and hold on for dear life.

Ferrari built another box-shaped car in 2002, but this was no kit car. The elongated wheel arches, thinly veiled F1-style front wing, and butch rear end with its flared spoiler generated nearly a ton of aerodynamic downforce at the tender speed of 186 mph. Another flick of the sequential gear paddle behind the steering wheel teleported you to a top speed of 218.

They originally produced only 349, later agreeing to 399 after a lot of begging, before finally adding one more . . . for the Pope.

Designation: F60—aka Ferrari Enzo.

Engine unit: 6-liter V-12.

Power: 650 horsepower, *no turbos required*.

Handling: *biblical*.

This was the only car Ferrari deemed worthy to adopt the name of its founder, Enzo Ferrari. Like the F40, it bore a Spartan interior but nonetheless weighed 440 pounds more than its grandfather.

The steering wheel bonded to my hand like the hilt of Excalibur, feeling both light and deadly accurate thanks to the carbon fiber construction and leather grips at the quarter-to-three position of the wheel face.

In terms of performance quality it reminded me of the mighty Porsche Carrera GT minus the demonic frenzied howl of its V-10 engine. The Ferrari V-12 had the mature boom of a cello at low revs, turning more alley-cat-locked-inside-a-steel-drum when you gave it some hammer time. Unlike the F40, the Enzo's flexibility of power throughout the rev range offered phenomenal control for every millimeter of throttle.

Big brakes annihilated my speed efficiently enough to dislodge unwanted nasal hair. I eyeballed the curve across a panorama of red bodywork and Excalibur took me there effortlessly. In the middle of the curve, the Enzo developed a reassuring moment of front tire scrub, resisting the true direction I was aiming for, but that soon balanced as I opened the tap on the V-12.

The crisp steering connected me to a magical four-wheel drift, with one minor design fault reminding me that I hadn't died and gone to heaven: the honking of the rather inappropriately wheel-mounted horn.

Handling: biblical.

Shifting Gears

2.5 STEERING

"If boys saw at the wheel or jab at the brakes, you just know they'll be hopeless in the sack."

—Vicky Butler-Henderson

The aim with steering is to be able to place the car precisely where you want it, whenever you want to, and without any hassle.

Believe it or not, steering technique is the subject of furious debate in the driving community. As I get under way with this section, police driving instructors and test examiners are sharpening their pencils, dipping them in poison, and preparing to fire them into my eyeballs. "This is heresy, burn him!" they cry. Read on at your peril.

Your choice of style ultimately boils down to what makes you feel most comfortable. Here are the different options:

THE SHUFFLE

This is the technique we Brits learn by rote to pass the test—passing the wheel from one hand to the other at points in its upper hemisphere to turn the car in the desired direction. The hands generally operate in the ten o'clock to two o'clock positions. For many, it's the simplest way to get from A to B, and a method that lasts a lifetime.

For very tight maneuvers in city centers and supermarket parking lots, shuffle steering is a simple and effective means of progress.

The shortfall is that you lose a sense of balance and the ability to gauge how much steering has been applied, which in turn can affect your reaction to an incident. And, unless you're really slick, making a turn tends to be a jerky series of direction changes rather than a smooth curve.

I find it pretty impractical for anything other than the most basic applications, but it didn't do Simon Cowell any harm. Simon shuffled his way to two record lap times at the helm of *Top Gear*'s Reasonably Priced Car. He was so comfortable with it that breaking the habit would have done more harm than good. And Simon generally gets his own way.

Steering technique is the subject of furious debate in the driving community.

However, when he tried his hand behind the wheel of a 450-horsepower Noble, we ended up heading backward into a field at 120 mph—the result of too much steering with a precision instrument that required finesse, unlike the old Suzuki Liana, which I'll get to later.

THE PUSH AND PULL

This is the time-honored system of the British Police, the Institute of Advanced Motorists, and many others—a more formulaic version of the Shuffle. Scandinavian rally drivers refer to it, a touch unflatteringly, as "milking the cow."

Going into a left-hander, the left hand rises up the wheel and pulls it down. As it does so, the right hand slides down the other side, until it comes level with its partner in crime. If more steering is required, the right hand pushes the wheel up, while the left hand slides up the wheel, ready to pull down again if required.

When Cottenham designed Police Roadcraft in the 1930s, you had to man-handle a wheel big enough for an America's Cup super-yacht, without the benefit of power steering—and the castor angles made them excruciatingly heavy to turn. Pulling and pushing was the only way to make a turn without breaking your wrists.

The Roadcraft system encourages anticipation of corners by readying the hand positions in advance, but in my view it's completely outdated, overly compli-cated, and inefficient for skid control because it forces steering activity to alternate between the lower and upper hemispheres of the wheel, making it harder for the human brain to register the subtle forces feeding back from the tires.

Crucially, you also lose a sense of balance by pulling into a corner with one hand rather than two—and, as we'll see, how you enter a corner has the greatest effect on weight transfer and stability.

Scandinavian rally drivers refer to it, a touch unflatteringly, as "milking the cow."

5. Rotational Steering

This range of steering is adequate for the majority of turns on the open road.

Where further steering is required for especially tight curves, such as hairpins, the lower arm takes a new hold on top of the wheel.

ROTATIONAL STEERING, OR HAND-OVER-HAND TECHNIQUE

Thankfully this is the method taught by most driving instructors in the United States. If you asked Dale Jr. or Mario Andretti which method he uses to hold the steering wheel, he would stare at you for a very long time. It would never occur to either of them, or any other pro racing driver, to control a car in any way other than this: Your hands grip the wheel in a fixed position, opposite one another at a quarter to three on the wheel face, where they have the best leverage. Your thumbs latch over the top of the wheel spokes for added grip—unless you're Jean Alesi, who used to hold the wheel farther up, to match his aggressive driving style.

Rather than changing your grip position to pass the wheel from one hand to the other, you just turn the wheel and allow your arms to cross over. Your hands balance each other, keeping the wheel steady over bumps, potholes, and other forces that might act on it.

With both hands on, you have far better control if the car slides or pitches. Most crucially, by keeping your place on the wheel at all times, your brain registers precisely how much steering has been applied. It provides a physical cue when the front tires are starting to skid.

It also means that unwinding the wheel couldn't be easier—or smoother. As we will see later, straightening the steering is essential if the rear tires skid.

To negotiate especially tight corners and hairpin bends, you release the lower hand and carry on turning with the uppermost arm, replacing the redundant hand as required. It balances the weight on the steering wheel equally to create a single graceful turn rather than a sequence of clunky shuffles.

A study by the UK Department for Transport examined how these last two techniques performed in terms of matching the steering to a visual target. It concluded that "drivers who used the crossed-hand technique significantly improved their time-on-target as compared with drivers who used push-pull" and that their performance improved more over time. The study theorized that rotational steering is probably a more natural way to drive, and advantageous when sudden steering corrections are required.

It is no coincidence that this is the technique used by race-car drivers worldwide, from Formula One to Le Mans, NASCAR, and World Rally. We use it because it works.

> *Your hands grip the wheel in a fixed position, opposite one another, at a quarter to three.*

When you hold the wheel, slightly spread your fingers so that you can feel the feedback from the road. By enhancing your sensitivity, you can learn to read beyond the vibration and tune into the slightest changes in grip via the weight of the steering.

HOT TIPS
- ▸ Many people jiggle the steering around for no reason. Less is more.
- ▸ Avoid rough, jerky movements.
- ▸ Lighten up on the wheel and feel the road.
- ▸ Avoid the "wide boy" technique: one hand on top of the wheel and the other hanging out of the window. I'd be lying if I said that I never drive one-handed, because there are times when it makes life easier, such as winding on full lock to navigate the confines of a parking lot. But for real driving, it takes two hands to tango.

After all that wheel work you're probably thinking that the steering actually turns the car. As with any good story there's a twist—because it doesn't; the tires do. Meet the real heroes.

We use it because it works.

2.6 *BRAKING*

Understanding the marvels of physics taking place on a molecular level when you hit the road helps you to comprehend the part that you, the driver, play in the process.

If it weren't for grip you would never leave the driveway.

If it weren't for grip you would never leave the driveway, the wheels would spin hopelessly, and you would just be sitting there inside an expensive smoke machine. Tires are gripping all the time, even when you're driving straight. You only become aware that they are working on your behalf when you put a force through them by turning the wheel or pressing a pedal.

As we saw in the first section, the rudimentary tires of yesteryear have evolved into their own form of suspension, working closely with the mechanical features of the car to balance and control the demands of the road.

These donut-shaped bags of air cling to the wheel hubs with bands of steel wire called *beads*. They can withstand enough pressure to carry the weight of the car owing to their immensely strong, but flexible, construction of textile cords bonded to a rubber matrix of vulcanized elastomers, themselves composed of entwined chains of molecules called polymers. The sulfur that Charles Goodyear accidentally added back in 1839 acts like a glue to anchor these molecules in place—and their structure supports the black carbon and sticky silica in the tread blocks that get on with the job of gripping and throwing water out of the way.

As the tire meets the road surface, it binds to it in two ways. The rough edges of the road material indent into the blocks of rubber and lock, while on a molecular level the surfaces on both sides are attracted to each other by adhesion. These bonds form, stretch, and then break faster than a *Dancing with the Stars* romance, allowing the tire to distort, develop grip, and create an elastic force for turning, braking, and acceleration.

When you turn the steering wheel toward a corner, it rotates a metal column connected to a pinion, which in turn swivels the wheel hubs on which the front tires are mounted.

When the hubs turn, the tires resist, causing them to stretch, and this creates the elastic force that pings you around a corner. The human eye never sees this, but the patch of tire, no more than the size of your hand, stretches away from the hub considerably when in contact with the road.

The degree to which this happens is called the *slip angle*—perhaps confusingly, because the tire isn't slipping; it's gripping. The "angle" is the degree to which the rubber distorts away from its hub without giving up and springing back to Mama—or *skidding*, as it's sometimes called.

The pull, or self-aligning torque, of all that stretching rubber creates turning thrust, the lateral force dragging the car in the direction in which you steer. The more elastic strength the tire can generate, the more grip you achieve. You can simulate this in the comfort of your own kitchen if you press the end of a rubber eraser onto a table and twist it. The harder you press down, the more you can twist the rubber—up to the point where it just breaks free of the surface regardless of how hard you push down.

But more on that later.

When the tires lose traction through, for example, a change in the road surface, they will stretch less, creating less torsion, and we feel the steering "go light." That's why smoothness is particularly important on a wet road: because the car is generating lighter forces than usual and is more susceptible to skidding.

Now we know how the tires work in conjunction with the basic elements of weight transfer. It's time to step it up a gear and explore the most challenging and rewarding skill that a driver can perfect: braking.

BRAKING FORCE

There are two kinds of braking: everyday and to the limit. If readers of this book unleash extraordinary new powers of the latter on the road, it is fair to say that insurance claims will skyrocket and my head will end up on a spike outside the Tower of London.

My view on this is that everybody, even the little old lady in the Honda, will brake to the limit at some point, and everyone would benefit from understanding

The harder you press down, the more you can twist the rubber—up to the point where it just breaks free.

what it feels like and what it means—but you'll need to turn to Part 4 for that. For now, let's just make sure we can pull out of the drive-through without spilling our milkshake.

EVERYDAY SMOOTH BRAKING

The goal for everyday driving is to be as smooth and progressive with the pedal as possible, and to moderate your speed in a single graceful exercise. To do this you deploy a widely accepted technique of *feeling* your way into the brake pedal, *firming* up the pressure to remove the bulk of your speed, and finally *feathering* off the pressure for a smooth transition.

I still set my standard by that of the chauffeur who once zapped me across the Italian Alps to work on 007's *Quantum of Solace*. He was so smooth that whenever we pulled to a stop and the springs began to rebound, raising the nose of his Mercedes, he bled the pressure off the brakes in the final few feet to perfectly counterbalance the effect. You could have performed open-heart surgery in the backseat.

I am considerably more accustomed to the bump and grind you get in the back of a taxi, where the guy bangs on and off the brake pedal like it's a tambourine. Observe your passengers. If their torsos are jiving back and forth like the crowd at an Eminem concert, then you are guilty of this most heinous crime.

By looking ahead and planning your braking phase, you should be able to squeeze the pedal gently without needing to come on and off it.

Let's just make sure we can pull out of the drive-through without spilling our milkshake.

6. Tire Grip Area

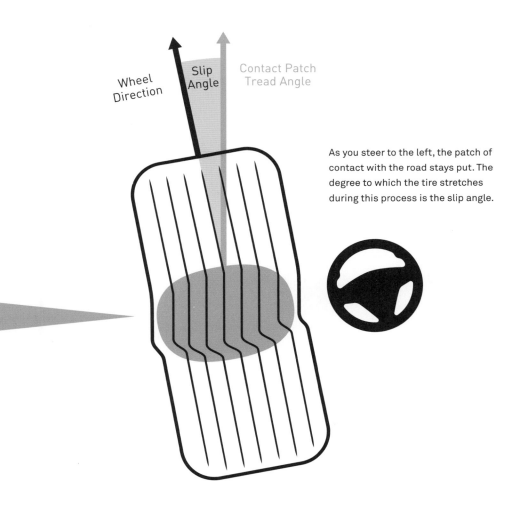

Wheel
Direction

Slip
Angle

Contact Patch
Tread Angle

As you steer to the left, the patch of contact with the road stays put. The degree to which the tire stretches during this process is the slip angle.

How Smooth Driving Can Save the Planet . . . and Save You Money

"It is amazing how many drivers, even at the Formula One level, think that the brakes are for slowing the car down."

—MARIO ANDRETTI, F1 WORLD CHAMPION, 1978

The media's conviction that *The Day After Tomorrow* spells global catastrophe means that eco driving is here to stay. I'll risk the curl of the Clarkson lip now and go into tree-hugging mode, because going vegan with your motor can also help you reduce your fuel bill by 20 percent.

Diesel is currently more fuel-efficient than gasoline (though hybrids are changing that), and cars with automatic gearboxes use around 10 percent more fuel than manuals—but the most important part of the fuel-saving equation is you. The harder you press the pedal on the right (*powerrrr*), the more gas you're using. If you're driving over the speed limit, you save time, but you're definitely burning gas and money. Driving at 70 mph uses up to 9 percent more fuel than at 60 mph, and up to 15 percent more than at 50 mph.

However, before you start driving around like a turtle and making yourself a target on the open road, here are some tips on how smooth driving can help your wallet as well as your cool quotient.

HOT TIPS

▸ Accelerate gently and read the road ahead to avoid unnecessary braking, because *the brakes are the enemy*. Every time you touch them, you're paying fuel tax. Try leaving a space behind the car in front so that you don't need to brake when it does, and roll off the gas early for red lights, upcoming traffic, pedestrian crossings, etc. The more you preserve momentum, the less fuel you require to accelerate again.

▸ Stay alert so that when you have to slow down or stop, you can decelerate smoothly by climbing off the gas pedal ahead of time and drifting to a stop.

▸ Shift gears earlier to avoid revving the nuts off the engine. Changing at around 2,000 rpm with a diesel engine or 2,500 rpm with a gasoline engine, when appropriate, ramps up your efficiency.

▸ Cruise control is an easy way to maintain a constant speed, and thus save fuel.

▸ Hills: Where cruise control fails is on varied terrain with hills, because the engine strains to hold a set speed uphill, burning a higher percentage of fuel. It is more economical to gas it downhill when the engine is hardly working, instead of coasting down, than carry the extra momentum into the hill. That way you need less power and burn less fuel on the way up the other side.

▸ Ditch the air-conditioning. At higher speed it doesn't matter so much, but at low speeds switching off the air can improve efficiency by 5 to 10 percent! In the summer you can always open the window and treat every drop of sweat like a dollar bill. You'll smell like a hermit, but a wealthy one.

▸ Pick your route. Optimizing your route and not getting lost is the simplest commonsense saver. When we filmed *Top Gear* for the 780-mile race from Switzerland to Blackpool on one tank of gas, route selection was the key to victory above everything else.

▸ Tire pressure. The love affair continues. Underinflation lets the tire's tread bulge, creating a broader contact with the road surface. The extra friction creates terrible rolling resistance, and your engine has to work harder to compensate, burning loads more fuel in the process. For the average family sedan, just a 6 psi drop in pressure leads to a 20 percent increase in fuel consumption and a 30 percent increase in tire wear.

Bad Ideas

▸ Coasting: Knocking the car out of gear and easing off the gas to save fuel is pretty harmless when pulling slowly up to an intersection, but there are major drawbacks on highways or around town. First, you lose the ability to quickly accelerate out of tricky situations because you are stuck in neutral. Second, without engine braking, you lose braking performance generally—and on mountain roads the brakes could overheat, and you might drive off a cliff. Money saved for the funeral, though.

Some folk turn their engines completely off while moving, which is plain dangerous. If you rotate the ignition key fully off it engages the steering lock, meaning you can't steer, precipitating your accident and much laughter at your expense. Modern cars rely on power-assisted boosters called *servos* to apply force to the brakes and the steering, and without them no human can push the brake or turn the wheel hard enough to get them to work properly. These servos work only with the engine turned *on*!

Modern fuel injection systems reduce the benefits of coasting, anyway. Unlike the old days with a carburetor, engine management systems control fuel and ignition electronically. The car's brain, the ECU, automatically cuts the fuel supply to the injectors when you stop accelerating.

▸ Drafting: This involves tailgating the car or truck ahead to benefit from the slipstream, the invisible hole in the air created by the lead vehicle, in order to save fuel. Unless your name is Cole Trickle and you're a NASCAR racer, drafting really pisses off other motorists and usually ends badly. That's why NASCAR races nearly always involve a massive pileup.

▸ Turning off the electrics: In some parts of the Far East, I've seen people driving around at night without their lights on . . . to save the bulbs and reduce fuel consumption. Some people apply this logic to their heated rear windshield and de-mister. While turning them off saves a tiny fraction of fuel, it is generally considered more important to be able to see where you're going.

That's why NASCAR races nearly always involve a massive pileup.

BRAKING IN THE REAL WORLD

The best brakers have an acute sense of vision, which has as much to do with eye-sight as it does with forward planning. You look farther ahead and wider than the average driver. This guarantees you the time needed to form an accurate braking plan based on your speed and the landscape feeding your eyes.

For switched-on drivers, the physical operation of your foot on the brake pedal is preplanned on a subconscious level, based on the continuous assessment of the scene to ensure that you can always stop within the distance you can see is clear ahead.

As you approach the corner or obstacle, you adjust your braking plan according to any new developments.

STOPPING IN AN EMERGENCY

When you want to stop quickly there are several factors that will define the outcome:

- ▸ thinking distance: how quickly you react;
- ▸ stopping distance: speed vs. grip;
- ▸ your car—and how well your brakes work; and
- ▸ technique.

THINKING DISTANCE

This is the distance you travel during the time it takes to spot a hazard worth braking for and then to do something about it. Thinking distance is entirely linked to your powers of observation and your speed.

DMV drivers manuals suggest *thinking* and *braking* distances for bringing a vehicle to a stop from different speeds. Ironically, they vary considerably from state to state, with Nevadans allegedly taking three times as long to think about things than the rest of America.

Alabama's driving manual opens more ominously. No cheery welcomes from the state governor here. On page one, Alabamans are offered the opportunity to donate their organs in the event that they splatter themselves into recyclable chunks. Perhaps this direct approach explains why the braking distances quoted in the *Alabama Driver Manual* are shorter than any other state's—making Alabama's stopping distance from 60 mph 138 feet shorter than New Jersey's.

7. Thinking Distance

20 mph   20 feet   20 feet   **39 feet**

30 mph   30 feet   46 feet   **74 feet**

40 mph   39 feet   79 feet   **118 feet**

50 mph   49 feet   125 feet

60 mph   59 feet   180 feet

70 mph   69 feet

Note the difference in braking distance between 30 and 60 mph—at double the speed, it takes four times as long to stop.

(*Source: Highway Code*)

Average car length 13 feet	Thinking Distance	Braking Distance	Combined Braking Distance

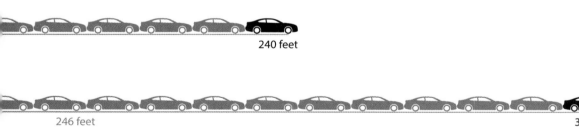

74 feet

240 feet

246 feet

315 feet

You're heading toward the wrong kind of rendezvous.

In reality, physics is a universal truth regardless of where you drive. With modern tires and a trained brain, you can beat the distances the government quotes. At 60 mph the average alert citizen's reaction time is 0.6 seconds. That's 53 feet, or about four car lengths. If you double your speed it naturally doubles your reaction distance, which is why you extend your vision at high speed in order to see things coming from farther away.

After a gut-busting meal or when you're tired, your reaction time edges closer to 1 second or seven car lengths, maybe a lot longer. With your finger up your nose and head craned toward a two-for-one offer at Dunkin' Donuts . . . you're heading toward the wrong kind of rendezvous.

The trick is to reduce the *thinking* distance closer to zero by anticipating the situation and covering the brake pedal with your foot, so that you're ready the moment you need to use it.

Expect the confused individual, or moron, looking for a parking space in front of you to anchor up without warning and you can't go wrong.

Anticipation replaces a reaction to an event with a true action. As for the unexpected, it pays to be decisive and controlled.

STOPPING DISTANCE

It's a battle between speed and grip. The important thing to comprehend about deceleration is that the process is not a constant. Our perception of the slowing process is linear because we tend to think in terms of time, and we generally shed around 20 mph for every second of braking. A car that doubles its speed will take twice the *time* to stop. And that sounds OK.

However, during that extra time, the car travels twice as fast and covers *four times the distance*. You might also think that a vehicle traveling at 60 mph would shed a larger proportion of its speed at the onset of braking. The opposite is true.

Over a total stopping distance of, say, 130 feet, over half the speed is wiped off in the last 30 feet, or roughly two car lengths. It takes 100 feet to get from 60 to 30, and just 30 feet to get from 30 mph to zero. That's scary when you put it in context with thinking distance.

You're on a freeway where everyone is traveling at 70, then you remember the chocolate bar you hid in the glove compartment and go for the grab. *Tick.* When you look back up there's a sea of brake lights across all three lanes. In the second that passed, the traffic ahead slowed to 50. *Tock.* By the time you react, they are doing 30 with a rate of deceleration that is a hell of a lot faster than yours. You can't match them, so unless you have the distance, you find yourself at the wrong end of the braking curve, and the last one to collide in the concertina.

This is Newton's fault. A vehicle builds up kinetic energy by a factor of its weight multiplied by the *square* of its speed, and as a result the braking distance increases exponentially. So if you double the speed, you quadruple the braking distance; a Fiat 500 moving at 40 mph hits with the impact energy of a herd of hippos doing 10.

This physics lesson matters for several reasons. Anything that postpones the onset of braking poses a similar problem. Locking a tire at a higher speed when you first brake creates immense heat and reduces the tire's friction just when you need it most. A lockup at a lower speed is far less punitive, and we'll explore this in the techniques section.

YOUR CAR

Your ability to stop will be governed to an extent by your car's braking system and the adhesion of your tires. Surprisingly, your car's weight has little to do with stopping *in a straight line*, but heavier cars will encounter greater trouble stopping on a curve. Weight is generally a bad thing.

Here's some lemon in the eye for the anti-fast-cars lobby. The fastest cars on the road also tend to be the best at stopping. Here are a few examples of sports cars:

MAKE AND MODEL	AVERAGE OF 10 STOPS FROM 62 MPH
Porsche Boxster S 3.4	100 feet
Audi R8 4.2 FSI	107 feet
Nissan GT-R	108 feet
Lexus IS 250C	125 feet
Alfa Romeo Spider 2.4	129 feet
Honda CR-Z 1.5 IMA	130 feet

If you double the speed, you quadruple the braking distance.

The fastest cars on the road also tend to be the best at stopping.

And for comparison, here are some others:

MAKE AND MODEL	AVERAGE OF 10 STOPS FROM 62 MPH
BMW X6 xDrive35d	112 feet
VW Polo 1.2	112 feet
Ford Fiesta 1.25	114 feet
Toyota Prius 1.8 Hybrid	132 feet
VW Caravelle 2.0 BiTDI	132 feet
VW Passat 1.8 TSI	132 feet
Mitsubishi Lancer 2.0 DI-D	133 feet
Mitsubishi Grandis 2.0 DI-D	136 feet
Nissan Murano 3.5 V6	137 feet
Land Rover Freelander Td4_e	138 feet
Chrysler Grand Voyager 2.8	143 feet

(Source: Which Car)

It's worth noting that even the *worst* performer, the Chrysler Grand Voyager, stops in nearly half the distance that is suggested by the DMV manual, which recommends 300 feet.

Assuming that your car doesn't fall to pieces, your main allies for stopping are your tires. Their ability to grip is loosely defined by the variable conditions of the road surface, over which you have no control, and by the quality of your tires, depending on their make, tread, and inflation, all of which you do control—admittedly not at the precise moment when you panic brake and the adrenaline is fizzing in your fingertips. But if you inspect your rubber once a month and don't buy cheap, then your odds of stopping short will improve dramatically when some wildebeest pulls out in front of you.

Boring but important:

> ▸ Underinflation can extend your braking distance by 10 percent or more if the car is loaded up with passengers.

TREAD DEPTH VS. BRAKING DISTANCE

Beyond that you'll need a parachute.

In wet conditions, your braking distance is about 40 percent longer when the tires' tread depth reaches the legal limit of 2/32"; beyond that you'll need a parachute. It's best to change tires when they wear past 3/32" on summer tires, and you want at least 4/32" on snow.

The simplest way to test depth is by inserting a penny headfirst into the groove. If you can see the whole of Lincoln's head, you've reached the legal limit and it's time for new rubber. For those of you who want more traction at 4/32" or more, shove a quarter headfirst into the groove; as long as the tread still gives George Washington a haircut, you're OK.

Here are some tire-test figures for the same car stopping from 70 mph to zero, riding on different tire brands. These are straight-line tests only, so if you were to add in any fancy moves, then the gap between the winners and losers would grow wider.

TEST 1: DRY

1. Michelin Pilot Sport 3	159 feet
2. Continental ContiPremium Contact 2	168 feet
3. Sunew YS112	171 feet
4. Goodyear OptiGrip	175 feet
5. Ovation VI-182	175 feet
6. ArrowSpeed CP661	177 feet

TEST 2: WET

1. Michelin Pilot Sport 3	195 feet
2. Goodyear OptiGrip	204 feet
3. Continental ContiPremium Contact 2	211 feet
4. ArrowSpeed CP661	224 feet
5. Ovation VI-182	249 feet
6. Sunew YS112	270 feet

(Source: MIRA c/o Continental website)

Yes, the tires with shorter stopping distances cost more, but you might as well shoot yourself in the face if it takes you longer than 230 feet to stop.

"When I slap
my clipboard,
I want you
to make an
emergency
stop."

TECHNIQUE

First, the basics. There are many braking styles with subtle differences for varying circumstances. We'll cover all of them, but let's begin with the moment when your driving instructor had that twinkle in his or her eye and said, "When I slap my clipboard, I want you to make an emergency stop."

After weeks of training, finally something exciting was about to happen. The street ahead lay empty bar a few parked cars and an old man checking his mailbox. The seconds elongated, your heart skipped a beat, and you wondered how hard you should actually . . .

Slap!

You lurched for the brake, possibly even remembering to apply the clutch to avoid the embarrassing shudder from the stalling engine, and came to a rest. A box was ticked, and off you went.

The above technique works fine for braking to a stop in a hurry. But I can almost guarantee that you could have stopped faster because the vast majority of drivers never push the brake pedal hard enough in an emergency.

The reasons for this lie in a conceit of technology called ABS and in people like me who preach smooth driving. When it comes to stopping in a hurry, forget smoothness. The objective is to stop safely in the shortest possible distance, and to do that you need to brake as hard as possible in order to make the most of the available grip.

BRAKING WITH ABS

Sixty-five percent of all cars have ABS, and most countries require new models to have it as standard. ABS stands for "antilock braking system," itself a misnomer because the system permits the tires to lock partially during heavy braking. "Locking" is when the brakes ask for so much slowing that a tire stops turning altogether and drags along the road surface.

Road cars typically assign 60 percent of their total braking force to the front tires in order to benefit from their rising grip level as weight shifts forward during braking. A fully locked tire provides no steering at all, and this is the point that ABS was designed to address. ABS works by sensing that one of the wheels has momentarily stopped turning, or is about to, and it reduces the braking force to that individual wheel, allowing it to rotate again and retain enough grip to steer or continue slowing the car.

In simple terms, all you have to do with ABS is press the pedal as hard and fast as you can and keep the pressure on. Ironically, when you do push hard enough, the pedal vibrates, snaps, crackles, and pops underfoot as if you had just stepped on a Rottweiler's tail, which can be disconcerting. So a lot of people take their foot off it and have an accident.

That snapping just indicates that the computer is doing its job by fluctuating the brake pressures up to fifteen times per second. The pulsing will be accompanied by mini lockups and squeaks from the tires as they scrabble between the stages of gripping, stopping, and rotating again. It's a weird sensation, so it's not a bad idea to try it out in the safety of an empty parking lot. Remember to check that nobody's following you.

In summary, ABS filters the effects of panic by preventing major wheel lockups that might otherwise reduce your stopping power and instead allows you to "stomp and steer." Stomp on the brakes as hard as possible, and steer around the terror.

For me that's where the honeymoon with this technology ends, because having ABS on board doesn't mean you can stop shorter than without it. In fact, we were safer as a species before its invention.

In the 1970s, vehicle manufacturers were either producing land yachts like the Buick Sport Wagon and Mercury Colony Park or muscle machines like the Corvette and Charger. These big beauties lumbered around roads like bulls in china shops and squealed through curves at the behest of men with dubious moustaches, bell-bottom trousers, and epic side parts like Ron Burgundy. It didn't escape the attention of software engineers that these mullets were getting bent out of shape whenever their owners were required to take evasive action on slippery roads. Skinny front tires would lock up under braking, and the driver lost all steering control as the fronts plowed along the asphalt, unless the leather loafer relinquished pressure on the center pedal to unlock them again.

Back at work with a fresh set of paisley-patterned underwear, mullet man would regale his colleagues with the story of his brush with death. A healthy focus group would dissect the incident with much tooth sucking on whether the brakes had been applied too heavily at the first touch for the slippery conditions, and how

The pedal vibrates, snaps, crackles, and pops underfoot.

ABS filters the effects of panic by preventing major wheel lockups.

Braking

one should always avoid severe braking in the curve itself. Those stories kept people informed and alive.

Meanwhile, the coneheads designed software that could control the brake pressure without macho intervention, so that in the event of a driver panicking and pressing the brakes too hard, the tires would lock only a little bit and he would retain some steering. At first there was a debatable safety improvement, but any benefit quickly evaporated. People felt safer, so they switched off their brains, followed closer, and started braking later.

The average crashing-in-a-straight-line-with-the-front-wheels-locked experience was replaced by a faster accident farther around the curve, with a higher and more dangerous chance of rolling over. But ABS is here to stay, alas, with more cotton wool in the pipeline.

COMMON MISTAKES

▸ The tires have fundamental limitations. If you exceed these with a combination of speed and heavy braking, ABS won't save you.

▸ ABS-fitted vehicles are not designed to run without it. When ABS develops a fault, the system usually sends too much braking to the rear, which can spin the car. Another fault is false recognition of a skid; the pedal goes solid without slowing you down. Been there, got the T-shirt. If you see an ABS warning light on the dashboard it genuinely needs love from your mechanic.

BRAKING AT THE LIMIT

As the phrase suggests, this means developing the maximum braking force from the tires up until the point where they stop turning. By virtue of the fact that this style avoids locking the tire, it is the fastest way to stop in a vehicle, with or without ABS.

A skilled driver with good observation skills and sensitivity underfoot to manipulate the pedal can apply an infinite range of brake pressure to match the conditions in order to stop the car in the shortest possible distance.

THE LIMIT

Instructions from your foot apply pressure to the braking system, which creates reverse torque at the wheel hubs, causing the tires to slow down just before the car does. When things are going well, the tires will be turning about 15 percent more slowly than your road speed before they begin to lock.

That point is the braking limit, the threshold beyond which the tire starts skidding.

The tires *streeetch*, and their elastic force pulls the speed off the car. As brake pressure increases, there comes a point where the tires begin to slip *before* the wheels actually stop turning and lock up. That point is the braking limit, the threshold beyond which the tire starts skidding.

Your brain detects these minute changes in physical forces through a mix of instinct based on experience of similar conditions, the varying pressure you get from your body pushing into the belts, and your sense of speed. It requires superb familiarity with your car, feel for the conditions, and practice in a safe environment.

The world's finest race-car drivers have an innate sensitivity for the available grip feeding through their backsides and the ability to tread the pedal with surgical precision, prompting the compliment "He was the last of the late brakers," often a reflection in the past tense, since the bravest brakers also tend not to live long. Sometimes it pays to be the guy who brakes first . . .

TECHNIQUE

It always pays to optimize the circumstances for braking. Wherever possible, you aim to brake in as much of a straight line as you can so that the tires can focus on one job only.

Your front tires perform 60 percent of braking, and to help them do this you want to transfer some weight onto them. Here's the trick, and it flies in the face of my philosophy about resting a glass of water on the dashboard: In dry conditions, you initially stab the brake pedal to shift weight forward onto the fronts, and then squeeze until you reach optimal pressure, modulating as required.

The nose dives as weight shifts quickly onto the front tires.

Stab: You dig your foot about an inch into the brake pedal and the nose dives as weight shifts quickly onto the front tires. The more weight bearing down on the fronts, the harder you can squeeze the pedal.

Braking very gently (like the *feel* then *firm* model) doesn't send enough weight to the front tires, and they will never develop their full braking potential regardless of how hard you brake later.

Squeeze: The first touch is immediately followed by a more gradual but firm building of pressure, hopefully based on the good foundations laid by the initial stab. You increase pressure to the point where you can feel the tire almost start locking. In your average road car the foot pressure is around 40 pounds, or the weight of two watermelons.

Modulate: Limit braking is based on constant, instinctive assessments of the available grip. When it's going well, you don't have to adjust the pressure too much once you reach the limit; it's just fine-tuning as you feel how much the tire is biting from one moment to the next. But on bumpy circuits with big surface changes, things can get quite lively.

The final item is bleeding off the brake pressure if you start to enter a curve, known as *trail braking* (see page 93).

8. Stab and Squeeze

Limit Braking

Feel/Firm/Feather

COMMON MISTAKES

▸ Those inexperienced with limit braking will master the stab, but reach a mental block after about 70 percent on the braking scale. Christian Slater was a prime example when he was competing to be *Top Gear*'s fastest "Star in a Reasonably Priced Car." His brain recognized that further braking force would exceed anything he had experienced previously and it refused to utilize the grip created from the generally good weight transfer he was creating. There are only so many times an instructor can shout "Braaake!" before turning into a crow.

▸ This initial stab does not mean slamming the brakes like an ape. The reason this technique separates the men from the boys is because it requires such sensitivity. To achieve this, remember to position your heel on the deck with your knee bent so that it's your foot doing the work, rather than your entire leg delivering enough force to produce diamonds from coal. Overdoing the stab at high speed and locking a tire carries a penalty equal to the potential gain, because a high-speed lockup has an exponentially detrimental effect on your deceleration curve. Some big words there.

Remember that the braking curve in relation to speed takes time, or distance, for the speed to fall sharply. The friction of a stopped tire when the vehicle is traveling at high speed creates an enormous amount of heat, and the molten rubber causes extra slippage. This kind of overload needs to be rectified early on by quickly releasing pressure on the brake and then reapplying.

ROCK, PAPER, SCISSORS

I took a lesson in brake modulation from a fire-breathing V-8 Supercar in Bathurst, Australia. The thundering V-8s boast over 600 brake horsepower (bhp) and achieve the highest road course speeds of any touring car racing series anywhere in the world, NASCAR included. They also run on tires so skinny as to make a lawn mower seem overendowed, not that you would notice beneath their flared wheel arches and aggressive contours.

Every year the V-8s assemble at the foot of a great mountain, Mount Panorama, the passage across which is fraught with more danger than any Tolkien chronicle.

The track climbs vertically from the pits before dropping over a crest so sharp that the wheels spin in fifth gear. You plunge down a way until your tailpipe clanks the asphalt and you veer uphill again to face a wall of asphalt bordered by solid concrete. You stab and squeeze the brake pedal, and the opposing force of gravity stops you dead in your tracks. The waist belt clinches you like a boa constrictor. The car shifts restlessly as the weight of the machine thrusts forward and the tires dig deep into the hill. You float into a banked right-hander with an apex curb high enough to put a van on its roof, shoot out of the curve toward a wall, and breathe again.

Squeeze up to the steel guardrail on the right to approach a sharp, blind left-hand turn. Only a fool would continue accelerating at this point. You floor it and change up a gear. You pass the last chance to brake before the curve, still flat out, squint, and point the car toward the wall on the left before finally applying the brakes, just a soft touch until the car turns, and you can straighten the wheel on the way out.

Braking is king when it comes to rock, paper, scissors. If you need steering, you can't brake hard, because the braking force will hog everything the tires have to offer.

Beyond the wall the road opens to reveal the orange hue of the mountain as the circuit cuts left and rises through a sharp curve known as "the Cutting." The wheels spin over hidden bumps, throwing you from one wall to the next, snaking and sliding as the camber of the road swivels and pitches, the speed ever rising.

An unhelpful thought from Bathurst winner Rick Kelly comes to mind: "It's just uncomfortable. You only have to go off line once and the show's over."

Pluck fourth gear, the rear shakes and wobbles out over the crest toward a left-hand turn and its metal "grate," a deep compression so severe that you have to turn away from it early to prevent the power steering from seizing. Still the throttle is mashed to the floor.

The car loads into the positive camber, a tiny lift, the tires are maxed, sucking you toward the wall until you jam the steering to the left and wait. Silence. The nose creeps to within a side mirror's distance of the wall and lazily peels away. You collect the throttle again and speed over another blind crest.

For me, getting to the top of the mountain is the easy part. It's all downhill from here.

As you aim for the skyline at about 120 mph, the only indication of a curve is the wall that meets the track on the right-hand side. You aim toward it, press the brakes, plunge downhill, and everything goes into denial.

Barely have you dealt with the crisis on the right when the flick-flack, left-right wall weave appears in the windshield. Gravity will punish the slightest transgression as it exaggerates your momentum, and your eardrums will blossom to the tones of the "squeaker," an electronic device fitted inside the helmet, that informs you in no uncertain terms when the tires have locked. As if you didn't know already from the fleshy rumble underfoot and by virtue of barely making the turn.

Each movement of the brake requires the delicate, immediate response of your foot on the pedal, and not the squeeze of a slice of lemon more to ride the limit . . .

Assuming you make it through, you descend into another slow double-whammy left-right called "the Dipper," listening for the squeak and feathering back the pressure by a slice or two before emerging and finally remembering what the gas pedal feels like. One last sharp hairpin and onto Conrod Straight for a well-earned rest while the V-8 winds you up to 185 mph.

The speed isn't such an impressive number until you arrive at the end and have to reduce it. Conveniently, the grass border on the left turns into asphalt just prior to the ridiculously fast, bumpy right-hand turn that drops you down into a relatively slow left-right chicane.

At the last moment you whip the rig across to the steel barrier on the left to benefit from the easier line this affords for sweeping into the right, then hit the brakes like your life depends on it.

Having spent most of my racing life in high-downforce cars that maintained a constant high level of grip throughout the curve, I expected similar support from the V-8, albeit on its skinny-ass tires. As I probed the limits of adhesion during practice, I postponed my braking point until the car was partway through the fast right and encountering the bumps at the crest. This was the prelude to my first, and hopefully last, 185 mph lockup.

At the first touch of the pedal, both front tires seemed to explode. The heat of dragging, locked rubber at 185 mph was phenomenal, and I was trailing more smoke than the Blue Angels. The lock and burn combined with all the inertia of a supersonic oil tanker was too severe for squeezing lemons. I had to fully release

Hit the brakes like your life depends on it.

the brakes, claim a moment of steering, and have another try at braking. And a few more tries after that . . . this was full disaster-recovery mode.

The gravel beds around the chicane were starting to welcome me like an errant golf ball departing the fairway, and my tires, now freshly minted million-degree quarters, were not cutting the mustard at all.

The wall on the right side looked uninviting, but the gravel looked thin on the far left, so I used my Xbox training to the full by giving up on the brake and straight-lining the whole deal at about 130. It was bumpier than on screen, but I made it.

I brought the car back to the pits, and the smoldering tires were removed and inspected by my old friend and crew chief Joe Bremner. His thatch was even thinner on top after a few extra seasons coping with the likes of me. He inspected the tires with their fist-sized holes and gurgled like Yogi Bear, "Havin' fun out there, are we? Fresh set for Mr. Collins."

Joe brought me a data sheet with an overlay of my speeds and braking inputs versus those of Rick Kelly, who was a bit of a legend down under. Old Rick had beaten me at my own game.

He treated the bumpy crest of the curve like a slippery surface and just lifted off the throttle to let his engine braking slowly transfer some weight to the front end. After the turn, as the car settled into the slope, he braked softly for a microsecond to let the tires soak up the load and then dropped anchor. The subtle loading made all the difference, and I never had a problem there again.

Bathurst demonstrates the full range of braking characteristics from the good to the bad and the ugly. The principles enshrined are thus:

- The brakes are king of the rock, paper, scissors game, so you try to brake in as straight a line as possible.
- In high-grip situations, you attain best braking using the stab-and-squeeze model.
- In low-grip situations (downhill, cresting, slippery surfaces), you dial back the stab and gently apply the brake.
- A locked tire at high speed should always be avoided and requires urgent redress.
- A locked tire at low speed is less of a problem and can usually be addressed by modulating foot pressure by a slice or two.

At the Silverstone driving school we used to compete to see who could stop shortest in an emergency from 40 mph. After a few tries we were all level because everyone dialed in to the available grip and stopped using limit braking. Prior to that there was a big divergence.

The guys who reacted instantly when the chief instructor yelled, "ALIENS!" locked up and screeched to a messy halt.

The clever ones who spent a second easing into the pedal and didn't lock up actually took longer to stop. Their advantage in braking performance was slighter at low speed, where a locked tire loses only 15 percent of its stopping power, and not enough to compensate for their initial delay.

I think I've made it clear that you want to avoid locking up, but when you need to stop in an emergency it is critical that you act quickly. Just remember that when the tires are locked you have absolutely no steering (also see Pulse Braking in Winter Driving on page 235).

TRAIL BRAKING

Trail braking in its pure form is a performance-driving technique for posting lap times. It allows you to brake later by extending the final phase of braking into the initial part of the curve itself. Limit braking wipes most of the speed off in a straight line, then you bleed off the pressure as you start turning the steering wheel. You have to reduce brake pressure to compensate for the tires as they juggle two jobs at once; otherwise you lose the ability to steer, or brake, or both!

For everyday driving, the benefit of overlapping a hint of braking as you turn into a curve is that the weight stays put and you get a smoother flow into the curve. It feels natural.

LEFT-FOOT BRAKING

Certain race cars with extreme setups require you to left-foot brake. In NASCAR, for example, the off-center axle has to be kept under constant acceleration to stop it from driving in the wrong direction. You continue to accelerate with your right foot while braking with your left foot to keep it stable. This specialized kind of oval racing is the only environment where I left-foot brake. Everywhere else, I always stick to the right foot.

On the racetrack, some drivers use left-foot braking and some don't, without any discernible performance advantage either way. At Le Mans a team of left-foot brakers would lose. The combined braking and accelerating burns a lot more fuel and chews up brake pads, so they would have to make an extra fuel stop and replace the pads more often.

Three-time British touring car champion Matt Neal races a front-wheel-drive car for a living and says, "It's gimmicky, you hear people overdoing it and the brake temps go insane, but really the benefits are neither here nor there. I'd never use it on the road."

Even in rallying, the role of left-foot braking has changed since the turbo era, when drivers used it to keep the revs up and work around problems in the suspension. These days it's more used for fine-tuning the weight around the apex of a curve where the car pivots most.

Left-foot braking on the road is as useful as an ashtray on a motorcycle, and don't let anybody tell you different. If you want to train your left foot usefully, keep smooth clutching. Transferring it to the brake pedal will only result in a clumsy push followed by a mouthful of steering wheel. It takes a lot of practice to prove otherwise.

Left-foot braking on the road is as useful as an ashtray on a motorcycle.

2.7 CURVES: THE ART OF TURNING A CORNER

"Man, this baby must corner like it's on rails."

—Julia Roberts, *Pretty Woman*

*It's time
for big-boy
pants.*

We've covered stopping, steering, and going—which, in that order, is effectively tackling a curve or turning a corner. It's time for big-boy pants.

The biggest misconception about race-car drivers is that our job involves piling through curves as fast as humanly possible. It doesn't. I'm not sure many of my passengers would have agreed when I took them for a ride as The Stig, but turning is about compromising. Some people find that harder to accept than others.

"Hammerrr!"

This is not the mating call of the lesser-spotted Stigasaurus, rather the piston-rattling caw of a primate better known as Jeremy Clarksonzilla. Jezza makes every car he climbs aboard look small, and they positively shiver when he turns the key.

Despite his sins as a car surgeon, Jeremy has quite a natural feel for the amount of grip a car has through a corner and regularly consumes it from start to finish. Flying in formation with him requires patience, lots of patience, and admitting to yourself that he can drive around the corner a little bit faster than you.

"I beat Steve Soper once, y'know," he remarked as we climbed aboard a pair of evenly matched sports cars.

Unaware until then that Jeremy had defeated a world-class touring car champion, I steeled myself as he described the manner in which he dispatched not just Soper but all manner of racing pros during a time attack around Silverstone's Grand Prix circuit.

"Soper was in tears," he continued. "He simply couldn't believe that some overweight journalist could possibly have beaten him. He drove his nuts off for the rest of the afternoon trying to clip my time, but he couldn't."

"How did you manage it?" I asked, kind of knowing the answer.

"I cheated, of course."

So off we went for a choreographed race and some tandem drifting around our favorite turns at the *Top Gear* track.

When you run super close to another vehicle, you learn to read its body language and to anticipate where it's going so that you avoid getting tangled up. From behind it's easy because you can gauge the attitude of the car in front by how much the front wheels are turning in the bend. If the fronts seem fairly straight inside the wheel arches, it means the car in front is oversteering as the rear tires lose traction, but if the front wheels are visibly turning a lot, it means they are resisting and beginning to understeer.

Even when I was ahead of Jeremy, I noticed his front tires twisting outside of the bodywork and could practically hear him swearing above the tire squeal. We pulled to a halt.

"You're too *fucking* slow into Chicago," he advised. (The Chicago corner is an increasing radius corner that should be taken at low to medium speeds.)

"No I'm—"

"*Yes,* you *are.* And it's making this car understeer like a bloody pig."

I studied the outside of his front tires, which admittedly were more grained than a photo of Jordan without touch-up. We swapped cars, and Jeremy's signature was clearly stamped all over the thousand-degree rubber-cum-molasses. Much to his dismay, I proceeded to enter the curves even more slowly to allow the molten tires to recover and effect a perfectly balletic flying exit. I tried explaining the racing credo of "slow in, fast out," but the resulting conversation would make a sailor blush. If you want to hear my side of the story, please read on.

VIEWING THE CURVE

In its simplest form, there are three overlapping phases of taking a curve: braking, turning, and accelerating.

To plan these phases, you must make a visual assessment of the approaching bend to gauge the sharpness and direction of the curve, then plan the appropriate speed and line for dispatching it.

Braking, turning, and accelerating.

You continuously update your view of the corner, road surface, and situation as you approach the braking zone. You squeeze the brakes and release pressure as you turn in, all the time looking through the corner to chase the vanishing point.

The vanishing point is the farthest point of the road ahead that you can see and is a good rule of thumb for matching your speed to the curvature. When your viewpoint is extending through a corner at the same rate as your speed, it means the corner is opening with you and matching your speed. If the vanishing point stops moving, it means that the corner is tightening up and you're going too fast.

On the track we say that the next corner begins before the last one finishes. In other words, we keep one eye permanently on the horizon, so we can plan the next turn well in advance and ensure that we are driving into clear space. Anticipation is another way we "slow down time."

RHYTHM

Taking a corner well depends on a number of factors, but these are all governed by a single principle: rhythm. Once you get a handle on the right way to position yourself for a corner, it becomes a way of life.

Bad positioning will make the car inherently unstable because it will be fighting you all the time and your erstwhile passengers will seek less dangerous pastimes elsewhere.

Timing the moves, swinging the controls, and seeing the situation develop ahead of time closely resembles some of our finest moments on the dance floor. And because there will be less commotion with the machine, driving it requires less energy, and you can focus farther ahead.

Race-car drivers use the rhythm of a circuit to develop a system that guides them from one corner to the next. We call that system the *racing line*, and although every driver has subtle preferences according to his feel for the beat, it is a universal language for describing the way to maximize a machine's stability through a curve.

9. Traction Circle

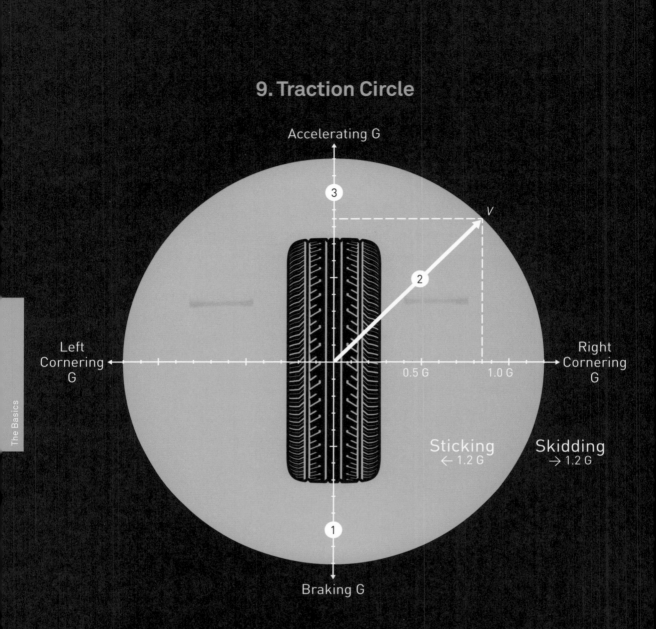

When a tire is strained beyond the orange limit, it starts skidding and you'll need to skip to Section 4 to deal with the mess.

The tire can generate a maximum force of 1.2G under braking or during turning—*but it cannot achieve 1.2G of peak braking and 1.2G of peak turning at the same time.*

When a tire contends with lateral turning forces as well as longitudinal braking or acceleration forces, it develops less grip for each task than when handling them independently. Line 2 describes the combined forces of a vehicle accelerating while turning right. The resulting vector V this creates has less grip on the scale as indicated by the dotted lines.

Although we view the tire's performance as a circle, the reality is that the longitudinal forces of braking and accelerating are the dominant players. If you overcook either of them during a turn, you start falling off the road.

THE PHYSICS OF TURNING A CORNER:
THE TIRE VS. ISAAC NEWTON

Sir Isaac Newton's Third Law of Motion asserted that no object could develop a force greater than that being applied to it. But by stretching in two directions (lengthwise *as well as* laterally) when introduced to a corner, the modern tire develops forces the *combined* value of which can exceed the loads being applied to it. Clever. However, while celebrating its capacity to multitask, one shouldn't forget that it can never do two jobs as well as it can do one. We therefore separate the process of taking a curve into three phases:

1. Best braking takes place in a straight line, because weight transfers to the front tires, which aids braking and initial turning power.
2. Best turning takes place with no braking or throttle. You reduce braking as you start steering. The body of the car will lean over; the weight transfers to the outside tires, creating turning power.
3. Turning power reduces as acceleration begins. Best acceleration happens in a straight line.

Pursuing this sequence is a whole lot more reliable, and comfortable, than dancing on the pedals.

Race-car drivers are known for being prima donnas with custard for brains and heavy right feet. But in 1958 one of the brethren, an F1 driver named Piero Taruffi, became momentarily possessed by some kind of Einsteinian spirit. His eyes rolled inside their sockets like the dials of a slot machine, and he spat out an equation for predicting the maximum speed of a car through any given curve—$F=mv^2/r$— then he skipped back to the swimming pool and demanded more sunscreen.

When you're taking a curve, your car's tires have four potential enemies, excluding your erratic enthusiasm: the nature of the road surface, the vehicle's weight, your *speed*, and the tightness of the bend.

In true game show host style, I will not reveal which of these vital elements is missing from brother Taruffi's equation until later on. For now, just consider that your tires have to create an equal or greater amount of grip than the centrifugal force—*F*—of cornering.

Your car's tires have four potential enemies.

WEIGHT: m

The weight of the car rounding an arc creates a centrifugal force, just like spinning a yo-yo around the end of a string. As any yo-yo champion will tell you, it doesn't pay to rely on a heavier yo-yo body for yo-yoing *or* cornering because the *heavier* the yo-yo, the greater the force trying to shear it away from the string and off into the neighbor's garden.

When you swing through a corner, the centrifugal force wants to throw the car off the road in the same way, but it meets resistance from your tires, which cling stubbornly to the road surface. If you were to let go of the steering wheel the car would instantly go straight, because the only things forcing it to turn are the front tires. The heavier the car and the more passengers you carry, the more work the tires have to do.

SPEED: v^2

Alarmingly, the effect of your speed on cornering force is exponential. In the turning equation, your weight is multiplied by the *square* of your speed!

BEND: r

In a perfectly planed curve, the apex is exactly halfway through the turn. On the opposite page, the example at the top shows a theoretically perfect radius (driving line) which with its maximum radius length offers the greatest cornering potential as far as equations are concerned.

In the example opposite, a driver could take this curve at a higher constant speed of 55.2456784 mph using line J by driving like Jezza. However, his tires would have spent all of their potential grip in the process, leaving nothing with which to accelerate onto the straight that follows. The time advantage you gain by traveling faster down the straights significantly outweighs any short-term gains from screeching through the bends. So although it's been fascinating to swallow a geometry book, you'll be glad to know that taking a curve is a lot more artful than driving by numbers.

10. Turning

Perfect Geometric Driving Line (as used by Jezza)

THE RACING LINE

The racing line is not geometrically perfect. It can best be described as a variable radius, because it sacrifices curve entry in favor of expanding the space available for the exit. You spend a little more time setting up for the curve by turning in a hint later, clipping the apex slightly farther around the curve, and reaping the benefits as you depart.

SLOW IN, FAST OUT

This means taking control of the biggest part of the equation—speed—by braking early so that you have enough grip in the middle of the curve to make a clean get-away. The tighter the turn, the harder the tires have to work until they reach their limit, so you brake earlier and harder to give them the stability they need at the apex for when you start to accelerate.

CUTTING CORNERS

When you look at a curve you might think that there's nothing to it in terms of choosing the direction you follow. But by making subtle adjustments, you can position the car so that it follows a gentler path.

Race-car drivers cut curves to shorten the distance their machines have to travel and increase the radius of their turn. They use the full width of the track because there's nothing coming the other way and thereby have the maximum possible amount of grip at their disposal. On a road with two-way traffic this is a dangerous and lazy move, and not what I'm suggesting at all.

Using the available space between the roadside and the white line, you can shape the curvature to your benefit. By turning in from a wider position, accurately cutting in toward the center of the corner, and gradually releasing the steering as you leave, you can potentially drive around it faster, or in safety terms will have more grip in hand to tackle irregularities in the road surface. A small uplift in accuracy provides a big benefit to the machine.

When I raced at Charlotte Motor Speedway in a NASCAR support race, the track conditions would change by the hour depending on the temperature. During the daytime I found that the fastest way around the kidney-shaped oval was to enter the two flat-out turns by turning in quite late, missing the apex by a few feet, and straight-lining the exit. However, at night, when the temperature dropped, the car became unstable and would "walk" toward the wall on my right.

"Get your ass down on that white line," came a voice from the Rodeo over the radio. It was my first night outing on an oval so I obeyed, ran all the way down to the white border, and listened to the motor perk up on the way out. Longer radius. Duh.

The voice belonged to the NASCAR legend who was Dick Trickle, winner of basically every race around a circle and infamous for smoking during the extended caution periods while the officials scraped the wreckage off the floor.

The tighter the turn, the harder the tires have to work.

This is a dangerous and lazy move.

BENEFITS OF "LATE APEXING"

Delaying your turn-in gives you a truer perspective of the curve. You have to make a tighter arc at the beginning, which forces you to reduce speed early, and gives the car (and you) room to breathe on the exit, and a straighter line for acceleration.

HOT TIPS

▸ The added bonus of the racing line is the enhanced viewpoint for seeing through the bend. You have a clearer picture of approaching traffic, for gauging the severity of the curve and planning ahead.

▸ To keep ahead of the game, you always keep a little margin in hand, especially on unfamiliar roads. Keeping your chin up and anticipating the road all the way should keep you out of the ditch.

PREMATURE EJECTION

If you crash out of a curve, in most cases it'll be because you accelerated and "apexed" too early. People often lament that their car "wouldn't make the turn" or "ran out of road."

Turning into a curve early is a common mistake; it feels great at first because it doesn't require as much turning force and the car feels stable because you have unwittingly created a gentle radius. That good feeling lures you into your second mistake: accelerating prematurely. If your speed increases, the radius of your arc has to get bigger too. Your life has been reduced to an equation.

Sadly, as the exit approaches you'll be required to do the exact opposite—to perform a second tight-radius turn in order to avoid the oncoming hedge, wall, tree, or fireball. Unless your speed reduces miraculously, you will be taking in some real estate.

That good feeling lures you into your second mistake.

11. The Tire vs. Isaac Newton

The Right Way

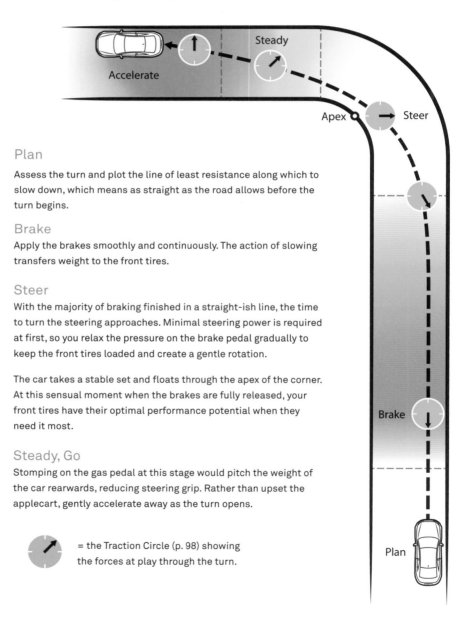

Plan

Assess the turn and plot the line of least resistance along which to slow down, which means as straight as the road allows before the turn begins.

Brake

Apply the brakes smoothly and continuously. The action of slowing transfers weight to the front tires.

Steer

With the majority of braking finished in a straight-ish line, the time to turn the steering approaches. Minimal steering power is required at first, so you relax the pressure on the brake pedal gradually to keep the front tires loaded and create a gentle rotation.

The car takes a stable set and floats through the apex of the corner. At this sensual moment when the brakes are fully released, your front tires have their optimal performance potential when they need it most.

Steady, Go

Stomping on the gas pedal at this stage would pitch the weight of the car rearwards, reducing steering grip. Rather than upset the applecart, gently accelerate away as the turn opens.

= the Traction Circle (p. 98) showing the forces at play through the turn.

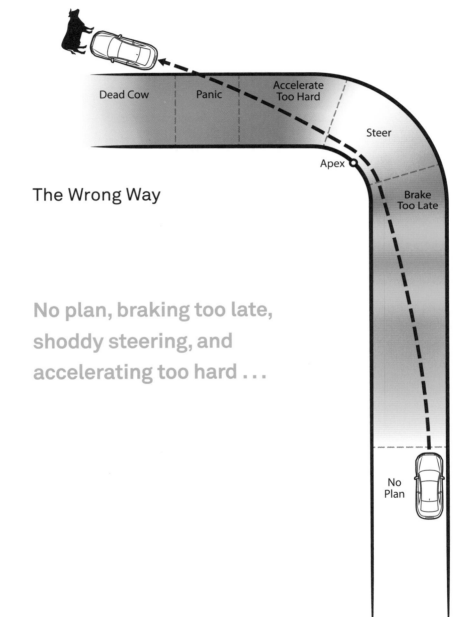

Dead Cow | Panic | Accelerate Too Hard

Steer

Apex

Brake Too Late

No Plan

The Wrong Way

No plan, braking too late, shoddy steering, and accelerating too hard . . .

THE REAL WORLD

Over the years I have noticed that curves, with the exception of the ones on PlayStation, don't have dotted lines on them showing you "the line." And you'll never need them to. Once you dial into the notion of accurately working an apex and pushing your gaze farther toward the exit of the turn, it becomes second nature.

Below are some garden-variety types of curves that should help you to identify what you're dealing with.

TYPES OF CURVES

An *increasing radius curve* is the easiest to handle because it naturally opens up on the exit.

But its evil twin brother, the *decreasing radius curve*, tightens up when you least expect it on the way out of the curve and wants to invite you to a party in the woods all alone. Train your eye to notice when the curve is closing you down.

The *double apex* at first sight might look like a long-radius arc. The easy mistake is to presume the curve is opening and accelerate after the first clipping point and then wish you hadn't. On closer inspection, the curve has two clipping points, and the last one always has priority.

Hairpins: On a track it's the slow turns like these that often cost people the most time, because this is when the car is most reactive to braking and acceleration in lower gears. Both can quickly overload the tires, and a little sympathy goes a long way, especially in the Alps. The common mistake is to rush into the curve too quickly or start accelerating too soon. By toeing the centerline, you take a fraction longer to slow the car and have a straighter, easier ride out.

Connecting curve: When one curve is immediately followed by another one. This is where it starts getting interesting. Rural roads are nearly always connected, meaning that the exit of one flows right into the next. Rather like the double apex curve, if you're too greedy or not paying attention during the first part, then you suffer in part two.

By keeping some margin in hand through the middle of the curve, you automatically set yourself up for anything that follows, be it the next turn, a clump of traffic, or that moose we keep reading about in the news that likes dancing with cars. Anybody taking the first part of the curve anywhere near 100 percent of the tires' capability could be in for a nasty surprise farther down the road.

But its evil twin brother, the decreasing radius curve, tightens up when you least expect it.

12. Curve Types

Increasing Radius Curve

Decreasing Radius
Curve

Double Apex

Hairpin Turn

Connecting/
Linked Curve

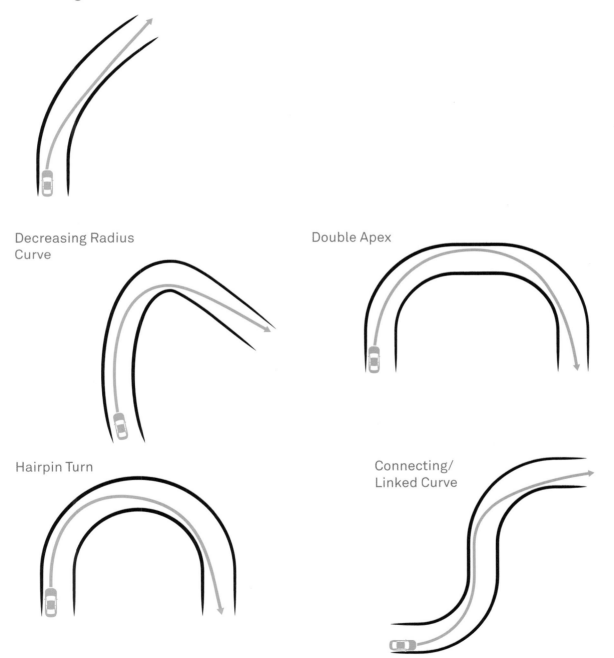

THE ROAD SURFACE
(THE MISSING LINK FROM TARUFFI'S EQUATION)

No curve is ever the same twice, and no equation can predict the *ever-changing* condition of the road surface. It's up to you to become the connoisseur, and thankfully this doesn't involve slipping your tongue into asphalt.

The primary factors that determine the grip of the road surface are: type, temperature, weather, incline, camber, and foreign bodies.

TYPE

The basic rule with asphalt is that the rougher the surface, the better the grip, because it gives the tires something to bite on. Conversely, the smoother or more worn it becomes, the less grip it has. Visually, when you notice a sheen on the surface, especially in warmer months, you can expect reduced grip. The problem is compounded when it rains.

Anti-skid surfaces come in a variety of colors and designs: red, sand, chevrons. They provide extra grip in hot spots, typically braking areas. They are expensive, so as they wear away they become bumpy, polished, and less supportive.

Concrete is the noisy stuff that drives you mad. It has a decent grip when it's dry, but beware of freezing water in colder temperatures and hydroplaning in heavy rain (see Tires in Rain on page 218). It is slippery when wet. In fact, it's slippery most of the time.

Bumps and potholes in the road shift the weight bearing down on your tires. Your suspension does its best to iron this out, but bumps nevertheless reduce road holding and makes the curves less predictable. As long as you're delicate with the wheel as you go through them, then there's no drama.

Some drivers swerve around potholes as if they contain anthrax, and a friend of mine destroyed his car doing this by hitting something far more solid instead. Common sense prevails.

Manhole covers and heavily painted lines can be slippery in the rain. Raised covers abound in the US, and the extra jolt to jelly-like suspension can put you in freefall for a second or two if you're not careful.

The rougher the surface, the better the grip.

The extra jolt to jelly-like suspension can put you in freefall.

Rough

Macro-smooth and micro-rough
road surface

Macro-rough and micro-rough
road surface

Smooth

Rough

Macro-smooth and micro-smooth
road surface

Macro-rough and micro-smooth
road surface

Smooth

Curves

Grip Levels

Effect of road surface variations on tire grip

	Grip Level %	
Dry surfaces	75–100	
Damp surfaces Macro- and micro-rough surfaces	58	
Wet surface Macro- and micro-rough surfaces Macro- and micro-smooth surfaces	50 16	
Snow	12	
Ice	4–8	

TEMPERATURE

Anything below 41 degrees affects the way your tires generate grip. The colder they are, the harder they become and the less reliable at gluing themselves to the particles on the road. Modern cars often display the outside temperature on the dashboard for this reason.

WEATHER

Rain cuts down braking and accelerating grip by a third, but it reduces cornering potential by *half* with a good tire. If you're driving on cheap rubber you could lose 75 percent of your grip. I'm not making it up!

Snow and ice coat the asphalt with an entirely new surface with further reduced grip. The right tire compounds really walk the walk when it comes to bite.

INCLINE

What goes up . . .

When you drive up a hill, the angle at which the tires meet the surface has the effect of pushing them into the road much harder than normal, providing more grip.

. . . must come down.

This wonderful boost in grip lasts only until the moment that the gradient reduces and the car "goes light." If you crest the brow of a hill at speed, all manner of weird sensations travel through the car as the forces of gravity affecting it flip into reverse.

HOT TIPS ▸ When cresting, keep the steering as straight as possible, no sudden movements.

When you travel downhill, everything works against you, with the exception of acceleration. Your gutless, good-for-nothing car will surge forth like a Lamborghini. Before you know it, you're experimenting with physics.

Gravity, the merciless overlord, accentuates the forces of inertia trying to push the car wide of the mark, and you need to throw a parachute to get the thing to stop. That's why everybody crashes on the way down hills. It's another reason to like engine braking because not only does it assist your brakes, the noise of the engine reminds you that you're speeding up.

CAMBER

The camber of the road is the level to which it slopes left and right on your horizontal plane.

Positive camber, the helpful kind that squashes your rump into the chair, absorbs some of the centrifugal force of rounding a curve and uses it to press the tires significantly harder into the deck, producing more grip. Negative or "off" camber, does exactly the opposite: it steals your turning ability and spills drinks from the cup holder. It pays to spot the difference early since failing to notice the latter can really bite you in the bum, especially when the road is bumpy.

HOT TIPS

▸ Most roads are crowned in the center to allow for drainage, which means that your average *American* road offers positive camber helping you into right-hand curves, and negative camber working against you in left-handers.

▸ Satan has a hand in shaping certain rural roads. He cleverly hides off-camber curves behind hills to lure you into his low-grip trap and he loads a sequence of innocent-looking bends with hidden bumps to throw the suspension skyward and spit you off the road.

Satan has a hand in shaping certain rural roads.

13. Road Camber

Curb   Crown   Curb

Rubber and dust accumulate on the outside bends
to form what are known as "marbles"—and they
are just as slippery underfoot.

FOREIGN BODIES

Oil, mud, wet leaves, gravel, dust, and sand can reduce the quality of the surface almost as much as ice. Observation techniques are vital to see these obstacles coming.

BIG BAILADEROS

The Dark Lord left his mark in Tenerife on the cliff road from the town of Los Bailaderos. It tracks the twisting coastline like a demented Scalextric circuit, relentlessly rising and falling around the crumbling mountain. Car-sized boulders continuously fall off the mountain and explode into the road, so it was finally closed to the public a few years ago. The carcass of road that remains is littered with all manner of dents and hasty repairs, giving it a sort of pummeled surface-of-the-moon look. But the views were "to die for," so they opened the road for us to film the opening sequence for *Fast and Furious 6*.

Fast 6 was like the *Jurassic Park* of car movies, and the primordial beasts at our disposal could shake the landscape with the roar of nearly 100,000 horsepower.

About two hundred cars met their maker during filming, mostly at the hands of the battle tank, which turned cars into confetti. During testing at the ever-gray Chobham proving ground in Surrey, we observed the effect of a glancing blow from the tank tracks on a small hatchback. The only recognizable component we could pick from the tank's teeth was a masticated steering column. Note to self: You touch the tank, you die.

Our skeleton stunt crew of Brits came under the charge of Greg Powell, son of the actor, stuntman, and boxer Nosher, whose legendary right hook must have passed onto Greg's right foot, because we never saw the man but for the plume of smoke from his cigar whenever he tore off in a motor.

Joining our gang was the sun-kissed crew from California, who greeted our weather as enthusiastically as a dose of herpes. Their rap sheet read like a Hollywood roll of honor, from the original *Dukes of Hazzard* to almost everything else since. Everyone felt a lot more comfortable when we shifted from rain-soaked Cold War airfields to the sunbaked coast of Tenerife.

We measured the route and worked out that you could make two cars fit side by side all the way around—just. Looks-wise, the black Dodge Challenger SRT that I was driving had one up on the Nissan GT-R running alongside it, and with 470 bhp under my right foot it packed plenty of muscle. Mark Higgins, my compadre for this

The Jurassic Park of car movies.

tandem mission, was wetting his lips with a mixture of excitement and dismay about the Nissan. "Too much grip."

With a helicopter chattering overhead recording every ounce of adrenaline for the camera, we set off around the mountain at a speed that was guaranteed to put the Challenger's comfortable suspension to the test.

At the midway point we emerged from an underpass before plunging downhill into a long, long left-hander that was slightly off-camber, and with a tightening radius. The Challenger up until this point had been wagging its tail delightedly at my inputs, and the opportunity to punch a spectacular high-speed drift for the camera beckoned.

On the run downhill I slipped past Mark, and with less weight on the molten rear tires, it was easier to flick the old gal sideways. I pitched into an arc that matched the curve as it began to develop, maxed the throttle, and everything felt great as the nose slipped past the cliffside barrier. Then something gray loomed into my peripheral, like a scene from a *Jaws* movie, as a patch of asphalt rose up from the road by nearly a foot.

The Challenger made a real meal of this, and its weight lurched everywhere but onto the tires. I had to contend with the tightening radius of the bend and worsening camber as I slid outside toward the angry mountain. I just about had it under control, when the outer bead of my rear right tire popped down into a drainage gulley and pulled the tail wider—and into a freshly fallen . . . *boulder.*

Mark had the bird's-eye view that afforded him a sense of humor.

"Coorrrrrrr, nearly 'ad that," he chortled, before consoling with: "Looked mega." My thoughts precisely. It was only a flesh wound, but the car was out of the picture. And I think it belonged to the producer.

That ordeal might sound like an unlikely extreme, but it demonstrates how the pendulum effect over bumps can combine with bad camber to dictate your destiny. Even at much lower speeds, innocuous-looking features like drains and roadside verges can quickly pull you into trouble, which is why accuracy with the steering is vital.

SUMMARY

The road surface is ever-changing, which is one of the things I love most about driving. As much as I admire its majesty, I always observe the revolving patchwork with a cynical glare.

Then something gray loomed into my peripheral, like a scene from a Jaws movie.

THE OPEN ROAD

3.1 AVOIDING ACCIDENTS

Now that you've spent some quality time with the beast and flung it around a few corners to warm up, let's take it out on the open road.

It's time to work and play well with others.

The one thing we haven't talked about yet, of course, is other cars and the dangers that come with them. It's time to work and play well with others.

STATE BY STATE

Where you live has everything to do with the daily challenges of the road. In order of risk factor, freeways are the safest places to drive followed by urban areas. Despite the fact that less than a fifth of Americans live in rural areas, more than half of fatal accidents occur there. The injuries you sustain are compounded by the remoteness of the area because it takes longer for emergency services to reach you.

That's why Montana holds the top spot for the most dangerous place to drive, with 98 percent of fatal accidents taking place on twisty country roads or unrestricted highways. Conversely, places like Massachusetts and Washington, DC, with mostly urban populations, had next to none. With their traffic, they probably never got past second gear.

But when it comes to fender benders, nobody does it better than the big cities. So before you squeeze out of the driveway and head into the urban sprawl, it's worth getting to know the width of your car and the design nuances by which you can judge your positioning. It could save some visits to the paint shop further down the line, and once we've mastered your sense of girth we can tackle the great outdoors.

MIND THE GAP

My driving instructor, Dave Clarke, was a diamond in the rough, and he taught me something that up to that point had had no meaning in my life: patience. Dave's Marlboro-hushed voice coached me in how to set off in a gear without ever touching the throttle, a simple lesson in sensitivity that I've never forgotten. And he egged me on when it was time to "Give it some rice, boy."

His advice on parallel parking was equally acute. He would get me to line up alongside the car in front of the space I wanted, reverse back until my head was level with the rear wheel of the other car and then turn into the space. He had me look over my shoulder and use the point where the rear wiper fixed to the windshield like a rifle scope to aim for the center of the empty space, then straighten the wheel, switch to the side mirror, and line up with the curb as I drove in. A hole-in-one every time.

Fixed features inside the car, such as the A and B pillars to the front and sides of the driver's line of sight, are a burden in the sense that they create blind spots, but they are useful when it comes to formation flying as you observe the movement of other vehicles relative to yourself, and for gauging distances to objects outside of your bubble.

In NASCAR, where you have over forty racers fighting wheel to wheel for a short stretch of asphalt, the drivers regularly annihilate their machines across the track whenever they misjudge their length or width. Every inch of asphalt counts when you're gliding past a concrete wall at 180 mph in a machine that handles and generally feels like a high-speed clothes dryer.

Brushing the wall is deemed acceptable up to the point that they classify as a "sticker rub," a streak of skin-deep scratches that would reduce you to tears if it were your personal ride, but a sign of accuracy in speed world.

Working through the pack of swarming racers is different gravy. On an oval circuit, everybody is slithering around on tires that are stretching physical boundaries, and a little kiss can turn into a catastrophe. You have to run exceptionally close to one another to benefit from the aerodynamic slipstream—so close, in fact, that your stomach shakes from the throb of the engine in the car alongside you, and the windshield is filled with the bouncing tail of the one in front, pressure-spraying your world with debris and exhaust fumes.

To prepare for this type of excitement I used to enlist my main man Vinny, who would stand patiently at different points around the car in the pit lane, at a top speed of 0 mph. It gave me the opportunity to stare directly at his proximity to the car at different points and acclimatize to that distance, then look ahead as if I were driving, and back to Vinny again.

A few of my competitors would snigger, but it was worth it. A dozen or so laps into one race at Rockingham Motor Speedway, I entered Turn Two at 160 mph and the whole track was blocked by crashed cars. There was a tiny space between one yellow car and the wall, and everyone ahead of me who tried to make it through was stonking into the concrete. I aimed my front left wheel arch on the tail of the stopped car, rather than focusing on the wall, held on to that view all the way, and cleared it.

Whenever I get in a new car I do the same thing. I never asked Clarkson to help because the temptation to run him over would have been overwhelming. If there's nobody around, you can do the same thing with a big cardboard box and practice driving up to it, or line it up alongside to test your width.

A common fault people develop is to continuously work the wheel for no reason and weave in and out of gaps between parked cars, simply because they failed to fix a course and stick to it. Aiming for a point in the distance makes it much easier to follow a smooth groove, and when you do find a challenging pinch, just kill the speed and allow yourself the time to handle it properly.

DEATH BY SLOW MOTION

As you drive into busy urban areas, it's time to start thinking about how to avoid taking out all those cyclists and pedestrians who are going to start running out in front of you. Who are these people? The very young and very old are most likely to be hit and least likely to survive—but just as dangerous are the rising numbers of zombies patrolling the pavement wearing iTuned earmuffs to drown any chance of hearing your approach. And that's before we even get to the drunks tripping over the curb in the evenings and on weekends . . .

Speed, pure and simple.

We'll look at some of the key triggers for accidents shortly, but I want to start by talking about speed, pure and simple. Doing 45 mph in a 30 stretch increases your chance of an accident by . . . twenty times! That's more risk than traveling the whole way from LA to Las Vegas at 100. Exceeding the speed limit in these areas by just a few miles per hour can mean the difference between life and death. It's all physics and biology.

Experts in the latter are Hollywood stuntmen like Batman's stunt double, Bobby Holland, who gets run over for a living. "Car knockdowns," he calls them.

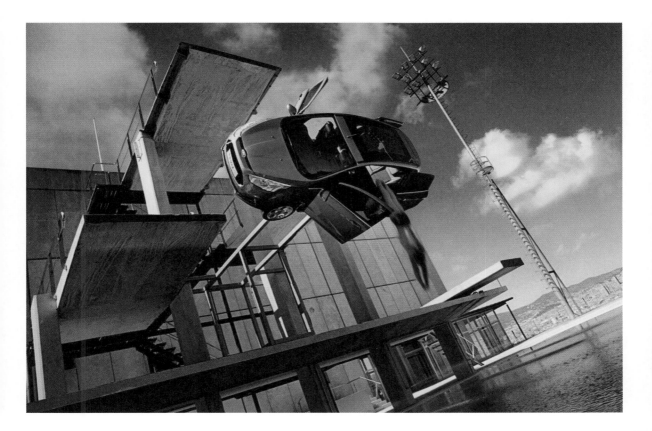

When Bobby's not diving over them, he's diving through them (Ford B-MAX commercial).

"I'm just glad I'm a dude," he explains while strapping a kneepad over the top of his gel-cushioned shorts. "The stunt women are worst off because they usually end up doubling some glamorous starlet in high heels and a miniskirt, so they can't pad up."

Bobby is built like a brick outhouse anyway, but by the time he's finished padding up he looks more like a medieval knight than your average pedestrian. His upper body is contained within another layer of neoprene, and all his pointy bits, like elbows and ankles, are encased in impact-resistant plastic. Once Bobby's final layer of clothing goes over the top, he is ready for action.

This week Bobby is playing the part of Joe Public who drops his mobile phone while crossing the street and gets run over when he doubles back in front of a taxi. Bobby eyes up the cab's hood and sucks his teeth.

"Yeah, gonna be tricky, this one, because I'll probably collect the windshield. What I really want is to get flicked over the top."

His main concern, however, is the taxi's speed.

"We never, ever do more than twenty miles an hour. Any more than that and you're guaranteed a trip to ER for sure."

The ideal speed for being hit by a car, he explains, is more like 15 to 18 mph. Bobby is a trained gymnast, is warmed up, and knows the car is coming at him. As the vehicle rolls in, Bobby starts crossing the street on cue, turns, and just as the car reaches his legs, slams himself into the hood by imperceptibly tucking his legs up at the last moment. He cartwheels over the roof and lands hard on the asphalt. And doesn't move.

A real paramedic rushes in like an Olympic sprinter.

"Get off the set you idiot, he's just *playing* dead!"

Bobby is fine.

The most dangerous US cities for pedestrians are Atlanta, Miami, and Tampa. The good news is that pedestrian fatalities like this are the easiest to prevent. As we already know from the section on braking, a car traveling at 30 mph can stop almost twice as fast as one doing 40. It adds seconds to a short leg across town, but it might save a life.

NOT NOW, I'M HAVING AN ACCIDENT

> *"I've gotten better now that I don't have to concentrate so much on driving properly."*
> —Freshly licensed driver

So, pedestrians aside, what are the things that we should be looking out for on the open road? Before we do that, let's dispel a myth. They say that most accident *claims* occur within five minutes of home, which is hardly surprising when most journeys start and finish there. Anecdotally, there's an element of truth that concentration might reduce as you near home. Oops, I drove into my house again.

Oops, I drove into my house again.

In reality, an insurer judges your risk profile by your zip code because it is a convenient method of gauging guilt by association: Their spreadsheet looks at a national claim database broken down by zip code and cross-referenced by credit rating. People with bad credit tend to claim more, so if you're unfortunate enough to live in an area where people tap their insurance in order to fund their new plasma screen, then wallop: Up goes your premium.

A driver's risk profile—your likelihood of crashing—is shaped like a horseshoe depending on your age. Young drivers account for a quarter of fatal accidents, as well as those leading to life-changing injury. Your likelihood of injury plunges as you get older, owing to the better decision-making skills that come with experience, until your risk spikes again in your sixties as your vision and reflexes dim, and perhaps a few bad habits come home to roost. Passengers make up a hefty proportion of casualties, and a startling 53 percent of those killed weren't wearing seat belts.

Although young drivers pose the biggest risk on the roads, they also adapt quickly, and their crash rate plunges during their first two years of driving. The vital knowledge that these youngsters acquire is a clue as to what it really means to be a good driver. Their experience of near misses and general observations develop into a broader, fuller view of the task.

That skill is grandly titled *hazard perception*. It means the ability to analyze the scene and prioritize the aspects or risks that might affect you and sort them by their importance. It means taking a busy road or a jammed street loaded with shoppers and being able to see the forest for the trees. A honed visual strategy and a simple system of car control make the job a lot easier. Time to learn from a master . . .

CHASING GHOSTS

North London, 10:22 a.m.—in hot pursuit. For once I'm the passenger, listening to a man in complete control of his vehicle, and the rolling reality in front of it.

Officer Silkglove, of London's elite Metropolitan Police Squad based in Hendon:

"Vehicle is failing to stop, it's a black BMW, outside weather conditions, it's 10 degrees F above freezing. [It feels colder when Silkglove drops the windows so we can hear the road]. Overcast with some light rain, no wind, traffic is moderate, risk at the moment is low given the road surface is dry, Hotel-Kilo-Six-Zero-Lima-Oscar-Juliet is engaging the suspect. Ident, Officer Silkglove, I am a pursuit commander in a vehicle suitable for a pursuit to take place in an advanced covert car. [It's an Audi A4—pimped, but not visibly so.] I'm a level 1 trained driver, and seeking assistance of the DSU [dog support unit vehicle]. In the distance the road bends round off to the left-hand side, row of tan brick housing set well back and pavement is clear, rain is spotting, headlights on for adverse conditions. . . . Mirrors, looks like he's going left, left, scanning right, mindful I'm lacking side profile equipment so traffic may not react, gear for speed now is 2 at 19 [mph], now at decreased speed it increases his options, easier for him to change direction. . . ."

I shift in my seat and quickly recoil to move away from Silkglove's side mirror as he rattles off information like an air traffic controller. His running commentary

The Who, Where and What of Accidents

Seventy percent of serious casualties are male,
although on a crash-per-mile-driven basis,
the gender gap closes.

The busiest traffic results in the highest incidence of crashing, so the rush hours offer notable peaks, especially the later one at 5 p.m. When your boss hands you a bigger-than-expected paycheck, be careful driving home, because when the economy picks up, so does traffic density and bent metal. The state, however, moves too slowly to react to the uptick in the economy and fails to build more roads.

More crashes occur as the week edges toward Friday and concentration levels drop. Your odds of piling in rise as darkness falls, regardless of day, in particular between midnight and 3 a.m. Teenagers have another crash spike from 5 a.m. because their body clocks work more like a werewolf's.

The most dangerous time of the week, however, is that part of Friday night that blurs into Saturday morning, at 3:18 a.m., to be precise. If you're driving at that time, you have your best chance of crashing into something, or being run over when you drop your double bacon cheeseburger into the gutter. The obvious reason why the weekend is so dangerous is that so many people are drunk.

Pay particular attention to schools and pedestrian crossings, especially those littered with parked or stationary cars that block the line of sight between traffic and pedestrians and lead to most of the trouble. That's why traffic enforcement officers go crazy if you park next to them. Driving a door's-width away from parked vehicles makes you less likely to hit them when the door opens, and affords a better view of these hot spots.

Black cars are the most likely color of car to be in an accident, and recently the most likely vehicles in which to meet your maker are the Kia Rio, Nissan Versa, and Hyundai Accent—unless you paint them dayglow yellow.

outlines the relevant details of the traffic picture *before* they affect him, forcing him to maintain an active visual search. Verbalizing every decision makes them accountable, if necessary, in a court of law.

"Cyclist ahead, he looks steady, and no wind to upset his balance, and past, mirrors, limit point is matched, speed at 84, steering set, straight before bend left, thumb up into fourth gear, limit still running, mindful of that greasy surface . . ."

The sirens wail, and traffic peels away to our left as Silkglove smoothly closes in on his target and snaps the trap shut.

"He's on his brakes, he's committed to the turn, one coming up behind me is signaling left, nothing inbound, so I can quarter him by moving across into his off side [Silkglove restricts the suspect from turning right], now I can fall behind, mirrors, off the brakes, back on the drive, no vision through the apex, applying a constant drive, to an intersection left, mirrors, he is braking, in second, gone left left, one inbound, so I'm now signaling, nearside mirrors and brake, left left, slippery, two-wide, caution for gravel, concealed entrance 80 yards, very large vehicles use this route, leave plenty of room for them, gently on the drive, in second at 30 mph, firming up the drive to a double bend, first left sharp deviation so mirrors full off the drive, 3,000 revs in second, limit point is now clear, opening toward the construction site, suspect is slowing, he's just twigged it's a dead end, moving in close now to reduce his options, he is braking, driver's door is opening. Hotel-Kilo-Six-Zero-Lima-Oscar-Juliet, suspect is on foot and moving toward the west side of the ACME plant on Leggit Lane. 10:55."

A youngish man sprints across the open ground, trying in vain to maintain the benefit of his gray hoodie. Silkglove, still calm as a weatherman, explains that it would be bad form to step out of the car before the dog team arrives. Besides spoiling the scent for the world's finest hunting dogs, you never send them home on an empty stomach.

During the debrief in the canteen at Hendon HQ, it dawned on me that these police were new guard. Their approach to pursuits bore no resemblance to the "Go Like F***" attitude of the '90s that saw police drivers in a state of tunnel vision, buzzing red lights and doing virtually everything you've seen in *Beverly Hills Cop* movies to keep up with the suspect. Yes, we drove quite fast, but speed was largely irrelevant, and Silkglove never lost control of the situation or endangered anyone.

When I asked the rest of the Hendon driving team about their thoughts on, dare I say it, some of the outdated police methods like push-pull steering, I wasn't prepared for their response. Most of them, though not all, said they would "drop it tomorrow." Suffice to say that a lively debate ensued.

Driving with a commentary like that was the ultimate, black-belted demonstration of awareness and anticipation. Beneath Silkglove's swan-gliding-over-water patter, the internal cogs of his supreme system of awareness were spinning like Catherine wheels as he acquired, prioritized, and addressed key information. If he could have planned my life for me up to that point, I would never have stepped in a dog turd or eaten a dodgy pizza. He was Yoda with a badge. His ability to read every situation before we arrived was phenomenal, and I can't remember a smoother journey. He passed the "glass of water test" and then some. Mind you, this was no ordinary driver. Silkglove was a thirty-year veteran, and nobody was slipping straight into those loafers fresh out of a multiple-choice questionnaire, least of all me.

You can always find someone else to blame if you end up having an accident, but all crashes are avoidable. Every near miss or hot flush when something takes you by surprise is a signal that you missed something. It pays to catalogue bad experiences and dwell on them, so that you can recognize the warning signs much earlier in the future.

I begin every journey by preparing for the worst and conduct myself accordingly. Hardening a few prejudices is really just honing your survival instincts. As sure as eggs are eggs, the man in the battle-scarred white van won't check his mirrors as you squeeze past—though, contrary to what Jeremy Clarkson seems to believe, not all Audi drivers are jerks. I know this because *I* drive one. (Oh . . . *now* I get it . . .)

I take it personally if someone else's bad driving interferes with my perfect execution because I should have seen it coming and read a vehicle's body language to see what it might do next. For example, a car lurking slightly off-center in its lane means the driver can't gauge the width of his car or is thinking of turning but hasn't yet put on his turn signal. Side-to-side motion is easy for the eye to detect, and if a car wanders all over the place, the driver is probably either drunk or plain awful. Harder to detect, and more dangerous, is movement forward and back. The image of a car slowing ahead just grows or shrinks slightly. Viewed from a distance of around ten car lengths, a change in proximity of one or two lengths is barely noticeable, a minor design flaw in the Mark 1 eyeball; more on that later. When someone slams on the brakes in front of you, the sensible gap you maintained up until that point should enable you to stop gradually in order to give the poor bugger behind a chance to recognize what is happening and make it less likely that he will whack your rear end.

Many drivers are oblivious to what takes place behind them and miss out on a rich palette of disaster. On one occasion in Pittsburgh I stopped at an intersection at the bottom of a hill with a truck coming up behind me. It wasn't slowing, so I checked that the light was still red, looked behind, and saw the big trailer was jack-knifed and inbound toward me. I drove up onto the curb and gave it space.

Clairvoyance came in handy when I worked in Johannesburg on the *Top Gear Live* show where we had a convoy of red Audis taking us to the venue. They drove too fast and too close for my liking, a military convoy but without the war or the training. After my driver conceded that his hometown was actually Cape Town, eliminating his only plus point in my view in terms of local knowledge, I rented a car for the remainder of my stay. Two days later I drove past the Audi group, with the leader firmly embedded into the sharp end of a flatbed trailer and the two sidekicks rammed up each other's exhausts like some kind of insect incest.

SUMMARY

There are drivers who cause accidents, those who share other people's accidents, and those who avoid them altogether. Good drivers learn to adapt to an imperfect world by accommodating and anticipating other people's mistakes until it becomes a habit. As Aristotle said, "We are what we repeatedly do. Excellence, then, is not an act, but a habit." If you can learn from Officer Silkglove, you will become the master of your fate—unlike these unfortunate "ultimate insurance fails":

> *"Coming home I drove into the wrong house and collided
>   with a tree I don't have."*
> *"I started to slow down, but the traffic was more stationary
>   than I thought."*
> *"I saw a slow-moving, sad-faced old gentleman as he
>   bounced off the roof of my car."*
> *"I was backing my car out of the driveway in the usual man-
>   ner, when it was struck by the other car in the same
>   place it had been struck several times before."*
> *"The pedestrian ran for the pavement, but I got him."*

"Excellence, then, is not an act, but a habit."

Avoiding Accidents

Channel Your
Inner Jedi Master

1. OBSERVE

Use your vision to create a 360-degree rolling map of the environment: the dog on the leash, the car speeding toward a side road, tiny feet visible behind a parked car, a sharp curve ahead . . .

Listen to the sound of the engine, the chirp of a tire, the protest of a gear change, and the sound of children getting out of school and spilling onto the pavement.

With your hands, feel the weight of the steering, how much it's turning and responding, looking for any telltale vibration from a loose wheel or underinflated tire.

Hear what your backside is telling you: This precision instrument has guided me through more situations than I can remember. The more elegantly you balance the car and feel it hug the road, the more eloquently your rump will squeak, I mean speak, to you.

Trust and develop your gut feeling.

2. INTERPRET

Filter the information coming in by ignoring the irrelevant and prioritizing the key hazards and road features along your path. The monkey smoking a pipe wearing pink pajamas in the back of that Mercedes as you approach a traffic light, however fascinating, is less relevant than the lights turning red.

Use your imagination to predict the paths and intentions of everyone and everything in sight. By projecting potential scenarios onto the scene, and creatively considering what might be around the curve, you won't be surprised by the guy picking his nose on the wrong side of the road.

3. ACT

Does the scenario you encounter actually require you to do something? If so, formulate an appropriate plan of action. Nothing too fancy. Calmly deploy a reasonable response while maintaining oversight of the bigger picture as it evolves with you. And continue to cycle the information stages every step of the way.

3.2 *INTERSECTIONS*

You've secretly been waiting for this section all along. Forget the thrill of conquering a hairpin curve or taking on a snowdrift, let's talk about rites of passage.

Let's talk about rites of passage.

For starters, the majority of car-on-car collisions occur at intersections and for one single reason: failure to look properly while a combination of converging speeds and optical illusions conspire to unseat you. Intersections lurk everywhere in all shapes and disguises, from the standard Mr. T intersection to its faster cousins at controlled intersections (with traffic signs and/or signals), and lately some foreign imports in the form of roundabouts. Conquer them with your all-seeing eye . . .

As you drive through town, you should become accustomed to looking along the length of the car to both fore and aft, using regular scanning and observation. The T-intersection throws up issues in the lateral plane, and with it comes new blind spots, while the oblique angles to opposing traffic make it harder to judge their approach speeds.

But that's nothing compared to leaving an intersection during rush hour and making for the far side of the road. As you inch out of your itsy-bitsy feeder road, you've got to establish eye contact with somebody who might be stupid enough to let you out, because everyone crossing your path will pretend that you don't exist.

Sweet old ladies, fresh from rescuing stray cats, whiten their knuckles and stare ahead with grim determination if you dare to pop out of your hole and try to join their ill-tempered crawl. They have right-of-way and never shall they yield.

The art of cold-shouldering will serve you well when it's your turn to punish potential mergers. But first you have to make it out alive, and to do this you have to perfect the halfway-house maneuver: that is, creeping forward with the tacit approval of incoming traffic until, surely for the love of God, somebody will play ball with you.

The key to defeating the cold shoulder is to point your melon in the direction of other drivers so that they realize you mean business. Humans find it hard to resist looking at another face, regardless of how ugly, and, once engaged, you quickly close the deal with an open-palmed salute and a Colgate smile. Then pull out.

Assume nothing.

Assume nothing. Make sure you have a reasonable-sized gap and delicately ease out while engaging with your fellow protagonists. On reaching the halfway mark, your odds of getting to the far side greatly improve as people realize you have the minerals to join their team.

HOT TIPS ▸ To gauge a car's speed as it approaches from the side, you either have to stare at it for longer and use background features like dotted lines or parked cars as a reference of distance or flick your eyes away to do a double take so that your brain can relate the distance covered between glances.

BOGEY AT SEVEN O'CLOCK

In lighter traffic you have to be even more careful because speeds and expectations are higher. This is when the "look right, look left, look right—whoa, is that Cameron Diaz behind the wheel of that jeep?—pull-out-and-crunch-into-the-unnoticed-car-from-the-left" catches drivers out.

The Diaz moment is what psychologists refer to as an *elongated fixation*, which is as naughty as it sounds. Something in the scene draws your attention for longer than it should; you lose track of the time that has passed since you scanned each hemisphere, and it leaves you vulnerable.

Besides thinking faster and looking more often to keep your information live, there are certain skills that improve your odds. When vision is restricted, you can often use reflections in shop windows to see other cars approaching, or look through the windows of parked cars to see what's behind. For tricky exits onto more open roads you can roll the window down and listen for road noise.

Ditto when you're on a suburban road; it helps to keep an eye out for side roads using telltales such as telephone poles and streetlights that suggest a side entrance, or scanning through open hedges for approaching vehicles. Expect people to come out blind from recessed entrances, and position youself toward the road center for a better view. Again, reflections help, as do shadows from vehicles hidden behind walls.

Intersections

133

15. Hazard Perception

Lampposts and telephone wires often indicate the direction and severity of an approaching bend.

Reflections, shadows, and sounds provide reliable clues for detecting the movement of other cars.

INTERSECTION ETIQUETTE

As you approach an intersection, whether you're leaving or merging onto the road, you check your mirror and position your car toward the side of the road that tells everyone around you the direction in which you're turning: right side to turn right, and vice versa. That way, nobody will be enticed to squeeze up your inside or try to pass (see Passing on page 140).

Here's the biggest piece of advice for pulling up at *any* intersection and preparing to cross traffic: Keep the steering wheel straight, with your foot on the brakes, until you pull out. Why?

Getting rear-ended at an intersection is as common as flatulence at a vegan BBQ. If your wheels are turned when you get bumped from behind, it will launch you head-on into oncoming traffic for an additional, much nastier, hit. If there's a car in front, leave enough of a space so that its rear wheels are visible on the asphalt. There are various reasons I like this drill, so take your pick.

Whether you're driving locally or around the streets of Johannesburg, the carjacking capital of the world, maintaining a space in front of you means keeping your options open so that you can move if you have to. At night it pays to creep slowly up to traffic lights so you spend less time stationary: a moving target is less attractive.

If the car in front breaks down or selects reverse by mistake, you can get around it.

In busy urban areas, leaving a gap helps pedestrians to cross. You were once a pedestrian, so you should sympathize with this terrible affliction, and clearing them away from the intersection will afford you a better view when you come to pull out. Karma works both ways.

Karma works both ways.

CONTROLLED INTERSECTIONS

As a European, it has taken me a while to acclimatize to the peculiarities of the big intersections dotted around the US. The infinite stop-starting as you hold up for a red and hopefully accelerate to the next green would test the patience of a monk. Red-light running is habitual in many places, and you need to be on your guard.

Unique to the US is the situation where cars turning left on a green, mindful of crossing potential light runners coming the other way, have to contend with arriving at their desired road to find pedestrians being instructed to cross in front of them. Contrary to popular belief, the pedestrians have the right-of-way. The

Winding up to 200 mph during the Le Mans 24 Hours in 2011 aboard the RML Honda HPD Prototype.

confusion is aggravated by the fact that three-quarters of us would walk across the road even when the sign is flashing "Don't Walk!"

The "right turn on red" law is truly enlightened, but it's a gauntlet if you're on foot. It's a long haul to cover ten lanes of traffic that never quite stops moving, so it pays to tighten your shoelaces.

Confusing signage that makes your eyes bleed.

Just when I thought I had intersections licked, I discovered the Jersey left, or jughandle. This special piece of road design means you peel off to the right in advance of an intersection, instead of making a straight left turn at the lights. Knowing where you're going is like solving the Da Vinci code while defusing a bomb. New Jersey lawmakers are trying to ban the jughandle, and I heard the FBI was putting out a warrant for its inventor: Wanted Dead or Alive.

In other news . . . a tidy little dance is making its way to American streets to overcome all of the above.

ROUNDABOUTS

The roundabout is like dancing a do-si-do but without all the leather. And according to the Insurance Institute for Highway Safety, there has been a 40 percent decrease in all accidents and a 90 percent drop in fatal crashes where a roundabout has replaced a traffic intersection, with further benefits in operational costs and fuel consumption.

Roundabouts are simple, and you approach them the same way as a normal intersection: Use the left lane to go straight, make a left, or hook a U-turn, or use the right lane to turn right.

To enter one you simply check your mirror, signal, and yield to traffic already in the roundabout, signaling as you leave.

Trucks tend to drive in the outside lane regardless of the situation because it gives them an easier turning arc, but is a notable reason for conflict over perceived rights-of-way when it comes to the exit. They should indicate their intention; but

Intersections

don't count on it. The beauty of the roundabout is that if you get cut off or make a hash of things, just go for another lap like Chevy Chase in *European Vacation*.

Which reminds me of the French . . . A roundabout is not the same as a "rotary" or a "circle." These abominations are of French origin. In France, traffic entering a "circle" can rightfully interfere with those already circulating, causing chaos and jams.

Vous n'avez pas la priorité.

Until recently, the French would dive-bomb a circle at maximum velocity with the horn blazing and lights flashing. That rule was recently overturned, unofficially, and cars entering French roundabouts now *cèdent le passage*, the same as the Brits, most of the time. If you follow in Chevy's footsteps and see the sign *Vous n'avez pas la priorité*, it means it's English rules, but if there are no signs or one of these bad boys ⚠ 🪧 then you can expect a wide-eyed Frenchman to come speeding toward you, waving a baguette. *C'est la guerre!*

There are no such warnings in America, but you'll be glad to know that the French way is being phased out in most parts of the country.

The very complexity of roundabouts and the way they force you to interact with other drivers, to make eye contact with a fellow human being, even, is what makes them work.

RURAL ROADS

As you leave town, the speed rises and the road starts twisting up hill and down dale. Single-lane highways like this and the rest of the "rural" road network are where 80 percent of *driver* deaths occur.

Mention "dangerous road," and I picture Indiana Jones dangling from the door of a runaway truck on some Amazonian mountain, rather than the idyllic alpine passage from Durango to Ouray in Colorado. Carved by hand in the nineteenth century, the road has no roadside barriers to stop cars from falling off the cliffs or spearing into a tree. It was nicknamed the "Million Dollar Highway" by residents who said it wasn't worth crossing it for less during the snowy months.

It's places like this where we see the greatest number of single-vehicle accidents caused by folks losing it on sharp curves all by themselves, or by misjudging while passing. The heady cocktail of turns, crossroads, and two-way traffic fuels too many opportunities to cross the path of another vehicle.

These roads cross the heart of the countryside and entail all the wildlife that goes with it. Trees kill about 130 people a year in the UK alone. You really don't want to hit one. Lampposts, telegraph poles, and other permanent objects such as bridges will beat you in a game of slaps every time. A friend of mine, a stuntman, drove into a tree head-on at 12 mph to see what it felt like. He told me he regretted doing it. Apparently it hurt more than doing a car hit at 45.

One in five young drivers will crash during their first year, mostly on these so-called minor roads. Taking curves (or skidding, for those who never read the label) is handled elsewhere. For now let's focus on passing.

As you leave town, the speed rises.

3.3 *PASSING*

Before Gary Powell had finished his question about the new Bond movie, I'd already said yes twice. Gary was a 007 veteran.

In *The World Is Not Enough*, he perfected flipping the Q speedboat on the Thames by jumping a smaller vessel—wait for it—onto dry land.

"At that speed, water's harder than concrete, basically . . ."

He also became inseparable from his T-55 tank in *GoldenEye*, power-sliding it around the streets of Moscow, through walls and anything else that got in the way. And you should see him drive a car.

Gary was the stunt coordinator for *The Quantum of Solace*, which picked up where *Casino Royale* left off. The script had a dark side to it. Bond's girl had been murdered at the end of *Casino*, and *Quantum* was about revenge. Gary was assembling a team of experts for what was being billed as the biggest opening sequence in Bond film history, with a visceral car chase followed by a bloody rooftop pursuit. The locations, vehicles, and stunt crew were handpicked to guarantee action, and the driving needed to put audiences on the edge of their seats. Which is where I came in.

The first stop was the Riva resort overlooking Lake Garda, itself overshadowed by the imposing and beautiful Dolomite mountains. The stunt team took a guided tour of the Gardesana Road, which rose from Riva and wound its way around the mountainside, punching straight through it in places to form the most spectacular tunnels and galleries that overlooked the restless pool of water below. We entered the mountain and crossed a gingerbread bridge that was wide enough for a horse and cart. It spanned a yawning abyss over a stream that trickled its way down to the lake. The road opened out into a cavern with a low bulging ceiling that could work metal like a pummice stone. Gary's assistant pointed this out as a potential passing spot.

My first call every morning was at 5:45 a.m. with the costume and makeup department for forty-five minutes of hair bashing and metamorphosing. I climbed into a Tom Ford suit that was customized for Daniel Craig and donned the Omega Seamaster watch. I remember thinking that I had a lot to live up to. Awaiting us down on set were no fewer than twelve Aston Martin DBS cars for Bond, worth $240K apiece, as well as six Alfas and a fleet of ND (nondescript) background cars.

I gulped down one last espresso: It was time to burn rubber.

Gary conducted the "stunties" with the tip of his radio antenna. "Ben, jump in the Aston. We're doing the high-speed stuff first, so make sure you're 'appy wiv it." With that, the DBS became my office. A 200-mph work station.

The DBS was one of the most sophisticated machines on the market, perhaps the best front-engine sports car ever built. Its graceful curves kept its brute performance covert; beneath the mature exterior was a recalcitrant wild child. It boasted six liters of devilish horsepower, totaling over 500 bhp. The V-12 engine responded to every hint of movement in the throttle, like an F1 car. It howled on full song but quieted to a whispering burble at low revs. The ceramic brakes clamped like vises, but with such sensitivity that you could modulate them at the limit of grip from its fat tires.

There was scarcely any visible difference between the DB9 and the DBS, yet the slightly lowered, delicately enhanced suspension turned the girl next door into a supermodel. Beneath her hemline, the heightened technology of the braking and traction control systems was streets ahead. Where most anti-skid systems prevented the tire from getting anywhere near to locking during braking, the Aston's onboard computer took it to the limit several times a second, and you sensed its work underfoot.

I selected the largely unmodified Car 5, running standard tires for maximum grip and outright speed. I climbed aboard and plugged in the crystal key to spark the engine into life. The words *power, beauty, soul* were thus illuminated on the dashboard.

I pulled onto the main road and joined the convoy en route to the first setup of the day. To check that the traction was disabled, I slammed the accelerator and steered right, laying two fat stripes of rubber across the pristine asphalt as I headed toward the Limone tunnel. The Italian *polizia* in their pretty blue-and-red-striped

The words power, beauty, soul were thus illuminated on the dashboard.

Passing

141

Doubling James Bond during the filming of *Quantum of Solace* in 2008—and treating the Aston Martin DBS with less respect than it deserved.

uniforms tugged at their crotches and cheered. The reverberating drumbeat of the DBS zapping through the wide-columned tunnel was majestic.

We gathered in a turnout overlooking a coiling stretch of road that plunged downward, following the curvature of the mountain. Each Alfa contained a driver and a passenger, and they would be leaning out of their windows to fire automatic weapons in my direction. Jagged rocks bordered the near side, while a thin line of Italian mortar stood between the road and a vertical fall into the bottomless lake on the right. There was no room to deviate either way, no quarter given for error.

At a normal driving speed, the curves were sharp enough for the rocky bluffs to block the view of the road ahead. We would be racing at full pelt through a convoy of trucks, box vans, and NDs spread around every turn, while timing our run for a near miss with traffic coming the other way. That meant leaving each move deliberately late, the last thing you would ever do in the real world.

Without line of sight, it was challenging to gauge the timing and movement of other vehicles in order to dodge between them and slide into a gap when you needed to.

A big dumpster truck would gallop uphill at 50 mph minimum. I would lead the convoy of three Alfas downhill and aim to pass the first box van after the apex of the second bend, then sneak into a space in the traffic as the truck swiped by.

In order for the near miss to look real, it had to *be* real. There was no CGI faking the stunts in a Bond movie.

Gary brought us in close. "Ben, whatever you do, you need to get back into the right-hand lane before Rowley comes through—or else you're wearing it."

As with any passing move, timing was critical. You practice the same thing every day walking past people on the street. They just weigh less.

Rounding the second curve too late would mean facing the dumpster truck dead ahead with the box truck blocking my escape to the right. Arriving early rendered the shot useless, and during the timing runs I found my foot creeping onto the accelerator whenever I disappeared behind the coves and lost vision. I had to hold back and count time; then the sequence clicked.

Rowley, a seasoned veteran, was behind the wheel of the skip truck, which gave me the confidence to go head-to-head with it, because he would do the same thing every time. But pity the Alfas. They had to find their own space between the traffic.

In order for the near miss to look real, it had to be real.

And with them on my tail, I couldn't just pull the ripcord and jam on the brakes if I mistimed the run without compromising their space. We were in this together.

I lined up next to a boulder with a face in it, my start marker, with the Alfas behind.

"Action, Action, *Action!*"

I feathered the Aston away to keep the Alfa group in tow, tight as a trailer. Bond's previous engagement with a truck earlier in the chase had ripped the door clean off its hinges, leaving me with an al fresco view of the craggy mountainside to our left.

We moved down the lakeside at a reasonable speed, and I counted the beats with Gary running a commentary from his cliffside balcony. I lined up behind the first car, jinked left and overtook it, ducked back in behind a van, passed it on the left, and stayed on the wrong side of the road for the agonizing length of time it took to round the blind bluff and start passing the box truck.

I cleared its front as the skip truck appeared large as life in my windshield. The top arm snagged the overhanging rocks above the road, shaking the rig and spewing shards of rocks and dust as it bowled toward me.

I zapped the throttle and swerved to the right to get out of its way. It passed my driver's side. With no door to deflect it, the dust from its wheels blew straight into the Aston. I surged down the hill until I was out of shot and then exhaled.

We made a few more runs like that and increased the speed. Each pass teased my nerve as I got as close to the truck as possible before swerving. When my retinas became the size of soap dishes, that was my cue to break off. Staying jacked was the best way to stay focused and instinctive, which was vital for self-preservation. Jackie Chan put it this way: "The worst thing isn't doing a stunt or not doing a stunt, but half doing a stunt."

Rowley managed to keep his foot hard on the throttle until he passed the Alfas. He was on the mark every time.

"Nice one, Rowley," Gary said over the radio. "Ben, you don't want to get any closer than that from where I'm watching, I tell ya."

The constant highs and lows were mentally draining, and we maintained a sense of constant alert. With so many vehicles, it was a case of keeping everyone in the zone.

I zapped the throttle and swerved.

Passing

We went over our timings and walked the route over and again. One of the Alfas had spewed oil precisely where I was dodging the truck, so we cleaned it up as best we could and cracked on. The surface change would delay my rate of turn by two seconds, so I factored this in for the next run. I braked a tad earlier, and the Aston slewed predictably across the wet surface in front of the truck, the rear end nipping out of the way as we crossed. It was the kind of high-octane driving I had always wanted to do.

Late in the day we were resetting the cars, and I was making a three-point turn under the watchful eye of the first assistant director, Terry Madden. He was effectively the producer's quarterback. You could be filming a movie about nocturnal animals and his wizened face would still be tanned from the previous shoot. As I nosed up to the cliff edge he sprang into action with a twinkle in his eye.

"That's far enough, you, just wait there."

The return up the mountain looked clear to me, and he clocked my expression.

"There's been more fatalities during resets than all the stunts in this business put together."

It was easy to forget that the return journey, despite being at half pace, bore the closest resemblance to the haphazardness of real life, where there are no practice runs or people with radios to tell you when to abort the run.

Passing is probably the riskiest and most complicated maneuver we undertake on the road. Perhaps that's why your driving instructor never taught you how to do it.

As a racing driver, there's nothing worse than listening to armchair heroes bang on about the lack of passing in a motor race. The last thing any driver wants to do is sit behind a slower car and miss the opportunity to squirt champagne in their eye. However, passing is one area where you may not live to regret a mistake, because once you commit to a move, it can be difficult to unravel yourself when things go pear-shaped.

For me the first consideration when assessing a potential pass is: Can I be bothered? If the traffic level is high, then it's pointless risking life and limb just for the opportunity to read a new license plate number.

If the answer to the first question is yes, then I need to come up with a plan that passes muster with the part of me that doesn't want to become an organ donor. That plan requires having the clear space and enough speed to pull off the

The riskiest and most complicated maneuver we undertake on the road.

move— simple enough, but it's the detail in arriving at that conclusion that requires your attention. These preliminary checks involve looking near, far, and wide for obvious reasons *not* to pass.

SPACE

You can usually get a better view of what lies ahead by favoring the center of the road next to the white line. However, if the road curves away, then you can see farther by moving to the inside line and looking past the passenger side of the car ahead. If you're following something big, always check both sides anyway to clock what you're getting yourself into.

BODY LANGUAGE

Check if the target car looks erratic, lost . . . or is slowing and might be about to turn off at an intersection, which is the number-one cause of passing accidents.

These crashes often involve younger drivers failing to anticipate when someone is about to make a turn, and older drivers making dodgy turns without signaling. There will be plenty of time to argue the latter point in the back of the ambulance or at the pearly gates if this was your final sin. Or you could read the situation better.

If you discover a train of cars ahead of you, the spaces between those vehicles will open and close like logs floating down a river. Passing one car may be futile in these conditions anyway, but if you go for it you need to be doubly accurate with your observations to ensure that the inviting space you're relying on will be there when you arrive. It really antagonizes other drivers when you force your way into a tiny gap, so don't expect them to offer you a steak dinner when they pull up alongside you at the next traffic light.

The primary method that racers use to predict traffic flow is by constantly judging their "delta" speed—the divergence in speed between vehicles. If the car in front of you has a high delta of, say, 30 mph closure on the traffic ahead, it probably means he is about to pass, close the gap, or have an almighty accident.

APPROACHING CARS: THE SECOND MOST LIKELY CAUSE OF ACCIDENTS

If a car seems to be far enough away that it won't affect you, keep tracking its progress, because speed is difficult to measure when you're facing an approaching target

The spaces between those vehicles will open and close like logs floating down a river.

down the barrel. Establish its speed in the context of background features that help to measure distance or do a double take to help your brain process the space it covered in that time.

If there's a curve in the distance, assess its severity to predict the exit speeds of cars that *might* potentially emerge from it during your move. Rehearse this imaginary relationship continuously throughout the process of passing, because at some point the ghost car will become a real one, and it should come as no surprise.

HOT TIPS   ▸ When you're waiting for an approaching car to clear, the point where it will converge with the target vehicle is predetermined. By measuring their rate of closure, you can anticipate this point and build your acceleration in advance of your move.

At some point the ghost car will become a real one.

Cast your eyes to the farthest point you can see ahead to ensure you have a comfortable space in which to make your pass before the next curve, obstacle, or approaching traffic. The common mistake people make is to misjudge the amount of time they have to spend on the wrong side of the road. It's better to imagine the single vehicle you want to pass as a row of parked cars because the effect is the same.

With a target traveling at 50 mph and you passing at 55, it will take 50 yards to get past it. That's ten parked cars. At 65 you can clear the same vehicle in a little over three car lengths—the smaller the difference in speeds, the longer the move takes.

GENERAL OBSERVATIONS

Trust nothing that you can't see clearly: blind bends, brows over hills, and undulations that can hide a car.

Beware any intersections or hidden entrances along your proposed trajectory, because cars can and will emerge from them without expecting to see you on *their* side of the road. These encounters make number five on the list of greatest hits.

Check for legal restrictions that forbid passing, such as solid or double lines, and other signs that, though not legally binding, might prove useful in the near future: railway crossings, traffic lights, single-lane tunnels, minefields, and intersections(!).

Make sure the road conditions are appropriate: Flooding or snow on the far side of the road might cause a problem. And finally, trust your gut feeling. If it doesn't feel right, it probably isn't.

16. Passing Line

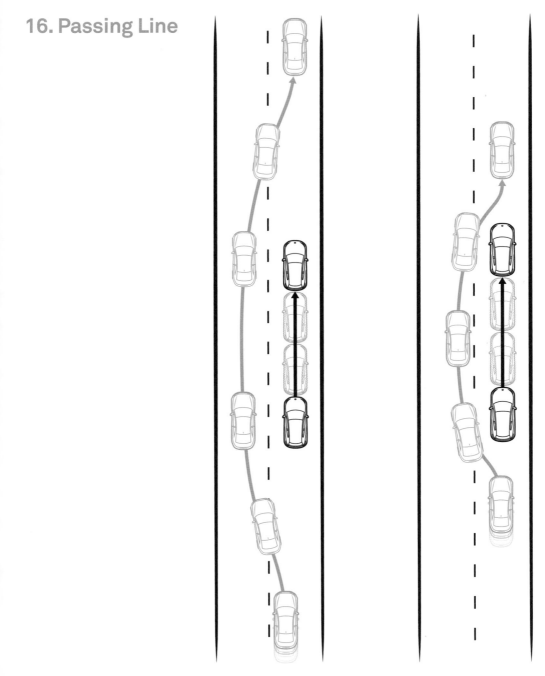

The Right Way

The Wrong Way

SPEED, MOMENTUM, AND POSITIONING

On closing behind a slower-moving vehicle, you analyze the situation from a distance to see if the move is on. The earlier you slow down, the better, because it gives you time to think while preserving your approach speed. Momentum is absolutely key to making a clean pass because it minimizes the amount of time you spend on the wrong side of the road with your foot to the carpet.

If you pull up to the target's bumper, you will have to slow right down to its speed and subsequently pass by gunning it from a standing start, albeit a mobile one, greatly reducing your acceleration power.

In situations where you need to be patient, it's best to hang back about three car lengths and match the target's speed from there. There's no point positioning yourself on its exhaust pipe because this limits your field of view and prevents you from rolling into the pass. This is especially true when following something big like a truck, when all you can see is "Wide Load" through a cloud of diesel.

Hang back about three car lengths and match the target's speed.

17. Reasons Not to Overtake

FINAL CHECKS

Select your best gear for power, ideally one that won't run out of guts halfway through the move and require a rushed, easily bungled gear change. Are you still sure that your car could rip the skin off a rice pudding at this speed and get the job done within the identified space? Check.

Mirrors: Are *you* about to be passed by another vehicle? No.

Sanity check: if you need to, you can ease onto the other side of the road to expand your viewpoint to double-check that the space ahead is clear before you commit to overlapping the target, or duck back to your side if you change your mind. Clear.

Go!

Be smooth, be decisive, flick your signal, and make your move.

Roll in: Accelerate into the move to build momentum and boost you past the other car, and if you need to abort for any reason, you still can before you overlap it.

Commit: The move is on, and you drive past the other car. Your focus is the farthest point ahead in search of an oncoming vehicle as well as the gap you're aiming for. Keep the target in your peripheral vision, give it plenty of room, and track your rate of progress until you're sure you're fully clear of it, then ease back to your side of the road.

COMMON PROBLEMS

- *Sideswiping* the car you're passing or clipping its nose is a common mistake. When a bad judgment call is followed by an overreaction to an approaching car or curve, common sense leaves the room, and people just cut across, hoping for the best. *Whack.*

- If you clip the nose of another car on reentry, the combination of your steering input with the impact on your rear wheel will likely cause you to rotate. Be accurate from start to finish.

- *Losing control* during the pass can happen. Most roads are crowned in the middle, and as you swing across it, the effect can cause the suspension to go light and destabilize. Combining that with rough steering or harsh acceleration can lead to a dangerous loss of control. This is naturally exacerbated by wet weather or a curve.

If you find yourself getting well and truly hung out to dry on the wrong side of the road with another car coming at you, then you need to make a judgment call. If you're most of the way past, and still passing, then floor it to get the job done. Otherwise, you need to abort your run by braking calmly and returning to your side.

The problem with braking can be that the person you're passing is actually a human being and has been watching your antics closely all along. On seeing the approaching tractor that you missed, he or she applies the anchors at the same time that you do, leaving you no room to return. I wish you the best of luck.

Assuming that you all survive, a sharp burst of adrenaline will raise your endorphins for twenty minutes or more, but don't be fooled into developing a super-hero complex. This was a big mistake, so be sure to log the experience and visualize where you went wrong.

Passing

HOT TIPS

▸ Practice using vision, space, and momentum to pass on dual carriageways or highways without the worries of oncoming traffic. Gauge your machine's performance at different speeds in different gears and develop your feel for timing.

▸ If in doubt, don't bother.

▸ *Boring but important.* Crosshatch marks—the diagonal stripes between two center lines—mean you can't cross them when their border lines are solid unless it's an emergency. The same goes for solid double lines. Sometimes the painted lines are white, sometimes yellow . . . depending on where you are and what color paint was on sale that day. Regardless of color, you can legally pass when the lines are broken, and many drivers are unaware of this.

▸ Dotted lines on your side obviously permit passing. When the broken center lines grow longer and the gaps between them shorter, it indicates a hazard up ahead.

Panic. *I mean: Don't panic.*

3.4 MULTILANE HIGHWAYS

For some, this is the moment they have feared since day one.

But with a little forward planning and gamesmanship you can enter the gateways to the world with confidence.

On the whole, dual and multilane highways are just like freeways, but with fewer restrictions. In one moment you might have a big three-lane road that looks and sounds like a freeway, and the next moment it can run into a single-lane passage with no central barrier separating your rig from whatever is coming toward you on the other side of the line. Highways lack controlled entry and exit access, and they often include controlled or uncontrolled intersections as the highway passes through towns.

Among the most notorious in America is US Highway 6 between Spanish Fork and Price in Utah. The recipe is ripe. High-volume, high-speed traffic mixes with heavy-goods vehicles passing up and over a curving canyon road, through pinch points as three lanes become two and with varying temperatures that are perfect conditions for black ice.

A technological breakthrough might prove to be the answer to the weather conditions (see Winter Tires on page 228), but from a driver's perspective, you should treat them like freeways but with your A-game anticipation skills.

Treat them like freeways but with your A-game anticipation skills.

3.5 FREEWAYS/INTERSTATE HIGHWAYS

In 1973 the Arab oil cartel OPEC stopped supplying oil to the United States, and President Nixon was faced with an energy crisis that slapped every American across the face and threatened to bring the economy to its knees.

Among other measures, Nixon enacted an emergency 55 mph speed limit for one year to improve fuel efficiency. As with all recessions and gas-price hikes, people drove less and had fewer accidents. Safety campaigners misused the information to make the double-nickel law last another *twenty-two years*.

In 1995 Congress bent to public opinion and repealed the speed limit to a cacophony of apocalyptic predictions from the safety lobby: "History will never forgive Congress for this assault on the sanctity of human life." But, gee whiz: The speeds went up and the highways became *safer*. The increase in the speed limit saved 200 million man-hours and two to $3 billion each year.

Why? Because the safer you feel, the dumber you drive.

In America, speed limits vary by state, but the majority of states now operate a 70- or 75-mph limit on highways, with one glorious stretch of 85 in Texas. Back in England, we have as much control over our laws as we do over the sands blowing in from the Sahara. Combined with toxic gases arriving from Northern Europe, our air quality has landed us in trouble with the European Union and led our government to reduce speed limits in "affected areas" to 60 mph. Common sense and safety are no match for good old-fashioned politics.

The safer you feel, the dumber you drive.

But I digress. The point regarding freeways is that they are *by far* the safest places to travel. The fatality rate is half that of other roads. The greatest danger you face on highways is dying of boredom and missing your exit. In fact, that is the biggest fear of motorists who travel along them.

Perhaps it's no surprise, then, that teaching freeway driving ranks lower with driving instructors than spending an afternoon with an incontinent student after a heavy tandoori. In some states, it isn't even covered by the driving test. Consequently, newly licensed drivers are terrified of the safest roads in the country and avoid them as much as possible. They shouldn't, because freeway driving is phenomenally easy. And, despite the high speed and volume of traffic hammering up and down them, it is by far the safest way to get from A to B.

I use the word "safe" with the guarded skepticism I hold for anybody preaching the safety of airline travel. When Dustin Hoffman refused to board the plane in *Rain Man,* I fully sympathized with his risk assessment because I don't like the thought of my person being reduced to a crater either. I don't like the fact that certain airline companies view the process as so routine that their pilots are denied a little extra fuel in the tank "just in case" they need it. And I sleep better thinking there's a former F-16 pilot at the helm, rather than some Xbox bunny with loads of sim-time.

The beauty of driving, of course, is that *you* have control. And it's perfectly sensible to respect the nature of high-speed traffic because when things do go tits up, it happens fast and there's precious little time to *react*. That's why I never rely on reaction time. Neither should you.

RULES

I follow some basic rules to keep myself clear of trouble on freeways and find the game of high-speed chess curiously satisfying. About half of freeway inhabitants play this game, and you can communicate with them on a quasi–Masonic handshake level. The other half are physically present but mentally abstaining. These people typically languish in the middle lane. Sometimes I join their group as well, usually in average speed zones, where my focus is obliterated by the need to strain at the needle lest it pass 53 mph.

And I sleep better thinking there's a former F-16 pilot at the helm.

WARM UP

Stretch your eye muscles and prepare to look *much* farther forward, toward the horizon. Your mental radar needs to become a 360-degree scanner, which means actively revolving your observation from side to side, forward and back, using your mirrors. Constantly.

You need to think several moves ahead, and concentration must be continuous to monitor the ever-changing flow of traffic.

THE FIELD

Freeways are gloriously suited to their purpose, with wide lanes and one-way flow. The slower traffic is meant to stay in the right lane, with passing taking place in the center and left lanes. However, it is fair to say that only a minority of Americans adhere to these rules. One of them passed away last year, leaving the remaining six in charge. Due to the nature of on- and off-ramps merging from both sides, lane discipline loses out to expediency.

THE SHOULDER

Nearly one in every ten cars that stop on the roadside shoulder is involved in a collision. Only stop there if you're in dire straits, not for picnics. The freeway shoulder is a kill zone. You are stationary, while everything around you is moving at high speed. Park as far over on the shoulder as possible, and turn the front tires away from the road. If you've managed to pull over on the right shoulder—which is by far the safest—get everyone out of the car, and move away from it and the road.

MERGING

By observing certain physical features, you can effectively predict changes in traffic flow. The on- and off-ramps are prime examples of where you can expect "displacement" from traffic merging or slowing to depart the highway. The resulting compression of vehicles in lane 1 causes a buildup effect that you can see coming a mile away.

Displacement is the buzzword that covers every scenario where a vehicle is *likely* to change speed or course. Your ability to predict how displacement might affect your progress will deeply impress Master Yoda.

Conversely, when *you* merge onto the freeway, you want to create as little effect on the surrounding traffic as possible. Your blind spot is accentuated by your angle of approach to the access road, a problem that is easily, though seldom, overcome by leaning forward and rotating your noggin like an owl so that you can look at what you're driving into. Check early and often, find a suitable gap, and maintain your speed. Combine this with checking your mirror, then signal and move into the right lane with all the confidence of John Wayne striding into a saloon full of Indians.

HOT TIPS

- ▸ Merging lanes that continue as part of the main highway often end up becoming exit-only lanes, so you find yourself being turfed out of the party shortly after walking through the door. You may need to make a lane change to stay on the highway.
- ▸ It is generally illegal, and inadvisable, to cross the gore point that separates the merging lane from the freeway.

Freeways are gloriously suited to their purpose.

18. Merging

Don't steal people's oxygen. Hold back to create a clear gap to the front and side, and work the traffic to your advantage from a position of strength.

19. Last-Minute Lane Change

In this scenario, both drivers will probably blame the other, but each is at fault.

> ▸ Anybody behind you is welcome to tailgate, but they should wait their turn. Just keep enough room to the front and ideally to the sides to avoid being squeezed by anybody. It's all about creating clear space.

EXITING

The problem with GPS navigation is that it crushes forward planning and makes thinking a crime. Freeways are still littered with quaint signage indicating the range to potential destinations, and assuming you're not too enthralled with your screen to notice, it means that you can plan an exit ahead of time.

Scan ahead frequently for forks in the freeway to prevent inadvertent road trips in the wrong direction. Identify your exit lane early to see whether it's an "Exit Only," or a plain off-ramp. Don't be the last-minute lane switcher, and beware kamikazes diving for the exit.

At Le Mans we spend 85 percent of the time with the pedal to the metal, and the average speed is above 140 mph. My brain becomes so accustomed to it that when I've finished a three-hour stint behind the wheel, I can close my eyes twenty minutes later and still see the dotted white line flashing past my retinas.

As you enter the pits, a sharp curve around a sand pit physically enforces the speed limit of 40 mph. It feels so slow, the world seems to stop turning, and there are more tears than sand in that pit from drivers who overcooked it on the way in and cost themselves the race. You have to flip a mental switch and remember that the world just got a lot closer, smaller, and slower.

Boring but important:

As you exit:

- ▸ Do mirrors and shoulder checks.
- ▸ Check the speedometer.
- ▸ Prepare for two-way traffic.
- ▸ Prepare for sharper curves.
- ▸ Beware slippery spillage deposited where the off-ramp meets an intersection.

THE GAME

The freeway game is just like musical chairs.

The freeway game is just like musical chairs, with long periods when nothing happens followed by sudden bursts of activity. If you can still remember, the winning strategy with musical chairs was to hold back a little and let the herd in front bunch up. You kept your eyes on the prized empty chairs, and listened. Then, when the music stopped and everybody slammed on the brakes, you quietly slipped into the empty space, assuming that you weren't rear-ended by the kid with braces who kept slugs in a jar.

Freeway speeds are higher than other roads, but the traffic flows at *relatively slow* speeds of vehicles to one another. The speed differential, the delta, between lanes might be less than 5 mph but when the music stops, or if someone cuts in front of you, then relative speeds can change quickly.

Rather than reacting to slowing traffic, the trick is to anticipate change well before it happens and create an opportunity with enough space to handle it. Using this fluid map of your surroundings means you can pick your moments to pass other vehicles without being cut off, while staying out of the way of those passing you.

Look out for hazards like speed cameras or the shattered remains of a crashed car that prompt lesser drivers to deploy a negative G emergency brake and rubberneck at the scene. Debris such as detached bodywork or a shredded truck tire also tend to spook traffic. Lane closures and other roadwork will also compress traffic, causing it to slow.

The trick is to anticipate change.

HOT TIPS ▸ Everything should be happening more slowly for you at high speed. Turn the steering more slowly, take longer to do things, and allow more time for people to register your intentions.

SPACE, TIME, AND RELATIVITY

The space in front of you acts like a buffer zone that gives you the room to maneuver and the safety to stop in a hurry. The space required to perform the latter governs the amount of buffer you need to maintain. By forward planning you also burn a lot less fuel—and money—than jumping on and off the throttle.

Most officials measure this safety zone using time, but I really prefer distance, because the brain recognizes these instantly, and time cannot be trusted.

When you brake from any speed, you shed roughly 20 mph every second in dry conditions. Your perception of slowing in relation to time is that the process is constant, but, as we saw in Stopping Distance on page 80, this doesn't hold true on the ground.

The way in which speed reduces across a distance varies *drastically*, and it takes much longer to shed higher speeds than slower ones. The result on a freeway when the music stops is that the early adopters of the middle pedal end up decelerating at a considerably faster rate than the ones who didn't see it coming. The late brakers cannot possibly slow down in time, and they all get smashed up, hence the term *concertina*.

For that reason it's a good idea to keep an eye on your tail, too, especially if a big, heavy truck has taken a shine to your rear bumper. Generally, tailgaters have one of two intentions: to pass you because you're in the way, or to sit there idly because their brain is in neutral. Switching to an outside lane should resolve the first problem. If it doesn't solve the second, then you can gently roll off the gas to encourage your new best friend to find another attraction.

FOLLOWING DISTANCE

As a general rule my following distance is at least the length of an articulated truck, increasing to two trucks for freeways and three if the weather turns gnarly. A semi-truck is about 57 feet long, so this equates to a distance of 114 feet for freeway driving.

If you're following a car of similar size, by positioning slightly to the side of the vehicle in front you can see well beyond it as well as through its windshield for a meaningful glimpse of what you're heading into. It also gives you space within which to back away from slowing traffic, or gradually build acceleration to pass, which saves fuel.

From this enhanced vantage point you can see the world ahead in all its glory and predict the future. Anticipation of an event reduces your reaction time to an incident considerably. Assuming that you see it coming, the delay in your foot reaching the brake pedal is roughly half a second—call it 50 feet at 70 mph. That length of thinking distance is fine when you're monitoring the flow.

If your observation is less than constant, a few missed seconds suddenly translates to 250 feet driving blind. It then takes a minimum of one full second for the brain to calculate your rate of closure to the incident and *then* react. You've traveled the length of a football field, and by now everybody in front is decelerating faster than you can. Good luck.

Predict the future.

20. Following Distance

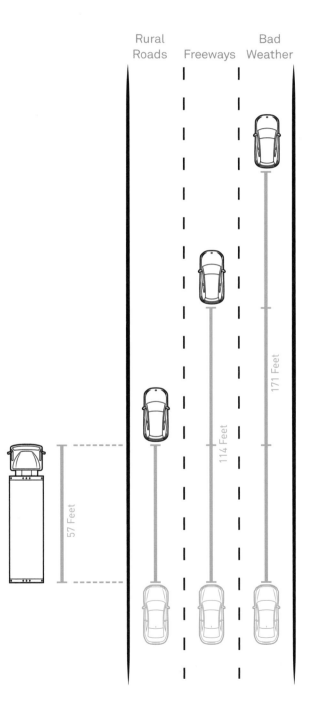

Rural Roads · Freeways · Bad Weather

57 Feet

114 Feet

171 Feet

▸ Be fast and fleeting with glances at the radio or gorgeous passengers, or suffer my fate from "King of the Road" (see page 27) you will, young Jedi.

▸ Tailgating the car in front denies you any situational awareness; you're just a sheep.

COMMUNICATION

Drivers communicate with each other by sharing of information nonverbally. Your focus should be twofold: to make your intentions clear and to be seen. Don't loiter in people's blind spots, and use signals with plenty of warning before switching lanes.

If someone isn't paying attention and strays toward your lane as you run alongside, give them a short blast of the horn. Anything longer might be mistaken for a request to partake in a duel at the next service station.

Besides the obvious signs you might receive when people actually signal, this is a game of innuendo. Study the other players for potential signs of movement as they close up on each other in front and as they approach you from behind. Relative speeds and traffic compression provide the best clues as to when vehicles might switch lanes.

Body language such as a turn of the head or a wobble of steering might suggest an impending lane change, or it could just be the second coming of that steak-and-ale pie. When a vehicle strays from the center of its lane, it suggests the driver isn't switched on and it might also intimate a lane change. People often turn the wheel and signal at the same time, which rather defeats the purpose, but you get used to it.

BLIND SPOTS

I love it when Europeans describe the business of NASCAR and oval racing as "shoving your foot down and turning left." It reminds me that the secrets of driving at continuously high speeds are known only to a few.

When you stand on the straight part of a two-mile superspeedway, it looks like a very long corridor that runs into a wall. You start driving along it with every intention of running into the apparition of banked asphalt at the end with your foot completely nailed to the floor. Sadly, there's more than enough time to debate this strategy several times during your journey . . .

You expect the wall to open into the longest and most forgiving curve you've ever seen, but it really doesn't. There's an abrupt camber change as you enter, plus bumps of the "Je-sus, why the f*** didn't somebody tell me about those?" variety that would loosen the bowel of the stiffest stool pincher.

The extra G created by the banking squeezes your delicate juices firmly into the chair, and if you didn't swallow enough air before going in, your next draw of breath results in a feeble whimper. The steering goes so heavy you think it might snap, and, as per tradition for a first oval adventure, your knuckles will whiten around the wheel in an attempt to force it to stop frightening you. This creates a tighter arc around the turn than necessary, followed by a savage response over the Jesus bumps and a far-from-pleasant "lightening" at the rear as you exit.

Misery loves company, and there's plenty to be had when the green flag drops to start the race. Forty cars join the party, packed so tightly around you that there's no space for wing mirrors, so you only have a head mirror. Your saucer eyes spend almost as much time there as they do facing the cars filling your windshield.

As the swarm veers into the turn, it carves through the air, leaving a messy vacuum in its wake. An invisible god called turbulence reaches deep into the pack and slaps you all around. With inches to spare to the car in front, one on your ass, and lanes of shuffling traffic huddled close to either side, there's precious room to spare when your car squirms and kicks in the jet wash.

The most sensitive part of your operation is the one bit of the car that you can't see: the rear quarter. Unlike on the open road, your melon is so tightly tethered with safety harnesses that you can't physically look over your shoulder.

With your vision naturally prioritizing the tangle in front and directly behind, it's easy to forget the blind spot and creep over into a lane of traffic traveling at a different speed from yours. At high speed the platform has to remain stable, and contact with the rear quarter usually results in a spin followed by a thump.

To cover this vital base, oval racers have a dedicated spotter high up in the grandstands who chain-smokes while watching your progress through some binoculars. He provides continuous dialogue via radio about everything taking place in the blind spot, offers moral guidance, and chivies you along with a narrative of what is approaching beyond the range of your head mirror.

Spotters are expensive creatures that require constant rehydration at the bar, so in real life you can save yourself a lot of money by looking over your shoulder before you go for broke.

When you stand on the straight part of a two-mile superspeedway, it looks like a very long corridor that runs into a wall.

21. Freeway Blind Spots

Eliminating the blind spot is as simple as looking over your shoulder—but don't be the joker in the bottom car loitering out of sight, waiting to be sideswiped.

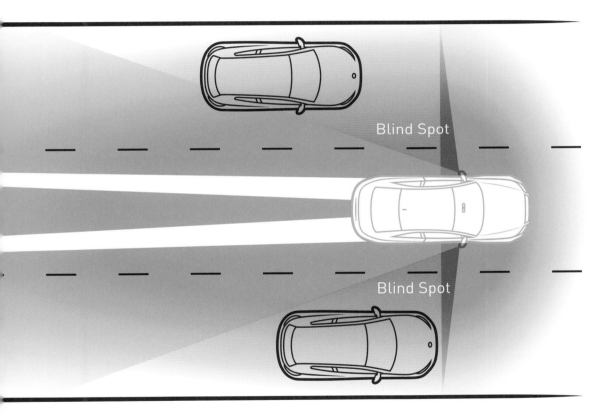

Blind Spot

Blind Spot

THE PLAYERS

Like any sport, the players bring out the best and worst in each other. Your own self-interest should remain your prime objective, but unless you deploy some courtesy and cater to the needs of others you will either cause pileups or find yourself being French-kissed by a hairy paramedic. If you find yourself jumping on the brakes a lot and making last-ditch maneuvers, I'm afraid this means you.

The biggest players on the field are the heavy-goods vehicles that float up and down the transportation arteries like icebergs. They have their own game, called *drafts*, which involves slipstreaming one another and occasionally making the slowest overtaking maneuvers known to man. It's like turtle sex, and the whole freeway comes to a standstill until it's over.

The majority of trucks are well driven, but you don't want to bet your life that a thirty-four-ton semi can stop if you cut in front of it and climb on the brakes. It can't, not even by half. Trucks may only make up 1 percent of the vehicles lumbering along American roads, but they count for nearly a fifth of fatal multicar pileups. A single truck doing 70 mph carries the equivalent force of a car doing 361 mph.

Owing to their size, trucks have enormous aerodynamic drag, and this vortex can shove your vehicle around. The effect is pronounced on windy days, and if you don't pay attention the effect can be magnetic, meaning your paths collide.

Boring but important:

- ▸ Keep checking your mirrors. The police take a dim view of following a driver for ten minutes with their sirens wailing.
- ▸ Own the blind spot.
- ▸ Note the air temperature: Below 40 degrees, there might be ice.
- ▸ Scan actively: A fertile imagination for potential scenarios will boost your attention span and buy you time to anticipate, rather than react to, situations.

MERGERS AND ACQUISITIONS

Lane hopping in busy traffic, spurred by the powerful instinct to get ahead of the pack by finding the lane of least resistance, is strong juju. But it's a fruitless pastime that makes you more likely to crash.

However, a closed lane that requires traffic to merge is a different game altogether, one that really separates the philanthropist from the predator. Typically,

Heavy-goods vehicles that float up and down the transportation arteries like icebergs.

the warning sign of pending lane closures ahead prompts a sort of dash for the last splash at the watering hole.

You either form an orderly queue with the rest of the righteous or motor on regardless until the last moment, then force your way in. Vigilantes spring to life to defend the sanctity of "their lane" by straddling the white line to block your entry or reaching for the Glock 9mm.

Research has shown that lane-merging is no more a moral struggle than a shoal of fish negotiating a reef. Merging "late"—when the lane ends—shortens the distance spent in reduced space and avoids the backup from a premature queue. By adopting the live-and-let-live policy, this should make traffic converge as seamlessly as a zipper. On average, late merging is faster for everyone. Don't shoot the messenger.

GAME-CHANGING WEATHER

Weather is dealt with in Part 4: Skidding, but it would be remiss to ignore the significant part that weather plays on freeway driving before you pull off for a well-earned coffee break.

SUN

Low sun in particular zaps you right in the eyes, particularly when combined with grime on the windshield. I'll never forget a teammate of mine launching out of the pits for a qualifying session at the Lausitzring speedway, hammering down the pit straight at 170 mph and driving straight into the wall. When he told the team manager that he was blinded by the sun, we didn't know whether to laugh or cry.

Drop the sun visor and slap the shades on. If the sun is behind you and reflecting off the mirrors, adjust their angle.

FOG, SPRAY, AND SMOKE

When your visual range is restricted to less than 120 yards, or the length of an American football field, your ability to predict the future suffers. Below that distance, you should run headlights. Run fog lights *only if* there's fog, otherwise they just blind other drivers—there's a reason these are illegal in many states.

When people can't see, they always slow down, so be prepared for this if you enter a flash storm or a bank of fog, spot glare from the sun beating off a wet surface, or approach a wall of smoke . . . since people still love to light a bonfire close to the road.

RAIN

When it turns moist, the freeway punishes fumbling fingers. With reduced vision and grip underfoot, you need to avoid coarse steering, jumpy braking, or harsh acceleration, which are more likely to upset the applecart.

So long as your car is maintained, it will actually brake quite well in wet conditions. What it can't cope with so well are lateral movements. Swerving will cost nearly half of your grip.

At 70 mph, the braking distance in wet conditions for a *good* modern tire is roughly 25 percent longer than in dry conditions, but you should still extend your following distance by the length of a semi. Why?

You can't see as much, and other motorists are more prone to making mistakes in bad weather. Steamy windows making it hard to shoulder-check the blind spots, mirrors obscured with drizzle, and worn-out wipers smearing the front windshield—all these combine to make it ever so easy to reach out and touch someone.

Giving more space to the car in front reduces the impact of its spray and provides better strategic oversight of everyone's relative speeds and positions.

Another reason for needing more space is to allow you to scan the road surface for standing water that could cause the car to hydroplane. If enough water forces its way underneath your tires, it lifts them off the road, and you lose control over them. Hydroplaning occurs almost exclusively at high speed, and if your observation skills are good, then you can spot these shimmering shadows before they greet your tires. For more detail on hydroplaning please see Avoiding Hydroplaning on page 218.

SNOW

Snow is less aggressive than ice but seriously reduces grip on standard summer tires. The snow often builds up quickest in the fast lane as people migrate to the perceived safety of the slower lanes.

Before the snow gets compacted, it fills up with slippery powder. So if you pile into an uncleared lane to pass slower vehicles, it won't be pretty.

Other motorists are more prone to making mistakes in bad weather.

Beware the sludgy ridges that form between lanes, which make life interesting when you try to cross them. If the ridge is small enough, and your speed is low enough, you can turn across it gradually to switch lanes.

The challenges arise as a result of the way in which the sludge interacts with each wheel as it makes contact. It builds at the head of the front tire, acting like a brake, transferring weight to the front and off the rears, and then when the rears encounter the sludge, well . . . you already know, they lose grip and probably slide.

To counteract this issue you can take more than one bite out of the apple by steering gently into the sludge, straightening the wheel as the car decelerates on the thick stuff, then very gradually inching your way across with micro-movements on the wheel.

BLACK ICE

These conditions are thankfully rare on highways, where regular sanding puts them out of business. But if the temperature drops rapidly, as it can at night, water may freeze and become "black ice." Ice tends to be silent underfoot, so the road noise will suddenly go absent, but if you're even questioning it, just get off the throttle and let wind resistance take your speed off. Be gentle with the steering and avoid braking until the car lands.

To check for ice, and assuming there's nobody close behind, you can dab the brakes in a straight line to test for traction. If there's a hint of trouble or the ABS light flickers, then Jack Frost is paying you a visit!

Braking distances extend by up to ten times in frozen conditions, and the surface grip varies from one yard to the next, so you need to extend your focus at least three times farther forward to anticipate events.

Jack Frost is paying you a visit!

3.6 *IN THE ZONE*

"Good morning, Mr. Stig," purred the dulcet tones of Gavin Whitehead, the Scottish producer of *Top Gear*.

"We're gonna V-max a bunch of supercars with you and Hammond out in the desert in Abu Dhabi, so we need to organize a recce and map out the runs. Have you got any special requirements?"

"Water, tons of it."

Gav scratched some notes, "H—2—O. You're a cheap date. One thing we've flagged is the cat's eyes out there are really big. The concern is that if you strike one at 200 mph it might cause a puncture. What's your view?"

"At ten thousand dollars a tire I think we should be OK, but we should make a rule not to drive over them. I'm more interested to see if the roadside verge drops away and check for things like trees, bridges, and roadwork in case we get a blowout."

The end of the line went silent.

"Yeah, that's pretty high on the agenda this time."

Just three years prior, Hammond had nearly lost his life at the helm of a jet car propelling him down a runway at 330 mph, when the front tire blew out. A big investigation followed, but the lasting impression was that hindsight was a poor substitute for 20/20 forward planning. We left no stone unturned for *Top Gear of Arabia*.

Stepping onto the asphalt at Abu Dhabi International Airport, I thought the rubber soles would melt off my shoes. Hammond was rocking a seriously bushy hairdo and absorbing a piss-take about a scene of him riding a horse across the dunes. The producers squeezed some gems into the risk assessment: "Ears flat back means 'I bite.' Watch out for big, heavy hooves, stamping on your feet."

Our first stop was a palatial building owned by one of the sheikhs with close ties to the royal family. It turned out that this building was just a garage for his car collection. I counted about eighty to-die-for models, including three Bugatti Veyrons: one red, one blue, and one in chrome. We were borrowing the red one.

Gav invited me to give it a once-over, and I walked around it like a sommelier judging a fine wine by the shape of its glass. Veyrons usually have a two-tone color scheme, but this beauty was dipped in bloodred from head to toe, accentuating its hunched shoulders, steely eyes, and bulbous rear end.

"I'll take it," and with that I was handed the keys to a $1 million car without even signing a form.

Down at the docks a precious cargo was being unloaded from its container and driven onto dry land by a man wearing white rubber gloves. The owner, Rowan Atkinson, would have preferred a full-body condom to anybody driving his beloved McLaren F1. He spent twenty minutes pacing me through its working parts in the UK and was excruciatingly particular that I "b-b-be very careful with the clutch," the severity of the words bringing out a Mr. Bean–like stammer in an otherwise perfect monologue.

We took the two titans to our designated three-lane highway, closed off by our very own escort of armed police. The one-mile drag strip was bordered with palm trees and ornamental grass in an otherwise barren infinity of sand dunes and blue sky.

We lined up the red Bug alongside the deep-purple Mac and admired the shimmering view of two radically different examples of engineering perfection: modern vs. a relic from the 1990s.

Hammond took the Bug, which was fully automated and had every gadget known to man for planting 1,000 bhp safely to the road through its four-wheel-drive system. Traction control prevented any slippage from 0 to 60 mph, in 2.5 seconds, and hydraulics whirred tirelessly to tune the car's considerable aerodynamic stability on your journey to 252 mph. Antilock brakes brought you back to earth, as did an air brake that deflected enough air with its wing to put over half the earth's gravity through your coccyx. That alone was more deceleration than most cars achieve with standard brakes. And it even had a launch control system for . . . pulling away from traffic lights in a hurry.

I took the Mac. It had three pedals and came with rear-wheel drive only. It did 0 to 60 mph in just under four seconds and topped out at 240. Basic, but bombproof.

The camera team was ready and had developed a disturbing penchant for stripping off whenever the sun broke cover, gaffer-taping their shorts into a sort of diaper-thong thing to spread the tan. You could probably be shot for lesser offenses in Arabia, but they felt the risk was worth it.

Basic, but bombproof.

In the Zone

McLaren F1 Supercar, built in 1992. Only the brave should enter these doors, and only then wearing Kevlar boxers.

Gav told us to stand by over the radio before signaling the local chief of police: "Please ask your men to hide themselves behind the trees and stand by to shoot."

An unfortunate choice of words, perhaps.

The race would be initiated by countdown. The amateur waits for the lights to change to green before accelerating, adding hundredths of seconds to the departure time. A pro eyes the red and pulls the trigger as soon as the first photons start to dwindle.

"Three . . ." The Bugatti belched a monotonous drone as Hammond floored the throttle and the launch control held his revs precisely on the red line.

"Two . . ." I held the McLaren's banshee V-12 at bay with 5,000-ish revs.

"One . . ." The clutch nudged the biting point.

"G—" I let slip half an inch of the Mac's hair-trigger clutch; she nosed up and belted forward. The rears bit perfectly, and the engine note stayed crisp until I reached a healthy enough speed to let the clutch out fully, causing the rears to chirp in the final moment of first gear with a satisfying *cha-cha-cha*. Rowan had insisted we only make one hot pull away. It was all I needed.

As something red faded from my window, all my hair stood on end. Unencumbered by technology or the weight that goes with it, the McLaren dusted the Bugatti to 60 and beyond. It finally succumbed to the irrepressible volume of power from the Bugatti's W-16 engine, the equivalent of two V-8s strapped together.

Though the Bugatti and the old McLaren F1 both head rapidly north of 200 mph, the experience inside the cockpits at those speeds couldn't be more different. In the Bugatti you are thinking about where you might like to have dinner that evening, while in the McLaren you are basically shitting yourself.

Its demented engine tone and otherworldly floating sensation from the chassis tell you that if you screw this up, your face will be flat-packed into the dashboard tighter than a wallet at a Scottish auction. The Bugatti has every stability control device known to man, and tires sticky enough to turn asphalt into molasses. *Yet more have crashed in their short history than the old McLaren.* I'm not suggesting we turn back the clock, but I prefer the McLaren because it really talks to you. Technology cuts off the connection between man and machine, numbs the senses and dulls the mind. And I don't trust it.

All my hair stood on end.

Gizmos like ABS have not made us safer.

Twenty years ago your car's air con came with a handle, and you only got GPS in the *Millennium Falcon*. By 2020, there will be well over a billion machines talking to each other and making decisions using artificial intelligence.

Google seems determined to take the fun out of things by producing a car that pretty much drives itself. Meanwhile, real car manufacturers are dabbling with partial automation to warn you of the presence of other road users using radar and a suite of onboard safety systems. They indicate invaders hiding in blind spots off your starboard bow by flashing orange lights inside the wing mirrors, with "lane change assist" causing the wheel to vibrate and resist your steering input if you mistakenly turn toward one. In the models I've tested, the lights flash all the time, so you learn to ignore your mirrors. Forward-facing radar can trigger the brakes if you doze off and run too close to the back of someone, and the GPS will command you when to actually do something yourself.

Like the *Falcon*, however, I regularly find myself transported to the wrong side of an asteroid belt with greater frequency than I care to admit. The almighty Cloud is as reliable as a South American currency, which makes the prospect of seeing flocks of driverless cars filing around the countryside in the hands of Cybernet seem unlikely from an insurance perspective, let alone a practical one.

Gizmos like ABS have not made us safer. Why? The misconception is that ABS enables you to brake later, which it doesn't. This leads drivers to follow one another too closely or brake too deep into curves. And skidding off the road at higher speeds into immovable objects such as trees, or barrel-rolling in the roadside shoulder is worse for your health than a locking wheel.

For now, at least, I can't help feeling that we should be the masters of technology, not the other way around. If you could have given Mozart a synthesizer, he wouldn't have let it play him.

So now that you're a hardened Garry Kasparov on the open road, your inner chi is braced for impact, and you've signed the waiver, it's time to channel your full potential, switch off the autopilot, and unleash your greatest asset: your mind. The next few chapters aim to demystify the mental and visual assets that race-car drivers use to chase perfection, to get into the zone, and bring it to a road near you.

3.7 FREE YOUR MIND (AND THE REST WILL FOLLOW)

The Mark 1 brain continues to outperform supercomputers in a range of complex tasks from instant facial recognition to observing and dissecting complex patterns, analyzing situations, and forming decisions.

It can multitask physical operations while prioritizing safe and threatening scenarios, form a plan based on that information, and act. All while consuming less energy than a lightbulb.

We take this miracle and pack it so full of rubbish that it fails the task of driving. The main drain on the mental system is human emotion. I'm not talking about people who cry when their cat sneezes; it goes deeper than that. There are key emotional triggers that interfere with the cognitive process and they need to be eliminated to cleanse the mind, Buddha-like.

Nearly a quarter of all drivers involved in fatal crashes—and more in straight fender benders—had been upset by an incident or an argument during the six hours leading up to the accident.

Stress and the emotional baggage it brings with it come in many guises, and it's sometimes hard to see it coming. It could be a fight at home or just hearing Kanye West's voice on the radio, but anything that makes you twitch like a psycho or feel negative will affect your decision-making process. Negative thoughts make you feel like the world is against you, so why bother? You abrogate responsibility for your actions, and mistakes follow. It makes it easier to personalize conflicts that don't exist and lose the context of a situation. With adrenaline, you have the happy kind of excited as well as the angry kind. Both can cloud your judgment but none more so than the red mist.

Cleanse the mind, Buddha-like.

EMOTIONAL BAGGAGE

For those perfect souls out there for whom nothing could penetrate your ice-cold demeanor, here are a few examples that might still rattle your cage without you realizing.

TIME PRESSURE

The perception of being "out of time" can turn you into a time bomb. We've all been to IKEA once in our lives, a black hole of vapid timelessness until you come out the other side with your pride in tatters as you try, and fail, to condense the rich pickings of the last four hours into the back of your wagon. You settle divorce proceedings on the back of an object you could never possibly put together and try to make up for lost time on the way home.

Your entire focus is enslaved to the clock, with nothing left for your surroundings. You become totally uncompromising, shutting down your willingness to adapt to the road conditions or anyone sharing them. In short, you've become a cabbie.

Time pressure also finds traction during a race. As the final laps tick away, drivers start to worry about that extra place on the podium, and that pressure feeds irrational behavior. The solution? I wish I had one. We are always in a hurry these days; just try to suck it up and smile.

PERCEIVED WRONGDOING/RAGE

The guy in front deliberately failed to signal at a roundabout so that he could hold you up on the way to work. And it's a BMW, which means he's one of those arrogant bastards who is probably on the phone. You're just reaching for the 9mm. Then the car shakily peels off, and you realize he was a granny and she was lost.

Stay cool because you'll live longer.

Stay cool because you'll live longer.

COMMUTED

Stress is the mind killer, the sense of being overwhelmed by a set of circumstances that you are powerless to overcome. Apparently long-distance commuting exerts so much stress that it's a miracle we survive the journey. One psychological study concluded that a third of commuters traveling three hours daily in Germany were, "from a medical point of view, clearly in need of treatment." Their condition was cited as "terrible" and included a blend of dizziness, sleep deprivation, and bodily pains that could only be brought on otherwise by watching *The Jerry Springer Show*.

Other studies show that driving stress raises blood pressure and increases the likelihood of heart disease. The only consolation is that users of public transport are more likely to contract infectious diseases or be assaulted for their choice of music.

The trick is to remember those Antarctic penguins. You feel sorry for the poor buggers stuck on the edge of the colony, freezing their flippers off—but they know their turn in the wind is about to end. They're only a flipper away from being able to shuffle into the middle for tea and sardines. The end of the traffic jam is usually a lot closer than you think, so crank the tunes, plan a vacation, and relax.

DISTRACTION

It's no wonder that people driving while jawing away on mobile phones are a nightmare. Kimi Räikönnen said it best when his team kept distracting him on the radio during a Grand Prix: "*Just leave me alone!* I know what I'm doing." It's fair to say that the clearer the mind, the clearer the road.

The all-pervading screen has infected every aspect of our lives—and making a call or, worse, texting while driving makes you twenty-three times more likely to have an accident *and* make a spelling mistake. It so saps the gray matter that a study in Utah reckoned it was safer to drive drunk. (That is most definitely not a recommendation, by the way.)

GPS is little better, and that blinding screen in the center of the dashboard with the hypnotic powers of Criss Angel is turning motorists into zombies. "Turn left," and moments later one woman had driven her $150,000 Mercedes SL500 straight into a river. No amount of telling her to "turn around where possible" was getting her out of this fine pickle.

Remember when Luke descended at breakneck speed into the canyon of the mighty Death Star amidst a frenzy of fire? The rebel base was in the crosshairs, and Luke only had one bomb with which to defeat the Empire, so he switched on his targeting computer. Obi Wan knew that the pressure was on and that the damned screen was ruining Luke's night vision. He persuaded Luke to trust his instinct and turn the computer off. The rest is history.

"Just leave me alone! I know what I'm doing."

22. Distractions

Sending a Text — 70 / 30 — 10 seconds

Looking at SatNav — 70 / 30 — 8 seconds

Applying Lipstick — 70 / 30 — 5 seconds

Glovebox Snack — 70 / 30 — 3 seconds

TOUCHDOWN · 10- · 20- · 30- · 40- · 50 · 40- · 30- · 20- · 10- · TOUCHDOWN · TOUCHDOWN

120 yards

240
yards

360
yards

DEAD WEIGHT

We sometimes forget that the most burdensome—and distracting—weight in the car is the passenger. Every time you add one up to the age of twenty-five, you *double* the likelihood of having an accident. And peer pressure is a continuing nightmare. If I had a pound for every time I've heard someone say *"Go on!,"* that Ferrari Italia would be sitting in my front drive. As well as goading you to drive faster, young passengers in particular press too many buttons and affect your ability to focus. And in small hatchbacks, standard issue as a first car, the combined weight of your passengers has an exponentially negative effect on the vehicle's ability to handle a curve, or to stop.

As for children, God love them, but they are the worst. There you are, working the wheel, urgently wiping urine and chocolate off your shoulders while a bag of wet wipes silently slips underneath the brake pedal, and all they can do is complain that *Dora the Explorer* isn't on or, worse, make happy noises.

HOT TIPS
- Square away all the children, the climate, the audio, and GPS before you move. Stay cool: You're doing an important job.
- You are the mission commander, so if anybody has a problem with that they can take alternative travel of the two-legged variety. If passengers distract you, tell them to be quiet and pay for your fuel.
- And careful with the mascara during rush hour. That goes for men too.

DRUGS AND ALCOHOL

You can't be in control of yourself or the machine if you're drunk, drugged, or sick—no matter what you tell yourself. Saturday is the most deadly day of the week for one reason: That's when everyone drinks the most.

ENVIRONMENT

Weather, traffic, noise, discomfort—these are all triggers that build muscular tension, which impairs the natural flow of blood through your arms and legs and stiffens your responses and buttocks. The resulting lactic acid creeps up on you and ultimately degrades your mental state too.

Blasting around Phillip Island, Australia, in a V-8 Supercar at speeds of up to 180 mph (and in temperatures of around 80 degrees), I noticed after an hour or so that the car wasn't slowing well into a hairpin. There was nothing noticeably wrong with the brakes; the problem revealed itself only after I took the checkered flag.

I knew my seating position would be uncomfortable because I had to make allowances for my vertically challenged teammate Nathan Pretty (aka Randy Corners). I failed to notice that it had entirely cut off the blood supply to my right leg.

The instant I crossed the line, my body finally gave up and exacted its revenge. My right leg went into spasm. It was so dead I had to make it back to the pits on my left foot and hobbled around the paddock like a lopsided cowboy for the rest of the day.

The most burdensome— and distracting— weight in the car is the passenger.

3.8 *VISION*

> *"If you are in a good state, psychologically speaking, your sensitivity of vision is so much greater, so much more accurate, it makes everything else much more natural and easy."*
>
> —Ayrton Senna, triple Formula One world champion

Earlier on, we highlighted how important it is to look around you and spot potential hazards, but let's go a little deeper into the techniques that distinguish the great from the merely good. Cleansed of all cerebral impropriety, it's time for your head socket to plug in to God's greatest gift.

THE MARK 1 EYEBALL

The most advanced piece of tech riding on board with you, 24/7, is the human eyeball. Fitted with night vision, it can detect movement at distances in excess of two miles. Your eye can switch focus from a close object smaller than a pinhead to a panoramic view in just 0.04 seconds.

Being hardwired to your brain, the most advanced of processors, the eyeball can not only read incoming signals but actually predict them. Vision and control are the driver's two most important functions. You can't manage what you can't see. And wherever your eyes lead, your hands generally follow.

US Air Force hero Chuck Yeager was arguably the greatest pilot of his era. In his words, the key to his success was survival. He had the ability to think one step ahead because he looked *much* farther into the distance than his contemporaries.

Analyzing the scene from farther away means that it takes longer to materialize; time and speed effectively slow down, giving you the strategic advantage to control events. On the road it pays to think like Yeager and stay one step ahead by reviewing the foreground, the middle distance, and the horizon.

PERIPHERAL VISION

"When you look up, look wide, and even when you think you are looking wide, look wider still."
–Robert Baden-Powell, founder of the Scout Movement

Look up, look wide.

Baden-Powell was talking about observing the natural world, and his teachings are wholly relevant to driving. The modern world encourages us to be near-focused on everything from TVs to computers. Our field of vision is constricted, and so our shoulders tense up, because it's unnatural. Going wide will be life-changing.

Samurai warriors learned to use the wider-focus technique in combat with multiple opponents. Rather than maintaining a hard focus on one individual, they relaxed their vision, allowing the edges to blur and extending their field of view. Peripheral vision is strongest at detecting movement, so by shifting their awareness around the scene rather than moving their eyes, the warriors were able to monitor multiple attacks.

Extreme sports offer fine examples of soft focus, arguably none more so than ice hockey. The extreme accuracy required to hit the puck into the net is matched by the predatory aggression of the competitors. Wayne Gretzky, aka "The Great One," chalked up his legendary ability to see everything and everyone simultaneously to: "Fear. When you're 170 pounds playing with 210-pound guys, you learn to find out where *everybody* is on the ice at all times. If not, you'll find yourself forechecked into the mezzanine."

To master this technique you don't need black pajamas or a hockey stick. Stick your thumb out in front of you and look at it closely: Your thumb is now in sharp focus at the expense of the wider scene. Now ignore your thumb, and look straight ahead to absorb the 200-degree field of vision without fixing on anything in particular. Move that thumb around and track it using your consciousness *without moving your eyes*. Now you're looking like a ninja and you can process ten times as much information.

It is simply not possible, nor recommended, to locate every threat or hazard on the road using a fixed stare. When you do need to move your head or your eyes to analyze situations, the aim is to flick across to make observations and return to the core peripheral view.

Vision

▸ A great way to improve your peripheral vision is juggling, and if you do it in public you might even get paid. Tracking each ball's path is impossible, so you pick a comfortable focus with occasional flickering glances at the wayward passes. If you find that easy, try doing it on an exercise ball.

THE VISUAL STRATEGY OF A RACING DRIVER

A scientific study carried out by the Biological Sciences team from the University of Sussex revealed that when we drive, our eye movements and steering inputs are tightly linked:

> *We studied the eye movements of a racing driver during high-speed practice to see whether he took in visual information in a different way from a normal driver on a winding road. We found that, when cornering, he spent most of the time looking close to, but not exactly at, the tangent points on the inside edges of the curves.*

For driving on curves, *peripheral* vision creates a much more fluid landscape than you can achieve using a series of hard focus points. That's the secret to being an effective driver for coping with speed on the racetrack as well as for everyday driving. The enhanced spatial awareness boosts your perception of speed and distance.

In biological terms, the Mark 1 eyeball has two types of receptors on the lookout for incoming light rays: *cones* and *rods*. Peripheral vision relies on scattered rod cells, which provide a loosely focused but broad impression of the world outside, great at detecting movement and providing night vision. That's right: Soft focus is how you drive at night.

Night-vision rods are housed around the outside of the retina at the back of the eye, which is why stars look brighter at night when you view them slightly off center. They are highly sensitive to bright light, so it benefits them to shield them from anything that dazzles them. The center of the retina is instead packed tight with cones, which provide hawkish, focused visual acuity—the type of vision we use for reading signs, or sending a text message.

Inexperienced drivers with less eye discipline use this type of vision when making turns by moving their gaze rigidly from one point to the next along the curb or the roadside. Alternatively, they focus on the area directly in front of them or on

Soft focus is how you drive at night.

the tailpipe of the next car, reacting passively to situations as they develop, rather than actively anticipating and controlling them. Put simply, they are missing the bigger picture. This is quite a natural way of adapting to being in a big, wide car for the first time, and developing the hand-eye coordination to avoid running into stuff. But it puts a major dent in your radar.

Fighter pilots refer to this practice as *target fixation*. On numerous occasions, pilots have chased their bombs into weapons factories or mistakenly taken Iceman's advice too far by literally following the wingman into the ground during formation flying.

Growing into the wider view takes practice, and it is worth noting that when the shit hits the fan, even experienced drivers will often revert to the series of fixed points.

The problem with big eye movements to pull focus, or to use the technical term, *saccades*, is that the eye can see only once it stops moving, so it takes a few tenths of a second for it to land and refocus. That may not sound like much, but it adds up and gets compounded by speed, because you travel a considerable distance in that time.

Race-car drivers do something else interesting. They flicker. I don't mean middle fingers to tell the other guy he's in second place. They flick their eyes rapidly at a scene, without drawing focus, and return to the main view. It's not accurate enough to read a sign, but it suffices to check for something alarming in the rearview mirror, or just to reestablish the general landscape.

HELL IS OTHER PEOPLE

When you drive in circles for a living, it's hardly surprising that what goes around comes around. It's been proven that if you put a man in uniform and hand him a stick—as in the classic 1971 Stanford Prison Experiment—he will push and poke people around with it. Not so many years ago, I was handed the keys to a really big stick and sent to race it in the FIA World Sportscar Championship as well as at the Le Mans 24 Hours.

My car had 800 horsepower, the hunter-killer look of a stealth fighter . . . and weighed less than a Mini Cooper. As if these Le Mans Prototypes, or LMP1 cars, didn't look fast enough sprinting down a French boulevard at 225 mph, the race organizers honored the spirit of endurance racing by allowing different, slower classes of car to compete for the same piece of asphalt.

The GT class, or cannon fodder, was made up of things like Ferraris, Porsches, and Lambos that routinely shuddered every time an LMP1 scythed past and blew their doors off. I could slide out of a curve in my beast, see one of these lowly creatures approaching the next curve, and still have time to dive-bomb past it at the last moment before veering off and leaving it behind like a static dot in the mirror. These close shaves would occur up to twelve times a lap, and you couldn't afford to show mercy, not even once, otherwise the other vultures would end up on your tail. When the team manager congratulated you on a "good job passing traffic," it really meant that you had been a splendid bastard.

Fast-forward to this year, and with an irony that would delight my list of former victims, I find myself driving a roadblock with a Ferrari badge. At Silverstone your vision is naturally extended by its long straights and sweeping curves, but the bastards still come at you from out of nowhere. Just as in everyday driving, you need to start growing eyes in the back of your head.

I found myself in the unfortunate position of leading the GT race aboard a Ferrari 458 when the rain was trying to decide whether to just cock its leg or summon Noah. Hot on my trail were the factory-run Ferraris driven by a brace of spritely Formula One test drivers, James Calado and Sam Bird. I drifted the car out of Copse in fourth gear and groped for an extra lump of steering as the rear tires spun on the AstroTurf. While dealing with that little emergency, I remembered to check *all* my mirrors for what must have been the sixtieth time that lap, looking for the piercing white flashes of something predatory.

Suddenly, two prototypes roared in out of nowhere. The 458 twitched a little sideways as I exited out onto the Hangar straight, the greasy surface affording me some advantage at first as the heavy hooves behind clambered for traction. I felt the thrum of their engines, then the cabin pressure rose as two Prototype missiles skimmed past on either side. The Porsche LMP1 to my right, possibly piloted by Mark Webber or some such rocketeer, shaved me so close that his rear wing amputated my mirror.

The severed limb left a scent of blood in the water. With no way to see what might be attacking my right-hand side, life on a clockwise track became challenging. Sam probed and pushed that area, and when he disappeared into my gaping blind spot during a manly showdown at another fast section, I had to cede him passage rather than risk a collision.

As a poacher turned gamekeeper, I found it fascinating to work the traffic in the opposite direction. Some drivers want to fight the world and waste time and energy defending their position when they are passed. In the battle of the classes between GT and LMP cars, it pays to help the other side as much as possible. When I see a faster car approaching, I gauge its speed by looking two, three, or even four times at the mirrors. Those snapshots are the only way to rate its closure in a straight line and decide how best to be "taken." If he's close enough, I ease off the throttle to help him pass before we even reach the curve so that both of us can take it cleanly. If my team manager congratulates me this time, it won't be for being a hard-ass, but for cooperating and playing well with others.

These close shaves would occur up to twelve times a lap.

3.9 *NIGHT DRIVING*

Picture a section of the most dangerous freeway you've ever seen, loaded with LA-style traffic and no manners—a road that dives down a blind bend, through a fairground, then rushes away toward the horizon, and all the while drivers are crushing past one another, headlights flashing and bodywork ripping.

The asphalt is crowned by years of abuse and littered with bits of gravel. It dumps you into a series of roundabouts without any warning, then catapults you along a tree-lined alley where you can't drive slower than 180 mph—and most folks prefer it above 200.

One missed gear shift can blow the engine. Failing to spot a passing car in the mirror can be fatal. And timing your bathroom break is *essential*. You have to maintain a high level of concentration over an extended period of time just to survive.

The hardest part is undoubtedly driving through the night. Your vision becomes severely limited at the point when your eyelids weigh most heavily. To prepare for a motoring marathon, be it the Le Mans 24 Hours or a late trip home from the office, it's good to know what's taking place in your mind and body so you can develop a diet and sleep strategy to deal with it. This is a rather long-drawn-out way of saying: snack more and take naps.

Our bodies follow a daily routine, based on a *circadian rhythm*. Crudely put, it judges light and dark, then pumps hormones around our system to switch our brains and guts off at night and wake them in the morning. That's why jet lag makes you feel sick and dehydrated.

We also follow longer energy cycles during the week. They vary from individual to individual, but don't we all hate Monday mornings?

In addition to the evening sleep, there's a secondary dip in alertness after midday, exacerbated by how much and what you eat, because blood flow diverted to your stomach leaves less for your brain. For adults, who have slower metabolisms than teens, this stage of the day is a danger zone for falling asleep at the wheel. The morning period brings on drowsiness among teenagers, because they produce more melatonin, the sleep hormone, later in their sleep cycle.

Sleeping at the wheel is the most common cause of vehicles leaving the road. Most sleep-related crashes occur between midnight and 8 a.m. (especially between 4 and 6 a.m.)—and between 1 and 3 p.m.

Dopey accidents are often fatal because the driver rarely decelerates before hitting something solid. Even if you do wake at the last moment, your reaction time and thought processes will totally suck. Eighty-five percent of those responsible will be male and young, because we do more miles and in our manliness believe we can push through the sleep barrier. I know several race-car drivers who met this fate.

Although most normal crashes happen on a Friday, sleepy ones generally occur on Mondays.

This is where *The Le Mans Diet* kicks in:

DRINKS

Water, little sips and often.

EATS

The Le Mans Diet creates the platform for enduring energy. Maintaining that balance from the beginning of the day is a far more reliable strategy than fighting off fatigue later on.

You can get away with being slightly naughty at breakfast, but by lunchtime you should definitely avoid fatty foods and unnatural sugars.

The overarching principle to maintaining energy is never to feel "full," hence the old saying "Hunt best on an empty stomach." It doesn't mean wobbling around with low blood sugar and a headache, but consuming less means you save a ton of energy that would otherwise have been expended on digestion. And pound the water like an Olympic athlete, because if you dehydrate you fall asleep. Water also enhances your metabolism, which in turn promotes mental and physical performance.

Breakfast: like a king only if you're about to earn it. Whole-grain cereal, oatmeal, fruits and veggies, and nonfatty protein. Haddock and poached eggs all the way. Tea, coffee, and juice are fine. Never miss the first meal of the day, otherwise your body thinks it's been abandoned in the Sahara and starts storing fat.

Snacking: nuts, dried fruit, and fresh fruit—all day long.

Lunch: good carbs like pasta, rice, or potatoes. White meat is best. Vegetable soups are good. These slow-burning sugars are complemented by faster burners such as bananas, gingerbread, and stewed fruit.

Dinner: Treat yourself like a Gremlin, only never eat after 8 p.m. Anytime I'm due to drive I follow the light-lunch routine. If there's time for a proper sleep after dinner then I might spoil myself with a little extra meat, and some chocolate—foods that are higher in calcium and protein promote sleep. Then it's lights out, phone off, and sayonara—always remembering to tell your crew chief where you are in case your shift starts early.

Refined sugars are like rat poison. Throwing sugar down your neck triggers insulin and leads to an energy crash, plus dehydration as your body tries to expel the excess the only way it knows how. And, trust me, you don't want to experience that on the Mulsanne straight where there're no more toilets, than there are on the freeway.

Good eating and drinking should preserve a balanced energy level throughout the day, but then again we don't live in a perfect world. When your body talks about sleep, you'd better listen.

SLEEPS

Tiredness has a way of creeping up on you unnoticed. The effects include blurred vision, heavily reduced peripheral vision, reduced awareness, and therefore a reduced ability to react. It also wreaks havoc with your emotions, which interferes with your decision making.

Your body will start going into a series of auto-shutdowns. These are known as *microsleeps*, lasting from one to ten seconds. You come to without being able to account for the time that just passed, but you cover about 100 yards in three seconds on a highway, so this is no micro-adventure. Micros identify themselves as a head nod, the hypnic knee jerk (usually painful if a desktop or dashboard is nearby) or suddenly becoming aware of closure with another vehicle or object. Alarm bells . . .

On a monotonous freeway I've tried pretty much everything to stay awake: windows open, chewing gum, loud radio, self-harm, wrenching out nose hairs, and shouting. But before I start looking like a Sweeney Todd victim, I head for the pit stop, because life's too short to arrive dead on time.

Most of us subscribe to the notion that sleep takes place at night in a single six-to-eight-hour block. Most animals, babies, and our siesta-loving Mediterranean cousins enjoy the benefits of *polyphasic* sleep, or power napping. The power nap is used by military pilots and sleep-deprived professionals to restore energy levels. A nap of six to ten minutes during times of fatigue throws the brain into a semi-deep sleep, quickly restoring a high level of alertness and cognitive response afterward. Ironically, sleeping longer than thirty minutes can put you into a deeper sleep cycle, and you wake feeling groggy and disoriented. This "sleep inertia" can last up to an hour, so it's no good for driving.

When I need a boost I set my alarm, down a coffee, and fall asleep. The coffee takes longer to digest than the sleep lasts, so you wake up like a newborn warrior. Even small amounts of sleep can be rejuvenating, so it's good to steal a wink wherever and whenever you can.

Sleep deprivation is cumulative and can creep up on you. Avoid big meals, beware of things like cough medicines and other drugs that would tranquilize a horse, and try to respect your energy levels.

When your body talks about sleep, you'd better listen.

3.10 BASIC INSTINCT

It was the night before Le Mans, and I couldn't sleep.

I had forgotten to pack my fireproof lederhosen.

I had forgotten to pack my fireproof lederhosen, my race license was out of date, and there was every chance that my alarm clock would fail me. It did.

I arrived late for the qualifying session. Other drivers were locked inside their rockets and pounding laps to the delight of the exultant crowds, team owners, and sponsors filling the pit lane. The race steward looked me up and down, shaking his head. Everyone was staring, probably because I was stark naked and my feet were superglued to the floor.

Then my real alarm went off, and I woke to the relief that it was a month before the actual event. I duly checked the location of my license, ran an inventory on my fireproofs, and noted that I was short of a balaclava, so I ordered one and went through my training regime for the following weeks. My body knows from experience that silly mistakes cost races, mistakes grow from distractions, and distractions are created by chaos.

Forward planning alleviates the chaos and frees the mind to tackle the challenge ahead. That's why nearly every race-car driver I know is afflicted by a strong streak of OCD. Everything is neatly stacked in its rightful place, compartmentalized, so that it can be picked up and replaced with the minimum fuss—physically *and* mentally.

Lotus F1 driver Martin Donnelly, one of the fastest men ever to grace Nomex, was notoriously anal about the way he folded his civvies before climbing aboard his race car and flicking a switch inside his brain, the switch that turns off emotion and turns on perception. As he blasted along the pit straight of Brands Hatch in a Formula Ford at 115 mph, his mechanics thought it would be hilarious to dangle his jeans and shirt over the pit wall as a prank. Something in Martin snapped. He lost focus and crashed as soon as he could.

A tiny error in judgment can spell disaster.

People often ask me what it's like to concentrate for a twenty-four-hour race, where a tiny error in judgment can spell disaster—or, worse, someone else might drive faster.

The pit lane gets frantic, nearly sixty crews running around with wheels and fuel hoses, and drivers running amuck in the melee. On track it's much calmer, and you work at your rhythm, in spite of the constant dicing with your competition, until you get to about 5 a.m., when some inconsiderate fellow lights his BBQ at Arnage corner half way around a lap of Le Mans. . . and throws on the hickory-smoked bacon. The waft of flavor tickles its way up the hairs inside your nose, and an intrusive voice asks, "Where's breakfast?" By then you've galloped along another 500 yards, which means it's time to take a deep breath and crank the wheel into the über-fast Porsche Curves.

There are two types of thinking going on during these moments: the jungle reflex and the conscious thought. The caveman in me smells food and wants me to pull over to grab a burger. The human element, the weaker part that I try to think with, orders him to shut up. Thanks to an extensive conditioning program, the caveman obeys. Usually.

The jungle reflex is powerful. A newborn baby will fling its arms and legs out like Spiderman if it senses it is in danger, or falling. The response is instinctive, preprogrammed, and occurs within milliseconds by virtue of evolution, which prepared our ancestors for the real possibility that they might fall out of a tree and have to grab a branch before hitting the deck. Where the hell is Ben taking us with this, you wonder . . .

There's no way that I can think as fast as my jungle brain can. But cavemen can't be allowed to drive without a responsible adult, though they often do. The jungle brain specializes in identifying threatening behavior through body language or familiar patterns that suggest danger. This gut feeling is useful radar for reading traffic on the road or the track, and a honed survival instinct is inventive at coping with tricky situations. However, Jungle Ben is a crude creature at heart: irrational, egotistical, competitive, always hungry, territorial; and he regards any invasion as a threat that should be dealt with aggressively. When someone cuts me up, Jungle Ben takes it personally and wants to teach this enemy a lesson he'll never forget, and his reaction registers first before my intellect kicks in. With a ton of metal in hand, any physical response is likely to lack any sense of proportion.

Le Mans . . . by night, with *dipped* headlights.
For "full beam" there's a blank white page
somewhere.

These basic instincts are hardwired, so you can't get rid of them, but you can mold them to suit a purpose by cultivating an active thought process. Self-discipline is the only thing separating you from a poo-slinging primate. To harness the jungle power you have to identify and banish intrusive thoughts, which are usually childish and obvious, and act on genuine instincts. Repetition turns this effort into a pattern of behavior.

For this process to flourish, the weaker part of the brain, your intellect, needs rest; otherwise your body defaults to the stronger jungle mode. Ideally I take twenty minutes to find my inner self and get some sleep before the race starts. I stare at the wall and allow my subconscious to drift and vent its concerns, rather than letting them fester, so that I can address them in an orderly fashion.

In one of my early races at Donington, I knew that I was lining up alongside a rival named Darren Malkin, and we always pushed each other to the edge. Jungle Ben really latched onto this and prepared all kinds of apocalyptic predictions. I visualized all of them in full until I felt that all my bases were covered, including the eventuality of being struck from behind at a lurid high-speed curve called the Old Hairpin. The lights went green, we both ripped away, and Darren tapped me in the gearbox, the tail end of a single-seat race car, at *exactly* the curve I predicted. My car half spun, and I instinctively swung the steering until it banged into the bump stops, then corrected the slide, and stayed in front. The mother of all battles ensued, and our fathers even squared up in the pit lane. Like I say, cavemen.

Harnessing the subconscious is extremely powerful for fine-tuning complicated tasks that the human part of the brain tends to overthink, or is unable to imagine, and you hear yourself whining: "I *can't* do it." You usually can. If you picture yourself performing a task better than you "think" you can, your subconscious will find a way to make it happen. We call it *visualization*, which is really active dreaming, focusing on something you want.

Millions of years ago, humans mostly wanted to catch food without being eaten, which is why we still dream about running through molasses and being chased by a man-eating Cyclops. Dreaming is deeply rooted in our survival instinct, and it's no coincidence that it connects directly to vision.

I use this technique every time I set foot in a race car. I imagine what I'm going to do, then do it, and then I fine-tune it in my brain and do it better. Anybody can do it.

3.11 VISUALIZATION: THE PERFECT LAP

I always pretended not to care too much about the guests on *Top Gear*, when in reality I loved seeing them realize their full potential.

So when war hero Billy Baxter unfurled a white cane and started tap, tap, tapping it to find his way across the parking lot, I couldn't help cracking a massive smile. Billy may have been completely blind, but he had the eye of the tiger if ever I saw it.

He told me that he was prepared to do "whatever it takes" to achieve his goal of beating a sighted celebrity's lap time around the *Top Gear* circuit. The target was two minutes and six seconds, set by game show host Richard Whiteley.

Billy's military background gave me the confidence to lean on his self-discipline to help him achieve that goal. I was mean. I barked rapid-fire instructions at him and reprimanded him mercilessly whenever he made a mistake. It was the only way to help him build a virtual picture of his surroundings in his mind and keep him laughing with his foot to the floor.

Billy was hanging on my every word and reacting to my voice so that he could apply the right amounts of steering, braking, and throttle as we rolled along. The problem with that was clear. We ricocheted our way from one curve to the next and never followed the same path twice.

What I really needed Billy to do was to think farther ahead.

By the close of play on that first day, we still hadn't negotiated a full lap together without some kind of incident or me diving across the center console to grab an armful of steering when we veered off course. Whenever we approached the high-speed Follow Through curve at nearly 90 mph, the gap between the tire wall and the garden was just too narrow to let Billy handle the steering unaided. We were a long way from letting him fly solo. What I really needed Billy to do was to *think* farther ahead, even if he couldn't *look* ahead.

So . . . at the end of his first day, I created a voice recording of the perfect lap. I used all the familiar vernacular, four-letter warts and all, to paint the picture of the world Billy was trying to imagine, and I timed the recording with a stopwatch to match the circuit curve by curve until we crossed the line within the time I believed he could achieve.

Two weeks later, Billy was standing in the parking lot. He had memorized the recording by listening to it every day until it was burned into his mind's eye. We climbed aboard the gutless but reasonably priced Suzuki Liana and set off at a steady pace.

To my astonishment, we completed our first tour of the circuit without major incident. Billy's hands were shaking with excitement, and I was bursting with pride, but I knew there was a narrow window for Billy to achieve his best before exhaustion set in. We did one more "sighting" run and then went for it.

Billy gunned the engine and tore away from the start line with a shriek of wheelspin. There's something unforgettable about a blind man doing that.

As we twitched across the finish line and I clicked down hard on the stopwatch, I ogled the figures. It was a moment to savor.

"That felt like a good one. How fast was it, Stig?"

I opened with a confession. Halfway around, I had lied about covering the steering at the Follow Through, which meant that Billy had run the entire lap single-handed. Hard man he may have been, but there was more than sweat starting to trickle down that weathered face.

"Your time was one minute and fifty-eight seconds. You've beaten four sighted celebs, you legend."

The emotion gripped us both, and I'll never forget Billy's achievement that day. To put it in context, Boris Johnson, the mayor of London, barely eclipsed Billy's time by two seconds. To my deep frustration, Billy later had time added to his official score for "cutting a white line" by a few feet. Bureaucracy knows no bounds.

In a race the most dangerous time of all is the first lap, when the field is tightly packed. You have no option but to run wheel to wheel with all brands of crazies, and there's precious little time to react to signs of trouble.

As the pack of up to fifty machines streams into the first curve at 200 mph, three or four wide, inches apart and jockeying for position, they are dangerously close. The varying inputs of man and machine ripple through the field as the speeds reduce unevenly in the braking zones. The drivers' heart rates peak at over 180 beats per minute, turbocharging the senses with adrenaline and oxygen to *think fast*.

Your eyes are on stalks, searching for key indicators—a plume of dust as one car drops a wheel in the dirt, a screech of rubber, a puff of blue smoke from a locked tire or the sudden convergence of two racers, any recognizable pattern that might lead to a collision—and you're always mindful of what's coming up behind you. It's not a case of whether you might need to take evasive action, it's a question of when and how much.

To cope with information overload and to reduce thinking time, race-car drivers visualize things like the first lap many times over before the race begins. When you close your eyes, preferably not while driving, the link between the brain and the eyes is so powerful that you can still form crystal-clear images of real-life scenarios. This isn't quite the same as dreaming, because you consciously control the scene. In the safety of your own synapses, you can rehearse how to handle complex situations as many times as you like until your responses start to feel instinctive.

This is a powerful model for conditioning your mind and another way of seeing into the future without even needing the keys to a DeLorean. With your crystal ball in hand, now seems like a good time to pitch you some curveballs.

SUMMARY

You now have the keys to the freedom of the open road, and on a normal day, in normal conditions, are in control of your car right up to the limit of its capabilities. What follows are the DEFCON 1 skills and techniques that will keep the beast on the leash when it tries to bite you, from skids and hydroplaning to the absolute gold standard of Hollywood stunt car control. So buckle up, crack your knuckles, and Enter the Dragon.

Buckle up, crack your knuckles, and Enter the Dragon.

04

SKIDDING

4.1 THE LIMITS OF GRIP

A skid, beyond the reference to brown trousers, happens when one or more of your tires are pushed beyond their ability to cling to the road surface.

When the bond is broken, you go from gripping to skidding, and it can happen fast.

There are two types of skid: one that affects the front tires, and one that affects the rear tires.

When the front tires skid, the car has a tendency to go straight on toward the outside of a curve despite your efforts to persuade it otherwise. The car understeers.

When the rears let go, the car rotates into the curve far more than you asked it to in terms of the steering angle. It oversteers. This condition is generally also accompanied by a growl from your bowel: *"Fuuuuuuu . . ."*

Trust me, you know the difference between understeer and oversteer.

The first thing to say is that preventing a skid is a far better strategy than working to correct one. We are back to the physics of the traction circle (see page 98): if you exceed the forces that the tires are capable of handling, they will let you know all about it.

The dominant forces at play are longitudinal: braking and acceleration. These will always win the arm wrestle at the expense of the lateral grip required for taking a curve. That is why you should always apply them carefully. The purpose of the early chapters on smooth driving and techniques for handling curves was to put you in good stead on that account.

Nonetheless, you arrive here, at the point where the car is out of control, and you'd like to offer a more purposeful response than the airline pilot who lost it in a car at Brands Hatch. He let go of the steering and deadpanned to his instructor: "All yours." Then they crashed.

23. Over- and Understeering

Ideal Path

Oversteer

Ideal Path

Understeer

COMMON CAUSES OF SKIDS

You might have encountered a slippery surface, but usually *you* create the skid by doing something that pushes the tires beyond their limit, such as:

1. braking too late and without mercy,
2. having too much speed on a curve,
3. using rough or excessive steering, or
4. accelerating too early or too hard in the middle of the curve.

UNDERSTEER

The good news is that understeer is a piece of cake to deal with, which is why most carmakers design their cars to do it. A front-wheel-drive car is naturally prone to this because the front tires have to contend simultaneously with the jobs of steering around a curve and accelerating. You flirt around the edges of understeer on a daily basis pulling out of tight intersections.

If you push the gas pedal too hard then, you will lose some steering because, as with braking, the accelerator is always the winner in the game of rock, paper, scissors.

If you lose steering ability, the hedge draws closer. You could do what the airline pilot did, or you could just back off the gas pedal, recover some steering, and be on your way. Easy. Next chapter, anyone . . . ?

Hang on.

There's more to it than that. On a dry, grippy surface you're hardly ever likely to encounter any more drama than point 4 on my list above—but I will give you chapter and verse on the rest just in case! Bear them in mind when we head out into the rain and snow.

COMING 'ROUND THE MOUNTAIN

We're going back to Bathurst, Australia, the road circuit packed with ever frightening and tightening bends, where failure to turn on command results in your immediate introduction to "the Mountain" on which it is built.

I was halfway through the race, in the groove and swiping around a narrow double left-hander called the Cutting at 95 mph when a voice inside my head said: *Why won't it go around the curve like I'm telling it to?*

The steering went light in my fingers (see points 2 and 3 on my list above) as the front tires, always the first to encounter anything slippery, broke free of the surface. It didn't take a rocket scientist to realize that, unless something was done sharpish, I had an appointment with the barrier.

The mistake people make when the front skids is to turn the steering more, because, normally, "the more you turn the wheel, the more it turns the car." Once you go beyond the limit of the tires' ability to grip, however, adding steering makes understeer *much* worse, especially at high speed when the temptation to do so is greatest. Speed is the issue.

I was already off the throttle, which passed weight forward and added grip to the front tires, but it wasn't enough. I needed to get the speed (point 2) down. I gently applied the brakes (point 1), which made the understeer even worse . . . but bear with me!

This is a technique I call "pump and saw," and it's a survival strategy, not a lifestyle choice.

Pump: Squeeze the brakes to get some speed off—that's the most important thing—then release brake pressure to give it a shot with the steering.

Saw: Straighten the steering as you brake—that helps the tires slow you down faster—then saw at the wheel by turning and straightening as your speed reduces.

Each time you steer, it reduces your braking performance and vice versa, which is why you try to alternate them to balance the needs of making the curve.

By the final moments of my mini-adventure, my speed was down to a jog, and the steering worked, the tail lurched around, and I slithered past the rock face. As to the helpful guy who had dropped his gearbox oil everywhere, rest assured I thanked him later.

Having dealt with too much speed going *into* the curve, let's have some fun on the way *out* when you give it a bootful.

Some of the longest seconds of my life were spent running away from *Little Britain* star David Walliams as he turned through the final corner of *Top Gear*'s Dunsfold circuit. He wasn't exactly God's gift to driving, but he certainly wasn't doing it "like a lady" the day I met him. As I stood beside the track in the line of fire, I noticed the whites of his eyes bulging more than usual. He heaved the Suzuki Liana's steering wheel several times in the desired direction while applying copious throttle, which negated the car's ability to turn. Neither my hand gestures nor the grass and rock flying across his windshield convinced David that turning the wheel even more wouldn't save him, and he shot off the track like a torpedo.

The Limits of Grip

I strongly believe that in his mind David was pushing the brake pedal. His only mistake was that he neglected to first remove his foot from the accelerator. The front tires can only take so much abuse until they reach a limit and stall, like the wing of an aircraft once the angle of attack has been exceeded.

That is why you adopt the quarter-to-three steering position: by fixing your hands there, you tend not to add big gobs of steering long after the horse has bolted. An understeering condition becomes obvious because your hands are crossing right before your eyes.

As we dived for cover, David shot past us, steering ever more to the left but heading straight as an arrow. The moment his outer wheels dropped off the shoulder of the road onto the slippery grass, the whole dynamic changed. His rear tire went light as the road dropped away, then encountered the grass and skidded. All that steering finally found an outlet. The car slewed sideways and spun around like a top.

OVERSTEER

Oversteer is predominantly the preserve of rear-wheel-drive cars, where an excess of power through the rear tires causes them to lose grip. It can occur by virtue of their generally edgier handling characteristics. As David kindly demonstrated, however, it is also possible to destabilize a front-wheel-drive car.

Besides the common causes of skids, here are some more specific examples of throttle-related oversteer.

LIFT-OFF OVERSTEER

Applying the throttle has a dynamic effect in the way that it transfers weight within the car. Acceleration plants weight onto the rear tires and loads them with grip at the expense of the front tires.

During acceleration through a sweeping curve the rear tires start squatting as they absorb the weight of the car like an Olympic lifter, and the fronts may reach a point where they start to lose grip. If the driver responds using the corrective model for understeer by lifting off the throttle, it will effect a weight transfer back onto the front tires. Done gradually, this will restore balance to the universe, and the car will negotiate the curve smoothly.

Done gradually, this will restore balance to the universe.

If the driver snaps his foot off the throttle, the weight lurches forward, giving the front tires more bite to steer with just as the weight shifts off the rears, reducing their grip and causing them to skid wide. This is lift-off oversteer.

POWER OVERSTEER

With a rear-wheel-drive car, if you put excessive driving force through the rear tires, they will break traction and the car will oversteer.

This problem is often compounded by premature acceleration out of a curve, causing the rear to sit and provide grip *at first*. It feels good, so you accelerate harder without noticing that the front tires are skidding slightly up to the moment when the rear tires spin. The extra steering angle causes the rear to snap sideways *very* quickly.

To counter this, you need to remove the cause by releasing pressure on the throttle and steering into the slide to control your sideways angle, or yaw. If the problem is extreme you can cut all drive to the rears by dipping the clutch. For further detail, skip to Drifting (see page 265).

Whatever the cause, when your car suddenly rotates more than you're expecting and skids sideways, it will scare the crap out of you. What you do next will either be inspired or awful.

Here is the recovery technique that covers most bases.

OPPOSITE LOCK

Your instinct, other than to freeze, is to remove lots of steering because the car is turning too much. That's a good start, but most people overdo it. Keep calm and . . . SHIT!

> ▸ *S*—Steer into the slide, with catlike reflexes. (Or at least straighten the steering if you run across a slippery surface like Walliams did.)
> ▸ *HI*—Hold It. Let the car recover for a second, no more.
> ▸ *T*—Turn the wheel toward the curve again. Everybody forgets that part, and it causes all the mess. You have to unwind the corrective steering once the car recovers.

The steering has to be instant and intuitive; otherwise you might spin. If you can find the time and the money, get to a skidpad. It's as much fun as you can legally have with your clothes on and the best training there is for safe driving.

Keep calm and . . . SHIT!

Addendum: At the time of writing there is a degree of change regarding skid control and use of the brake. The old rule was that you avoided the brake at all costs during oversteer, because the negative weight transfer this created might worsen the problem or cause a spin. In high-tech cars fitted with the latest ABS and ESP (stability) software, this is no longer the case. These systems may actively cut in and trigger braking to individual wheels on your behalf to control the slide, or become activated when you press the brake during a skid. I've used this in conjunction with steering to recover seemingly impossible slides with Mercedes, Porsches, and Audis. It's worth asking the dealer what's under your hood!

OPPOSITE LOCK EXPLAINED

When the tail skids out to the left, as would *normally* occur if you overcooked your goose into a right-hander, then you steer left to counter it, and vice versa. All being well, the car will follow the curvature of the road, even though you're steering in the opposite direction to the curve.

OVERCORRECTING

In a small slide, the action of the tires scrubbing sideways can drag enough speed off the car to resolve the situation without much human intervention. In a wider, faster slide, immediate intervention is definitely required.

In a perfect world, where nobody panics in a crisis, you would calmly turn the wheel in direct proportion to the angle of the slide and not a fraction more, and then unwind it as the crisis draws to an end.

In reality you counter-steer, almost certainly too much, then hold the slide for a brief and terrifying intake of breath. The duration of this eye-of-the-storm moment varies depending on how dire things are. The rears recover grip as the speed drops, and this is the instant that separates the men from the boys.

You must reclaim control of your sphincter, which is now twitching faster than a badger's nose, and remember to *straighten the steering* and aim for the curve.

Perfecting that response might require the seat-of-the-pants connection you only find at the *Top Gun* canteen, but you can do it. Counter-steering is natural; just don't overdo it.

This is the instant that separates the men from the boys.

THE "TANK SLAPPER"

This secondary slide is far worse than the first.

You overdid it. Turn too far into the skid, lose your place on the steering wheel, and the tail snaps a second time—in the opposite direction. All too often, this "yaw oscillation" is the end of the game. It's like ducking one of Mike Tyson's jabs and planting your face straight into the uppercut.

When the rear balances, the back tires grip, and so do the fronts (which are now pointing completely the wrong way for the curve). If you fail to straighten the wheel, all the energy in the rear axle rebounds, and the added momentum created by the steering angle causes the rear tires to skid in the opposite direction. This secondary slide is far worse than the first. Good luck; you're back into SHIT mode.

HOT TIPS   ▸ Steer properly. Avoid jerky steering that might destabilize the weight of the car and cause a skid. With shuffle steering you lose track of how many times you turned the wheel. Using the "racing" method (see Rotational Steering on page 67) makes it quicker and easier to apply opposite lock and whip the wheel straight at the end.

RECOVERING FROM A SPIN

If all your attempts to wrestle your beast away from the jaws of oversteer come to naught, then you will go from sliding sideways to spinning backward and then . . . who knows what direction?

The old adage at this point is: "In a spin, both feet in."

You hit the brake pedal as hard as you can and put your other foot on the clutch. A maximum brake scrubs off speed in the shortest possible distance, and putting the clutch in will hopefully keep the engine running once the car comes to a stop, should you be lucky enough to drive away from this.

Don't be fooled into releasing the brakes until you come to a rest, because during the spin you will lose all sense of your speed and direction. Rotating on the road is a terrifying and potentially deadly experience, but remembering to floor the brakes could save your life or someone else's.

The Limits of Grip

In a racing situation, drivers treat spins a little differently. The aim is not only to avoid a collision but to regain control as quickly as possible. In order to do this we deploy a technique known in ballet as "spotting." During an intense spin a ballerina fixes her gaze on a spot to prevent disorientation until the rotation of her body requires her to turn her head and refocus.

In a spinning car you can fix your eyes on your line of travel, flicking your head around as it spins backward, and automatically bringing the car around with your hands until you face forward again. It goes without saying, this should only be practiced on a track with a good instructor!

"In a spin, both feet in."

4.2 DRIVING IN WET WEATHER

"There's no such thing as bad weather, just inappropriate clothing."

—Sir Ranulph Fiennes, polar explorer

One-fifth of our time on British roads is spent driving in wet weather, but it contributes to a third of all daytime casualties and over *half* of all casualties at night.

When it rains, the world changes instantly. You have to change with it. Driving technique in the rain is really no different from dry running, it just requires you to dial your reflexes in to the notion that things take longer, and the driver's inputs need to be slower and gentler to allow the tires to cope with reduced levels of grip. Put simply, you can't throw as much force around, and the secret to being a wet-weather ace is being silky smooth with the controls and keeping your cool.

The one element that is most different in terms of technique is the way you apply the brakes. In dry conditions, you can be assertive on the pedal and use an initial stab before you squeeze to load the front tires, and the car can accept greater forces. This doesn't apply in wet or low-grip conditions. You have to be more gradual with the initial application to create slower weight transfers. Throttle technique is the same, but you effectively have much more power under foot than normal. Yes, sir, even you in the Cinquecento.

Locking a tire at the start of braking in the rain can cost you as much as 70 percent of your stopping power, a problem that ABS is designed to handle. Nonetheless, in the wet, as ever, skid prevention is always better than cure.

I raced an Ascari GT3 car at Mugello with none other than the boss and owner of the company, Klaas Zwart. He's a fast driver and, by his own admission, slightly impatient.

The car didn't make the opening practice sessions, and by the time qualifying started, Klaas's foot was tapping a hole in the ground. As the crew fluttered around us, I insisted they cut air holes into the door for venting. Tempers frayed a touch, but I got my vents and joined one fully soaked circuit.

Forty cars churned the asphalt. Crazy people launched themselves at the track like a demolition derby, and the marshals duly counted them into the tire walls. Clouds of spray added to the downpour already challenging my one-speed windshield wiper, but the vents worked perfectly.

I picked an inside line at the end of each straight, avoiding the usual line, which was caked in glossy rubber, slipped my foot gently onto the brakes, and squeezed slowly until I felt the tire reach its limit. As the tires squirmed, the feel of grip permeated every sinew of my leg.

Walking on eggshells.

Despite walking on eggshells, when I shifted down the gears the rear wheels would occasionally lock over puddles, and the thunder of V-8 would be replaced with the deathly chatter of gearbox. I dipped the clutch and released it more slowly than a turtle swimming through molasses.

As the straight entered the curve, the rubber-coated racing line cut from the outside to the inside of the curve, so I did the opposite; I headed straight across the usual line to the outside of the bend. I released the brakes and, with no throttle, flew around the widest arc to benefit from the most unused, porous stretch of track, steering with only the lightest of touches on the wheel—feeling for a change in asphalt, and then crawling onto the throttle so carefully that I could barely hear the engine picking up.

Down the straights I sought out the shallowest puddles and splashed through dead center with the tires pointing straight, wincing as the rear tires hydroplaned and the tires spun in fifth gear, but the Ascari never wandered. By the end of the session, this tiptoeing exercise was worth pole position by one and a half seconds.

On the streets there's nothing to be gained by using "wet" lines because the entire surface tends to be equal in terms of grip, but you can feel the change from one surface to the next. Ah, but puddle watching, what sport.

AFTER IT RAINS

The road remains wet, and it's the surface condition that dictates the grip level. After the rain stops the conditions linger, especially on local roads that are sheltered from sunlight. Wooded areas continue to drip water long after the surrounding roads have dried, and a nice coating of wet leaves handles like ice.

Ignore the loonies who want to tailgate in these conditions, and keep a longer distance from traffic ahead so that you can see well beyond the immediate.

You have a quarter less grip for stopping and accelerating, 50 percent less on smooth, slippery roads, and *half* the cornering grip of dry running.

READ THE ROAD

"All that glisters is not gold . . ."
—William Shakespeare, *The Merchant of Venice*

During long periods of sunshine, cars lay down lots of rubber on the road surface. It becomes so highly polished by oily lubricants that it becomes less porous and reflects sunlight. The first droplets of rain sit on top of this layer and create a greasy film, which just sits there, waiting to undermine you.

In California, this happens a lot. There are ten accidents every hour in LA during peak traffic—add a little drizzle and it jumps straight to fifteen. After a long bake in the sun, our brains fail to acclimatize quickly enough just when the road is at its worst.

As soon as it rains, double your following distance. Look out for anything that shines, from manhole covers to cobblestones, and be especially mindful of regular stopping points such as traffic lights, off-ramps, bus stops, and taxi stands; they tend to get doused with slick lubricants, so leave enough stopping distance so you can feather the brake pedal for the last few yards in the wet.

"All that glisters is not gold . . ."

TIRES IN RAIN

As rain falls, your tires work hard in a number of ways to support your progress, and their ability to do so varies considerably, as we saw in the chapter on braking.

Pressure at the tires' leading edge cuts through the water and displaces it through the channeled grooves, yet traces of water remain. The edges of the sipes and tread blocks dig into the road surface, pressurize it, and actually break through the film of water to create *dry* contact.

If the water level rises on the road surface, the fronts of the tires plow through it, splitting the bow wave. Surface water is channeled away, and this process of cutting and squirting has to disperse the water quickly enough to prevent it from building up.

When the pressure of water meeting the tires' leading edge exceeds the pressure on the contact patch, the tires lift off the road, and hydroplaning begins. You are effectively driving a boat.

AVOIDING HYDROPLANING

Hydroplaning occurs almost exclusively at high speed, so you will experience it most on the freeway or similarly fast interstate highways. All you need to do to avoid it, therefore, is to slow down.

Heavy rain, the stuff that sounds like it's denting the bodywork, creates perfect conditions for hydroplaning within seconds. When the road becomes saturated it forms pools in the lower portions, filling troughs and worn grooves made by trucks, and any dips by the roadside. It also creates small rivers that cross slopes in the highway with no thought for your wellbeing. Persistent rain might take a little longer to form puddles, but the point is that you need to read the conditions to anticipate the presence of standing water and *moderate your speed accordingly*. Don't judge your speed by looking at other people, as their vehicles may behave entirely different from yours.

You scan the ground ahead and search for signs of standing water, which identifies itself by its shine and from the splash of incoming droplets. Noticing these signs in the daytime is hard enough with all the spray, so a healthy following distance helps. At night it becomes harder still. Usually you can make out two black stripes in your lane, which are the grooves from regular traffic filling with the deeper water.

By running slightly off the center line you can avoid the worst of it. The right lane is most affected by these grooves, the left lane less so, but the right-side shoulder may be flooded, leaving the center lane as generally the safest place to be.

Beyond these nuances, situations develop where the whole surface is covered with several inches of water. The tires become so saturated that they lift off the road.

Skidding

24. Tires in the Rain

View of the contact patch from below

Vehicle Direction

Bow wave
of water

Vehicle direction

Pressure at the tire's leading edge

forces water away, creating a bow wave.

Water trapped in the sipes is driven into the
tread grooves and channeled away.

FACTORS AFFECTING HYDROPLANING

Hydroplaning is directly proportionate to your speed, and a wide tire has to deal with a much larger flow of water. This feature has been well researched at Bugatti's secret test track in Ehra-Lessien in Germany, where I coached Captain Slow, aka James May, on the finer points of handling a $1 million Veyron. James showcased the one thing it was designed to do best by guiding 1,000 unbroken horsepower down a five-mile straight at a speed of 253.81 mph.

The heavens opened as soon as he finished, and it looked like playtime was over, but *Top Gear*'s director, Nigel Simpkiss, had other ideas.

"I'd just like to get some shots of the Veyron whipping up some spray over the top of the steel barrier. Do you think that would be OK?"

The Bugatti engineer nursed his chin for an answer to this innocently couched question before consenting for us to film "a couple of runs."

I strapped into the fitted leather throne, twisted the key, and felt sixteen pistons fizzing to life. The engineers checked the tire pressures, as they did every time the Veyron left their bosom, and I ventured out onto the gigantic highway.

I looped around a carousel and accelerated through a curve toward the straight where Nigel's camera team was stationed by the twelve-foot barriers to my right. Even at 60 mph the rooster tail of spray was kicking pretty high, but *more* is an ever popular adjective in the film game, so I squeezed.

The bony feeling you get from the Bug on a dry road makes it handle like it's on the proverbial train tracks. It sits on rubbers that are nearly fifteen inches across, making them the broadest tires ever manufactured. Throw in the four-wheel-drive and untold electronic stability systems, and you might be excused for taking a nap on the way to the yacht. So I squeezed the gas.

The 8-liter engine promptly replied, and I surged forward into a sea of shiny black asphalt, and a world of pain. All that tight handling evaporated the moment the water crawled under those fat tires. The Bug flicked sideways, and I found myself facing left toward a welcoming grass bank. They say it takes years to build a reputation but you can throw it away in a single moment. This was one of them.

The opposite lock went in immediately in an attempt to correct the extreme angle, or *yaw*, as pilots refer to it. Things seemed to be OK, but at nearly 2,200 pounds the Bug was projecting itself into yet deeper waters. I could feel the

Skidding

steering going even lighter, so I pressed the middle pedal to request a little customer service.

The ABS was thus engaged. It could perform the one task I could not, which was to activate individual braking mechanisms on each of the four tires and by doing so begin the process of addressing the slide sideways.

By adjusting individual wheel speeds and compensating for the tire that was struggling most, the ABS trimmed out enough of my rate of yaw to keep me from spinning. The speed slowly but surely bled off. Once the tires landed, the Bug snapped back into line, and because I had only applied a modest level of countersteering I could straighten it quickly; and the nightmare was over.

The nightmare was over.

Nigel crackled over the radio: "Could we get another one of those from a different angle?"

I took the car back to pit lane, pronto.

I mentioned my little moment to the Bugatti engineer, who exhaled and explained that they had lost three Veyrons up the grass bank previously during heavy rain. We agreed we should wait for the track to drain.

SUMMARY

- Speed and water level dictate hydroplane severity.
- Tread depth: If the tires are bald, you're toast. Good tires dissipate up to 7 gallons per second.
- Underinflated tires reduce the ability of the tire to cut the mustard.
- Vehicle weight is a positive factor, unless the tires are underinflated.
- The wider the tire, the more likely it is to hydroplane. It's the only time that driving a 2CV beats a Bugatti Veyron.
- In a rear-wheel-drive, wheelspin in fourth or fifth gear is not for the fainthearted. Hitting standing water with one side of the car during acceleration can cause you to spin. Lighten the foot.
- Turn cruise control off when it rains. It will try to accelerate when you hit standing water.

HANDLING HYDROPLANING

Hydroplaning in a straight line manifests as a tug at the steering wheel, a braking sensation, and the sound of water gushing inside the wheel arches. One side of the car might suddenly pull more than the other. If you are accelerating at the time you might hear the engine note rising unexpectedly, as if you pressed the clutch by mistake. That sound is the driven wheels spinning!

Serious hydroplaning only happens at speeds above 50 mph, so speed is what you need to reduce; but do it carefully.

Lift off the gas.

Keep the steering straight and grip it firmly.

Stay off *all* the pedals. The force of water hitting the tires acts as a natural brake, and once the speed bleeds off, the tires will touch down again. You recover control by effectively doing nothing.

HOT TIPS

▸ Sometimes hydroplaning will affect one side of the car more than the other. If you sense it pulling to one side, *gently* resist by applying *a little* steering to keep you going straight while lifting off the accelerator as usual. The steering won't actually work until the tires "land." If you panic and wind loads of steering on, it won't have any effect until the tires kiss the road again, which will cause the car to swerve or spin.

When a car hydroplanes *in a straight line,* I personally prefer not to brake, even with ABS, because it gets confused and drags things out by locking the tires, albeit slightly, and reducing steering power. I prefer to keep some steering in reserve in case it's required.

Hydroplaning in a curve is a different animal. The car becomes possessed, instantly losing steering and then pitching violently sideways as the tires lift off unevenly, and all this while your ejector seat is still being serviced.

If you do go sideways on standing water and you have ABS, this is the time to use it. Push hard and fast on the brake pedal, fix your steely-eyed gaze on where you would like to go, and put in the requisite opposite lock.

How much you drift across the highway will depend on your speed. Once you slow and the tires land, locate the nearest service station and dislodge excrement.

If you see a flooded curve coming at the last moment, dab the brakes and try to straighten the steering a little so the tire can plow better.

FLOODS

Near biblical volumes of rain have been turning our towns into Venetian piazzas. There's a temptation to battle the elements. Deep inside, we let rip a silent but deadly Mel Gibson war cry, *"Freeeeedddoommm,"* and within seconds the objections of our spouse are drowned out beneath two feet of water.

I was sizing up a flooded road last month when a rare moment of Bear Grylls–worthy self-preservation gripped me. I waded into the water up to my knees to measure the depth, crucially above the height of my car's radiator, and agreed with another driver it was a no-go. A third man thought better of it.

He reversed his newish Audi Q7 a considerable distance back up the hill, stopped, then gunned it toward the water. He must have hit it at about 50, the equivalent of slamming into a brick wall, judging by the way the hood exploded skyward. There was an impressive amount of steam from both engine and driver as he realized the reason the motor died on impact was that the water had taken out the radiator, then been sucked up the air intake. Mucho expensivo.

Avoid floodwater wherever possible, but if you give it a go . . .

HOT TIPS

- It's better to get your feet wet checking the level first than to rinse your wallet at the garage. Walk the full length of the crossing to make sure the road surface hasn't been washed away and confirm where the water level is lowest, which is often in the middle of the road. Ideally you want a depth of no more than 6 inches (the height of the center of your wheels).

- Don't drive across at the same time as oncoming vehicles, as their wake won't sit well in your lap.

- Take it slow and steady. Select a low gear and head through at a brisk walking pace so that you benefit from the bow wave created in front of the car. That way, if the standing water is deeper than you thought, you *might* still reverse out. It also prevents the water crashing into your engine's vital organs.

- Once you emerge, check the brakes a few times because the water tends to get stuck between the brake pads, preventing them from working properly, or at all. The same goes for extended periods of driving in heavy rain; check the pedal pressure periodically when it's safe to do so.

Seeing and Being Seen

Mr. Magoo sees better than most when it rains. Droplets lash at the windshield, and spray from other vehicles outpaces the wipers.

The white noise of water rushing around the wheel arches numbs your eardrums; and, before you know it, the windshield mists up.

Small mistakes that might go unpunished in dry conditions catch up with you in the rain. There are some technological assets available to counter the elements, as well as some clever driving techniques and strategies.

One of the biggest problems with driving in the rain is simply being able to see through the windshield when it mists up like a Turkish spa and the rain god opens its bladder in your face. Some of the biggest crunches on road and track occur when vision is compromised, because people generally don't get a chance to brake for something they cannot see coming.

Rarely, if ever, has a race-car driver stepped out of a rain-soaked race car and high-fived the crew to compliment them on the effectiveness of the wipers or de-mister. Yet the belts hold you so tightly to the chair that you can't reach the windshield to clear it. When Guy Smith raced his Le Mans–winning Bentley Speed 8 in the rain, it reached a point where he was gazing through a clear spot the size of a quarter. The mechanics eventually took pity and passed him a sponge-on-a-stick when he managed to find the pit lane.

De-misting is easier said than done if the inside of the windshield has never been cleaned, because the layer of your DNA stuck to the glass surface sucks in the moisture and creates condensation. Your smudgy hand, as you know, does little to wipe it away. A once-over with a cloth and some glass cleaner every decade makes life considerably easier.

You can follow your granddad's advice and keep a dry rag or chamois leather at hand or you can line

Follow your granddad's advice.

the inside of your windshield with a moisture-resistant agent called Rain-X Anti-Fog. Failing that, rub liquid hand soap, or any household soap, across the inside of the windshield with a damp cloth, leave to dry, then polish with a soft dry cloth.

Sorted. Vent as required.

VENTING

When it's cold you need hot air to heat the windshield and vaporize the condensation, then an open window to get rid of it.

Warm air can hold more water vapor than cold. Summer rain fogs up your windshield, then you blow hot air at it, which is full of humidity, and wonder why the windshield mists up more. Ideally you want to blast cold, dry air (air conditioning works best) with the windows open until the engine has warmed up

enough to produce hot air, then heat the windshield as quickly as possible.

Race cars use the same heating strips on the windshield that road cars have on the rear windshield, but sadly this hasn't filtered through.

HOT TIPS   Use Rain-X, the yellow bottle, for the front windshield. Wipe it on and the raindrops scatter faster than the French Air Force.

LIGHTS

Headlights on is a good idea—but *leave the high beams and rear fog lights alone*. It's illegal to use them if visibility is better than 120 yards, and dazzling everyone around you prevents them from seeing your brake lights.

4.3 WINTER DRIVING

A drop in temperature and a sprinkle of a frozen substance frequently turns the road into a demolition derby. If Santa Claus gave driving lessons, insurance underwriters worldwide could sleep much easier during the winter months. This chapter covers the skills you need to arrive, survive, and still manage a merry jingle.

SNOW AND ICE

If the thermometer in your car reads 45 degrees, you are driving in winter conditions. At anything below 40 degrees, you should expect ice. Daylight is in short supply during the winter months, road surfaces are 60 percent more likely to be wet, and as the cold weather sets in, the chances of ice or snow grow by 35 percent. The sun's arc tracks 30 degrees lower across the sky, and the grime from salted roads and condensation reduces visibility to a sub-marine opacity.

The vital ingredient is preparation.

The vital ingredient is preparation: five minutes to prepare the car and, with it, your mindset. Muscle memory, the reason you never forget how to ride a bike, lets you down with driving on snow and ice because we do it so infrequently. Grip levels are from a different planet.

At the lowest end of the scale you have ice, which is practically a frictionless surface at temperatures close to freezing. Ironically, as ice gets *much* colder it offers more grip.

Snow passes through various states, depending on the temperature and how much traffic has compacted it. If it looks hard and polished it will behave like ice. Fresh, deep snow provides better grip and as it melts away you approach something closer to a wet road.

The easiest way to transform yourself into the God of Winter Driving overnight is to buy a set of winter tires. En route to *Top Gear*'s Winter Olympics (car ice hockey, anyone?), our testosterone-charged convoy ventured across a snow-covered Norway to Lillehammer, until we ran into a little local difficulty: a steep, frozen hill at the base of a giant ski jump. Cars in ditches as far as the eye could see, faster than the producer could yelp "insurance premium," followed by much tire-kicking and ego-deflation. Then our twenty-four-year-old production assistant drove past the lot of us in her Saab Aero, the only vehicle properly decked out for the prevailing weather conditions.

PREP THE CAR

Start the engine rev at 3,000 rpm, and crank up the defroster.

Unless you're a tank driver, you need front, rear, and side vision through the windows, so clearing the snow from these areas is the first order of business. Clear the hood too, otherwise you get a face full of snow as soon as you depart. For clearing ice, de-icing liquid is best. Boiling water can crack the windshield, but warm water from a kettle is a quick way to clear ice and be on your way smartly with less fogging up.

Check and/or replace worn-out windshield wipers. Don't use them straight away; if they are frozen to the windshield in the morning, the brittle rubber can snap.

If there's time: Use freeze-resistant windshield washer fluid, which works like Kryptonite on freezing fog and sleet. (Do not use engine antifreeze, which strips paint.)

Like Kryptonite on freezing fog and sleet.

You need a fifty-fifty mix of antifreeze and water in the cooling system. It needs refilling roughly every two years and should be a part of your car's regular service. If your car runs out and it freezes overnight, there's a fair chance that vital parts of the engine, like the water pump and the block, will freeze too and then break.

Leave tire pressures alone—reducing them does not improve traction on ice, it reduces stability, unless you're on sand!

Weight: Unloaded vans and pickups are tricky in the snow, so it's better to add weight to help the tires bite into the surface. For rear-wheel-drive cars with a front engine and low-profile tires: good luck; put something heavy in the trunk.

PLAN A ROUTE

Unless you love stationary traffic, you want to avoid hills *at all costs*; they will be littered with crashed lemmings. The higher the road takes you, the colder the weather.

Assuming the roads are open, aim for major roads that will have been sanded or salted, avoiding the smaller roads that won't. Allow extra time to get there, and so what if you're late?

GET MOVING ON ICE.

Icy conditions make it easy for the wheels to spin when you accelerate. During a big freeze, even the slightest pothole can make leaving a parking space a major extraction.

Like Kryptonite on freezing fog and sleet.

Avoid hills at all costs.

Winter Tires

Fitting winter rubber might seem unsporting or a waste of money, but . . . improvements in the technology mean that you can run certain winter tires—decent ones at least—all year round without a major penalty in the summer months. They last as long as summers and are equally fuel-efficient.

At the time of writing, Michelin has just launched a "CrossClimate" tire with equal performance to their best summer and winter tires in both snow and dry conditions. These are game changers for those of us living in a cantankerous climate.

The secret's in the sipes. Winter tires have ten times as many sets of teeth and, unlike a summer tire, their jaws don't stiffen up in the cold. You cannot believe their effectiveness until you try them. Here are some comparisons on braking distances from quite low speeds; the effect at high speed is greatly exaggerated, as you know.

SNOW CONDITIONS, STOPPING FROM 30 MPH

Summer tires: 200 feet

Winter tires: 100 feet

ICE CONDITIONS, STOPPING FROM 20 MPH

Summer tires: 150 feet

Winter tires: 85 feet

Acceleration figures in dry conditions are fairly even between both tire types, but in the snow you benefit from a tripling in performance with winter tires when you pull away at low speed, and they work magic on hills.

Whether you get them or not is a close call. In the far north of England and Scotland especially, there's a ground frost for more than half of the year based on averages across the last thirty years. That means you're definitely better off on winter tires there. For the rest of the country, the frost falls to about a third of the time.

We have two cars in the family: one on summers, the other on winters, ready for the whiteout.

25. Summer and Winter Tires

I personally prefer to feel the conditions and always use first gear to pull away, but if you find my way too complicated, then use second gear to control the wheelspin.

Using very low revs and hardly any throttle, close to stalling, let the engine torque ease the car forward by gradually releasing the clutch to the biting point so that the car barely moves.

As soon as you get some momentum, the worst is over, and you can feather the throttle until you're clear. Keep your *front wheels* as straight as possible, otherwise they will spin.

STUCK IN A RUT

If you're stuck, it's time to deploy some rock 'n' roll!

When snow gets packed around your wheels you may need to dig yourself out. Clear away any ruts around the tires that will impede progress. Then jam something—like a piece of carpet, rags, or anything dry—underneath or in front of the driven tire to give it the initial purchase required for forward motion.

Endless wheel spinning only digs you farther into the mess. You need to rock the car forward and backward until you build enough momentum to crawl out. To do this requires timing and deft clutch control.

In first gear, ease forward using the engine torque at low revs up until the point of wheelspin, then ease off the gas, or clutch in, to let the car roll back until it meets resistance. And repeat.

It may take ten or more attempts, but each time you roll back, it builds a little ramp behind you, and from that platform you can eventually carry enough forward momentum to drive clear.

To make it a social event, you can invite friends to put their weight onto the driven axle. Tell them you'll buy them a drink later, and remember to hose them liberally with slush once they've succeeded in freeing you.

With a front-wheel-drive, get someone to sit on the hood on the side that is spinning most, and bounce as you accelerate. Weight is your friend on slippery surfaces, and the more you have, the better your traction.

Remember not to run over your savior in the process.

Skidding

Mud

Mud is another element with a sense of humor.

Always *let* your friend get stuck first, then smugly find somewhere else to park.

Inevitably at some point in your life, someone will invite you to "park in the field" as casually as informing you that the restroom is on the second floor.

I wouldn't dream of insulting your intelligence here, but . . .

Always let your friend get stuck first, then smugly find somewhere else to park.

Aim for the high ground to aid your departure.

Take as straight a line as possible and go in really fast with loads of revs; it'll sound great and you'll look cool, even if you sink straight into a quagmire.

As a general rule, if you drive backward you carry some momentum. By reversing a front-wheel-drive car uphill, it puts more weight onto the driven wheels and provides more traction. And once you've parked, you can drive straight out. This method is a proven icebreaker for the frosty driveway too.

If you do get stuck, apply the rock 'n' roll method as per snow.

DRIVING IN THE SNOW

Once you get going, make sure there's nobody behind and do a fairly abrupt brake test at low speed to see how easily you can stop. Then try it again without the tires skidding to tune you in to the available braking grip.

BRAKING

Planning ahead is everything. If you enter a curve too fast and try to adjust the speed later, you'll skid. Braking distances are up to *ten times* longer than normal, so although staging a curve feels like putting a date in the diary, it beats ending up in a ditch.

Use low gears to keep the engine rpm high so that, when you lift off the gas, the engine braking instantly reduces your speed without your having to touch the brake pedal. If you do use the brakes, use them sparingly so the tires don't skid. With enough anticipation of intersections and by leaving enough room between you and the cars in front, you can avoid using the brakes almost entirely.

Like the throttle, the brake pedal is super-sensitive on snow. Caress and squeeze it as tenderly as though you were treading onto your own genitals, allowing it enough time to spread away as you increase pressure. A delicate process to be sure.

When you're following other vehicles, a simple calculation of distance is four car lengths for every 10 mph. So if you're driving at 20 mph, you allow eight car lengths between you and the vehicle ahead. At 50, it's up to twenty car lengths.

As a last resort you can use the hand brake, sparingly, to slow down, but only if you're confident enough to do it. There's minimal weight transfer when you brake on snow, which means the rear tires have braking grip in reserve, so gently applying the hand brake can buy a few yards of stopping distance when you really need it. The idea is not to fishtail sideways like Starsky and Hutch!

Braking distances are up to ten times longer than normal.

Pulse Braking

*We looked at braking in detail earlier in
the book and established the fastest way to stop
in normal driving conditions.*

The picture changes when you accidentally cause the tire to skid under braking, and when driving on slippery surfaces.

Vehicles fitted with ABS are simple in this regard because the computer dictates your options. You press the brake pedal as hard as you can; this activates the ABS, and all you have to do is think about the direction you want to head in and steer toward it.

Without ABS, it gets more interesting. If you lock a tire at high speed or on a slippery surface, you will slow down eventually, but your braking loss is significant, and you will have no steering ability. You can sit there watching the world go by, or do something called *pulse braking*.

You quickly release pressure on the brakes to allow the tires to turn and then reapply them sharply. The tires lock again, and you repeat the process as fast and often as you can until you slow down.

Pulsing the brake in this way creates small windows of grip during which the tire takes a bite at the surface as it makes the transition from locking to unlocking, and the more such windows you can create by rapid pulsing, the better.

In the case of snow, ice, and gravel this method has been proven to stop shorter than ABS because the skidding tire is able to grind through the slippery surface and latch on to the crunchier stuff underneath.

When it comes to steering around an emergency, such as a moose or another car, you need to time your final release of the brake pedal so that the tires unlock before you turn the wheel in order for it to respond.

It takes great presence of mind to pulse-brake in an emergency, but it's worth it. Just as important is to consider the direction you're taking yourself. I know top drivers who swerved to avoid an animal, only to be killed on the other side of the road.

▸ Check whether your hand brake attaches to one or both rear wheels. If it's only one, then be aware it will be less stable for the technique described above, and it might not hold you if you stop on a hill (in which case keep your foot on the brake pedal to avoid sliding backward; four tires holding you are better than one).

▸ If your car has a parking brake in the footwell, it's best not to use it because the rear brakes will lock on until you pull the manual release.

STEERING

Less is more. By turning the steering wheel gradually, you become aware of the point where the tires start to skid. If you feel the front sliding, *do not turn the steering more.* That's like writing checks on an overdrawn account. Just wait for the grip to return.

With limited traction to steer around things, you need to focus, and to anticipate the movements of other road users and pedestrians.

ACCELERATING

Don't accelerate into curves, in curves, or out of curves. Coast gently through them with the throttle open a fraction to maintain your speed. Wait until the steering wheel is nearly straight and then squeeeeeeze. . . . On snow, your tires can only do one job at a time, so if you accelerate in a curve you will lose steering.

READ THE SCRIPT

Roads exposed to sunlight will thaw first, but shaded areas concealed beneath woodland, high hedges, or under bridges will retain freezing temperatures for much longer.

Bridges can be very naughty. They stay frozen the longest, because they have no contact with the ground, just cold air, which forms a lovely layer of invisible black ice. Other practical telltales include pedestrians performing involuntary cartwheels on the pavements, frosty foliage, the whiz of spinning rubber, and the crunch of bumper.

Winter Driving

Use your local knowledge to pinpoint places where water regularly runs across the road—it will have frozen.

As you cross ice, the road noise goes deathly quiet, and you might notice the steering wheel feeling very light. Keep your inputs smooth and to a minimum.

Above all, mind the hills.

HILLS

When I was five years old, my mum was driving me to school in her Renault 4, the "biscuit tin" of myth and legend. We crunched through a few icy puddles before dropping around a left-hander into a steep wooded area. At the bottom of the hill lurked a stone-walled bridge across a river, on which was strewn a selection of steaming, crashed motors. Between them and us was a perfectly laid sheet of black ice. We slid down and joined them.

From the point at which Mum applied the brakes, locked the front wheels, and lost all steering, there was little that could be done to avoid that accident— *at that point*. Even ABS couldn't have overcome the laws of gravity on a friction-less surface.

Like the men in Lycra, if you find yourself staring down something resembling the Cresta run, once you climb aboard there's no stopping until you reach the bottom. If the road is icy and steep you should avoid it because the car will be unable to defy the effects of gravity.

For gentler descents, bring your speed down early and hold the car with high revs in a low gear as you descend, using maximum engine braking to complement the brakes.

UPHILL

When approaching an incline, ensure you have enough speed and momentum to carry you all the way up. If you have to stop partway up, then you may not be able to get going again; or, worse, you may start sliding backward.

It's best to allow traffic to clear in front, for your entertainment as much as anything else. From your vantage point at the bottom you can decide whether to take a run at it or find an alternate route.

The car will be unable to defy the effects of gravity.

Skidding

ESSENTIAL GEAR

Even freeways get shut down when the weather creates a logjam. It pays to pack a few basics to make sure you're covered:

- food rations—especially water
- mobile phone, fully charged, and kept in a warm pocket to save the battery
- ice scraper and antifreeze spray
- folding shovel
- warm jacket and hat
- foil blanket
- tow rope and jumper cables
- first aid kit
- high-visibility safety vest or jacket
- cigarette lighter—in case the door lock is frozen. (It's better than licking; remember *Dumb and Dumber*)
- bright LED flashlight—for attracting attention as well as avoiding it in rough areas and
- duffle bag or, better still, a burlap sack (to throw the gear into and to place under your tires when you get stuck).

4.4 WORST-CASE SCENARIOS

Here is a series of terrifying situations with remarkably simple solutions. Well . . . simple as long as you remain calm, think fast, and do the right thing.

Think fast, and do the right thing.

TIRE BLOWOUT

Tire blowout is often cited as a terrifying ordeal—yet it couldn't be easier to deal with, or prevent. You basically do nothing.

The most common cause of a tire failure is underinflation, which massively overheats and cuts the sagging rubber until it explodes. If you whack a curb or something really thumps the wheel, then it can weaken the tire. A fault will reveal itself as a bulge or a cut in the sidewall, assuming you remember to check.

If you didn't check, you may find yourself flying down the highway some weeks later and experience a sensation similar to the shudder of a rumble strip. This signals imminent tire failure.

A tire blowout at the front or the rear demands pretty much the same response:

The car will want to swivel around the blown tire and introduce you to a world of pain.

- ▶ Keep the wheel straight.
- ▶ Climb *gently* off the accelerator and let the car's rolling resistance slow you down. *Do not brake* until your speed reduces to at least 50 mph—ideally, slower—and then brake with great care.
- ▶ Check your mirrors and ease your vehicle to safety on the hard shoulder using minimal steering.
- ▶ Exaggerate your speeds and heroism at the bar later.

If you hit the brakes, the car will want to swivel around the blown tire and introduce you to a world of pain. The same will happen if you steer sharply. Keep it slow and steady.

A rear blowout in a top-heavy 4x4 or SUV may cause the rear to crab sideways as the proportion of weight higher up in the vehicle acts like a lever; so you may have to work at holding a straight course until the speed drops and you are able to restore control.

In the case of a blown-out front tire, it may pull at the steering and cause the front to drop on that side. All you need to do is gently resist with the steering to keep it straight.

If you change to a space-saver tire, remember that they are rubbish, with a speed restriction and a limited range; they heat up, and don't handle worth a damn. Just saying, change it for a real one as soon as you can.

Keep an eye on your tire pressures, at least visually, if nothing else.

Check tires for damage, especially for a long journey with the family (when you double the payload).

Never buy secondhand tires. Garages sell them at a tempting price, and though not visibly damaged, they were discarded by their previous owners for a reason. Or, worse, they might be remolds.

STICKING THROTTLE

This happens when the car accelerates all by itself, either because the pedal is jammed or an electronics gremlin tells it to. It is most alarming, and not as rare as you might hope. In 2009 and 2010, Toyota alone had to recall over eight million cars; a combination of sticky throttles and ill-fitting floor mats caused the cars to accelerate against their drivers' wills, sometimes with fatal results.

A stuck throttle sends your brain into a tailspin because you feel powerless to control the engine—but that's not the case.

In a manual transmission, disconnect the engine by pressing the clutch pedal. Problem solved. In an automatic, shove it into neutral. The engine will scream like hell because the revs will hit maximum—but just ignore it and steer to safety.

Press the brakes, hard. This will counter the engine while you gather yourself and muster the sense to execute step 1, as just described.

Passengers take note, too—if the driver doesn't select neutral, do it for him.

Don't switch off the engine with the key until you stop—you will lose steering and braking (see following).

BRAKE "FAILURE"

The most common braking issue is getting something wedged beneath the brake pedal. If your car resembles a garbage dump, this slum dog might bite you.

Solution: Remove the old Coke can or copy of *Guns & Ammo* or *Cosmo* that is wedged beneath the pedal and resume business as usual.

Another possibility is that you struck a curb, pothole, or deep water splash. These can knock the brake pads away from the disks, and when you push the brake pedal it goes soft. It's called *brake-pad knockoff*, and my first lesson was expensive.

I rattled the curb at the Donington raceway, and the impact knocked the pads from their marks. When I pressed the pedal for the next curve, at 135 mph, it flopped to the floor. By the time I pumped it up and down to restore the system, I was airborne, and the brakes weren't much use anymore.

Solution: Pump up the pedal a few times and restore the brake pressure.

If you service your car regularly, the fluids that feed the brakes' hydraulic systems should be good to go. A quick pump of the pedal when you climb aboard should meet with firm resistance. If it feels increasingly soft, or moves farther than normal, you have a problem that needs fixing.

BRAKE OVERHEATING

Brakes use friction to convert the energy of inertia into heat—and in doing so they can get extremely hot, especially if you drive down a series of bends on a sharp hill. Using engine braking, and allowing the low gears to decelerate your rolling mass, can prevent overheating.

However, if you rely solely on the brake pedal during an extended downhill, the brakes may overheat and fade. You will notice that pressing the pedal has diminishing returns, and your car screeches at every curve. Assuming you still wish to stay attached to the mountain at the next hairpin, you need to:

Downshift through the gears to force the engine to reduce your speed. Progress down the gears until you reach first or, in an automatic, low. Buzz the engine if you have to and never mind the sad, uncomfortable, and painful jerking you feel as the car shudders from the violent convulsions taking place within the engine, like the car hates you and wants to die, because this is serious.

Force the engine to reduce your speed.

Pull up on the hand brake as far as it will go, because the rear disks won't be overheated like the fronts. Pull gently at first, then apply full pressure, but try to avoid skidding. If you have a modern push-button thing, you're screwed. Some American models have a "parking brake"—it works like a hand brake, but it's operated by your left foot. Get on it.

Park and let the brakes cool down, which could take twenty minutes.

Still not stopping?

TOTAL BRAKE FAILURE

This is rare, but it could happen if the pedal sticks or the brake lines burst.

If the pedal flops to the floor and pumping it fails to revive it, use the same drill as above for overheating brakes. If you're on a hill or you're still not slowing down, then you may have to come up with a Plan B.

Look for an escape route, an incline, an empty street, an alley, any clear space, dammit, where there's nothing solid to crash into. You may be able to make a few sharp maneuvers and thread your way through.

If you're approaching a curve and possess the ability (and mental agility) of Stirling Moss, you might consider doing what he did during the Mille Miglia in 1957. His brake pedal snapped as he slowed from 130 mph for an 85 mph left-hander. He turned the steering wheel several times more than normal, which caused the front tires to scrub the tarmac and act like a brake, albeit a limited one. The resulting friction from the skidding front tires reduced his speed enough to save his bacon. But for him, after years of similar experiences, it was instinctive.

Failing all of the above, you may have to consider crashing to a stop as an absolute last resort. Find some gravel, curbing, hedges or—worst case—a wall, or some steel barrier or a ditch that you can steer into and drag your speed down. Common sense must prevail.

PARKING BRAKE FAILURE

Leave the car in first or reverse gear and turn your front wheels in against the curb.

STEERING FAILURE

Anything that impedes your ability to steer the car in the desired direction is a problem. These days, the steering wheel is not likely to fall off in your hands; nor will the steering column sheer off, unless you've dodged your mechanic for several decades. When it happened to me, I felt the wheel lighten and was able to brake before it did anything more dramatic.

Power steering is the principal culprit for what we commonly call steering "failure" in a road car. Manufacturers these days are designing their vehicles' suspensions with phenomenal levels of caster angle in the front wheels—a bit like the extended forks on a Harley Davidson. The benefits include greater fuel efficiency and stability around curves, but at the expense of making the steering so heavy that it's practically impossible to turn the wheel without power-steering assistance.

If your power steering fails in a curve, it will be time to test those muscles and drag the wheel to where you want it. Power steering tends to fail in fits and starts, rather than all at once, so as soon as you notice the first heavy hints, you should get it fixed.

BREAKDOWN AT A RAILWAY CROSSING

Ah, the Swiss Alps . . . The scent of pine resin, the patter of clogs, the rustle of lederhosen . . . It's enough to put anyone in the mood to open up a few V-12 cylinders. A few years ago we shot Jeremy Clarkson's *Thriller* DVD along the mountain pass at Flüela in Switzerland, and the experience certainly lived up to its name.

On day one, the director shaved a couple of inches off the flank of his Maserati during a close encounter with a concrete barrier. Day two heralded the destruction of a sparkling Alfa Romeo 8C Supercar, on loan from Nick Mason of Pink Floyd. And they say that bad luck comes in threes . . .

I was chewing the fat with Jay Kennedy, our twentysomething cameraman (and my regular copilot for anything dangerous) in a brand-new Pagani Zonda Roadster after an exhausting day's shooting. As usual, I had been cajoled into using every last drop of fuel for "just a few extra shots" and was coasting down the mountain into Davos to find a gas station with barely a martini left in the tank.

With the pump in sight, and only a minor incline and a railway track separating us from victory, Jay heard himself saying, "Wouldn't it be classic if we ran out of fuel in a million-pound Zonda right in the middle of that railway crossing?"

And with that, we did.

As my rapidly pumping foot failed to introduce enough gas to the spark, I noticed a large red train homing in on our right-hand side.

"OH F*** . . ."

Jay had too.

I popped open the luxurious leather-lined door and looked behind us to see if we could roll back down the hill, but the German parked on our tailpipe was staring blankly ahead. Jay and I somehow summoned the strength of Samson to move the Zonda forward by a crucial two yards. Of course, it started right after that.

Nobody wants to see their pride and joy become a hood ornament on a southbound freight train; but no car, not even the Zonda, is worth more than your legs, let alone life. It's a pressure situation, and time dictates your choice of the following actions.

- Get out and run.
- Push the clutch in, turn the key *all the way* off, and restart the engine, then drive forward. That usually works.
- Get out and push.

Pressure makes you do silly things like trying to leave the car with the seat belt on or forgetting the person in the backseat. Don't let it beat you.

ESCAPE FROM A SINKING CAR

More people in Britain drown in cars than on boating lakes. Not many people do drown in boating lakes, but, according to American professor John Hunsucker, about 350 people die every year in sinking vehicles.

ROSPA (the Royal Society for the Prevention of Accidents) now agrees that the best survival tip is to get the hell out of the car, as fast as you can—rather than following the old-school theory that you should wait until it has filled with enough water to equalize the pressure.

The fact is, your options narrow by the second. You must take quick, decisive action to survive.

As soon as you hit the water:

- Release your seat belt and unlock all the doors (especially if you have passengers).
- Open the door and force it open, or roll the windows down if the water is too high already.
- Get out. Then you can help attend to others.

Get out and run.

350 people die every year in sinking vehicles.

What to expect:

- ▸ The electronics will fail—which is why you should unlock the doors as soon as possible if you have power door locks.
- ▸ The windows are also electric-powered, which is why you can't rely on them and should get the door open quickly.
- ▸ Panic: A friend of mine in the Royal Navy had to ditch his helicopter into the sea and, despite all his training for this situation, was stunned by the pace at which the water invaded the cockpit. He got his leg jammed on the seat, grappled with his breathing regulator, and finally crawled out. His survival made him the first pilot to ditch that particular aircraft and live to tell the tale.

You might run off the road into a river or, with changing weather patterns, be swept off the road in a flash flood. With things happening that quickly, your action may differ from a situation where there is more time, for example, if your car rolls down a bank into a lake.

Whatever the situation, if you are in deep water you will have to get out as quickly as possible; but you will need as much energy as possible to swim and, possibly, to fight the cold. If the car has submerged quickly, fight panic by switching on the interior lights (if they work) and breathing deeply.

A few other guidelines might also help.

When you release your seat belt it may not retract; take care not to get tangled.

If you need to escape through a window and it jams, you need to break it. Unless you happen to carry a window hammer, as I do, you will find it hard to break the windows by kicking. A steering wheel lock might work; or, if your headrest is removable, pull it out and wedge it down into the door seam of the window, and lever it until it pops the glass. Then smash through. Equally, if you have passengers in the back seats, this might help get them out.

The car will sink heavy-end first (i.e., where the engine is). In deeper water it may flip onto its roof.

In a car that sinks front first, there will be a bubble of air in the back; but you should stay in the front, as the front windows are often bigger and easier to get out of—for all passengers.

The car won't sink immediately, even with the windows open. However, you must use every moment to free yourself and your passengers and get out. Push children out first.

It may seem obvious, but don't try to save anything except lives. Computers, phones, purses, jewelry, etc. can be replaced—you can't!

If you are unable to open a window, there is the equalization option as a last resort. Keep your head. There should be enough air for the minute or two that it will take to prepare to escape. When the car is nearly full of water, take a deep breath and push a door open—you may need to do this with your feet (for extra strength). Note the wait: If you try to open the doors too soon, the water pressure will defeat you.

HOOD FLIES UP/BROKEN WINDSHIELD

Congratulations on checking your oil, but make sure you closed the hood afterward. I can't remember the last time a hood flew up in my face, but the instant blindness and sense of powerlessness came as quite a surprise.

Loose hoods are mostly a character flaw of an old banger. It's more likely that you will lose your vision from a flying stone or some debris cracking the windshield and filling the glass with a spider's web that you can't see through. In either event:

- ▸ Open the window and stick your head outside so that you can see.
- ▸ Hold the steering wheel steady on its original course.
- ▸ Reduce speed and casually get off the road.

Obvious tip: Secure your hood if it looks loose. If it flies up at speed, there will be a loud bang, the windshield will probably smash, and you may freak out!

Now that your adrenaline is tingling, it's the perfect moment to step into the world of advanced car control and learn to maneuver a car when you push the limits.

4.5 *STUNT DRIVING*

Once upon a time in the West, men with jaws of granite and Glocks tucked down their jockey shorts developed evasive driving techniques for dealing with mobile assaults by terrorists in parts of the world where you tend not to book summer vacations.

Around the same time, some stunt boys in Hollywood were doing the same thing because it was fun and looked cool on shows like *The Fall Guy*, *Knight Rider*, and *The Dukes of Hazzard*. By adopting an aggressive driving style that destabilizes the car, and then bringing in measured amounts of speed, steering, and brake, they learned to make a car *dance*.

I've taught some of these skills to law enforcement operatives, Special Forces, and even James Bond himself—but whatever you call them, these moves are only legal on film sets or if you're being shot at. In the real world, you'd only get to have a go on a closed parking lot or airfield with an instructor, but these techniques do represent the theoretical outer limits of what is possible and therefore deserve their place in a book called *How to Drive*. So join me, if you will, in a thought experiment: It's your first day on the set of *2 Fast, 2 Furious 27*, you've just been thrown the keys to a brand-new Aston Martin, and the director is about to yell, *"Action!"* . . .

DRIVE THROUGH

The goal of evasive driving is to evade the threat and flee to safety. Your aim throughout is to *keep moving*. In an ambush, your best chance of escape is to drive through it, or spot it early enough to change your route.

In *Spiderman 2* there's a scene where the villain carves through the city with a big towing rig, literally scything through traffic. I was one of thirty cops in hot pursuit, and we had to drive through the mess "no matter what," while preserving the cars as best we could.

The truck was turning cars into confetti, and squeezing through the maelstrom of flying debris and crashed cars was easier said than done, especially with half of New York's Finest trying to fit through the same hole!

When that hole was too small I needed to make it bigger, while avoiding the kind of head-on collision that usually kills radiators; so I would slap the offending blockage with one of the front-quarter panels and drive through. One trick I've used before is to ease off the gas just before impact and then accelerate through—it helps to lift the other car out of the way and preserves your momentum. It's still crashing, but with style.

They learned to make a car dance.

HAND-BRAKE TURNS

THE 180

If you find yourself in the unfortunate position of actually having the ball during a game of *Top Gear* "Car Football," then you can expect a visit from one crazy cat by the name of Richard Hammond. For him the ball is like a sack of catnip, and it's best not to get in the way when he speeds toward you with "that look" in his eye.

In this situation the hand brake turn is a lifesaving solution because you can get out of the way fast by spinning the car around and heading off in the other direction. Here's the garden-variety method:

- Slow to a speed of around 20 to 30 mph—at higher speeds things tend to get messy.
- Pick a spot ahead of you around which to pivot the car on the hand brake, bearing in mind that the car will shift across by roughly its own width.
- *Release the foot brake.*
- Rip the hand brake like you're tearing out a molar and hold it there until it locks the rear tires, and then steer so that the car rotates 180 degrees.
- *Push the clutch in and select first gear.*
- After the car spins around, you can brake if you need to, then accelerate away in first.

COMMON MISTAKES

- Leaving your foot on the brake pedal when you pull the hand brake—it prevents the rear tires from locking properly. You will just veer off in a cloud of smoke.

Skidding

26. The 180

25 mph

PREFERRED PARKING: STUNT 180

For pulling a 180 into a parking space between two cars I would advise practicing with vehicles of the rubber-cone variety before attempting it in your driveway.

The goal is to fill the empty gap between two cars, and to do this requires alignment, timing, and control. Repeatability is the key to perfecting this move, and that is achieved by using exactly the same speed and turn of the wheel every time. Throughout the move, you need to keep your eyes fixed on the parking space.

Line up facing the car you plan to turn away from. That way, when you make your hand-brake turn, the car will naturally rotate away from the car you're facing and rotate into the gap.

Drive straight toward the outer car and up to your set speed, then flick the car to the right, yank hard on the hand brake, and depress the clutch (or switch to neutral).

As the car spins, turn your head in time so that you never lose sight of the parking spot—this helps your hands, which are stupid, follow your eyes, which have a hotline to your brain.

A fraction before the car rotates 180 degrees, release the hand brake and straighten the steering to begin reversing. Depending on your distance from the space, you may or may not require reverse gear.

As long as you stay off the foot brake, the car should have enough momentum to carry itself backward into the space until you stop on your end mark.

HOT TIPS

▸ Pick a speed that is fast enough for the hand brake to work—around 35 mph—and still retain enough momentum to keep rolling at the end of the move, but not so fast that you can't control it. Every car is unique, and the hand brake will bite differently depending on your speed and surface grip.

▸ Allow plenty of space between the 180 and the gap until you can repeat it every time without swerving all over the place.

▸ Try to keep your steering hand in one position on the steering wheel so that you don't get lost and can straighten it the moment you start reversing.

Skidding

27. Stunt 180

35 mph

PARALLEL PARKING: STUNT 90

The stunt version of parallel parking is the toughest trick to master, and there is no substitute for practice, practice, practice. To pull the perfect 90 you need to focus on two vital dimensions: the arc of rotation and the landing.

As with the 180, your approach speed will depend on how the car behaves on the surface. The greater the grip, the higher your speed needs to be in order to break traction and skid into the space: 25 mph is about the max.

Lining Up: Pick a start point about ten car lengths away from the parking space, offset by roughly three car widths so that you have enough room to steer a gradual arc toward the space. This gives you a longer arc along which to turn and apply the hand brake so that momentum carries the car into its spot.

The key to this is arriving so that you can aim into the gap at a perpendicular angle. The incredibly hard part to judge is when to steer toward the gap and pull the hand brake.

You need to think everything through in slow motion and remember that, as the car slides, there is a delayed reaction to your inputs.

Key Markers: You need to determine an initial pivot point around which to start rotating, and this will vary depending on your style and the grip level. Generally speaking, the pivot point can be found one car length away from the center of the parking space.

It is important that you aim toward the center so that, as the car rotates, it has equal space to fill into at both front and rear, assuming your car doesn't have a vast overhang beyond the rear axle. Your line of sight should draw focus points on the space itself, as well as your distance from the rear bumper of the car you're about to slide up to.

Doing It: Fix your start mark to make the process repeatable. Choose one that gives you plenty of time to get up to a set speed.

Make a few practice runs at low speed to get a feel for timing the steering and pulling the hand brake without actually committing.

Once you're ready to give it a go, drive up parallel to the gap and make your turn. Just before the car is pointing directly at the space, pull on the hand brake and let fly toward the space.

28. Stunt 90

25 mph

W   W   W

As you enter the parking space you should sense whether the car will over-rotate and spill out of the space if the speed is a little high, or under-rotate if the car isn't sliding on the hand brake. To correct over-rotation as it's happening, you can ease on the foot brake. If the car isn't sliding enough, then pull harder on the hand brake and add a little more speed next time around.

Break Out:

In the event that you succeed in breaking the world record for parallel parking into a space an inch longer than your car, you need to figure a way to get out again. You could ask someone politely to move the other cars out of the way, but that wouldn't be very sporting.

No, what you need to do is pull the hand brake all the way up and turn the steering as far as it will go in the desired direction. Then select first gear, redline the engine, and release the clutch. With the hand brake restricting forward motion, the front tires will spin wildly and drag the car's nose out of the space. Release the hand brake and head off to buy some new tires.

J-TURN

A J-turn is a reverse 180-degree spin that requires a deft hand and good coordination at each step of the move.

The key to a good J-turn is how quickly you whip the steering through the twelve o'clock position to initiate the spin, and how efficiently you unwind that steering to complete the move.

To achieve both these goals, I hold the wheel at two o'clock with my left hand and look over my right shoulder (vice versa in right-hand drive), so that I can yank it through twelve with plenty of force and apply enough lock to swivel the nose of the car. At the end of the move, it's easy to return my hand to its original position so that I know the front wheels are pointing straight again.

Step 1. Line up: Stop the car, select reverse, and observe the view through the rear windshield to check it's clear. There needs to be enough space to accommodate the length of the car when it spins, so you should line up in the center of that space and fix your sights on an object in the far distance to ensure that you drive straight.

Step 2. Position your whipping hand at two o'clock (looking over your shoulder through the rear screen is generally easier), or ten o'clock for a right-hand turn, and reverse quickly, so as to load the suspension, up to a minimum speed of 20 mph, and ideally around 40 mph, to ensure that the front tires will skid when you want them to.

Step 3. Whip. Once you're up to speed, lift off the accelerator and crank the steering to the right from two o'clock to about eight o'clock and put the clutch in. The car will spin on its axis.

Step 4. Steer through. As the car's nose makes its way past 90 degrees you should be looking *through* the windshield and steering the wheel *through* to the left. This helps the car rotate a full 180 degrees into its new direction.

Step 4½. Gear and go. To be really slick with a manual gearbox, you need to have the clutch engaged by the time the car passes 90 degrees, before it starts going forward, so that you can calmly move the gear lever from reverse to second and drive away. Failing to do this will result in some disagreement between your transmission and the road over which way each one should be going. With an automatic you just flick the car into drive as the car rotates and peel away when you're facing the right way.

Stunt Driving

29. J-Turn

Whip the wheel

30. J-Turn Wheel Position

Stunt Driving

▸ If you don't steer fast enough initially, the nose of the car won't spin; it will grip, causing you to head off in a new direction. Brake before you hit something!

▸ Remember to steer through at the end of the move to prevent the car veering out of control.

▸ Don't steer too much. If you wind on loads of steering, it's easy to get lost. Keep your golden whip hand in one place throughout the move.

DONUTS AND BURNOUTS

To pull off the following maneuvers, you will need a car that allows you to turn off the traction control and stability systems—an endangered feature in these times of state intervention. It also needs to be rear-wheel-drive with a limited slip differential, or *diff*.

The diff connects the driven wheels together and does two jobs. In a curve, it allows the outside wheels, which have the farthest to travel, to turn faster than the inside wheels. When you accelerate, it also divides the amount of drive transmitting through them.

As the car leans into a curve, the weight bearing down on the outside tires gives them more grip than those on the inside. This makes the inner tire more prone to losing traction under acceleration, so in models with a very "open" diff, all their power slops through the wheel with the least ability to handle it. When the inside wheel spins, no power is transmitted through the other tire, and you don't go very far.

A "locking" diff limits the speed differential between the driven tires and thereby metes out the power more evenly across them, providing better drive and accuracy. There's only one way to know for sure . . .

BASIC DONUT

The garden-variety donut is as easy as walking out of your front door, as long as you have the space and don't mind abusing your tires. It's easier using a manual transmission, but still possible with an automatic.

From a static position in first gear, keep the clutch fully depressed, floor the throttle, and redline the engine. Let the cacophony sing for a few seconds and don't mind the engine, because the rev limiter will protect your pistons.

Turn the steering hard in your preferred direction and dump the clutch. "Dumping" means lifting your foot off the clutch faster than if you stepped on molten lava. The common mistake people make is to pull away slowly by easing out the clutch, which just fries the clutch plates and accelerates you forward when you want to go sideways.

When you dump the clutch pedal, the clutch plates grab hold of the engine and instantly transmit all its power to the rear tires. This overwhelms their tractive ability and they start spinning, which is good. The act of steering causes the car to pivot around its nose, and as long as you keep your right foot planted to the floorboards, you will rotate in a glorious cloud of burning rubber that will cost you around eight dollars a second.

That part was easy.

DONUT: THE BLACK BELT EDITION

This is much harder to do and may take a while to explain, let alone master. With the basic donut all you had to do was hit the gas and turn right, or left, to make the car spin as tightly as possible. The controlled donut is all about accuracy around a specific mark, which means keeping the beast on course using some fluid hand-eye coordination.

Before going any further, let's plan some geography. On a live stage with *Top Gear* I used a mark that was about 5 feet, 7 inches, with chestnut-brown hair, and the ability to do standing splits, making martial arts superstar Chloé Bruce a distinctive beacon to rest my eyes on.

Backstage, behind the blackout curtains, I was mentally visualizing the *arc*— the precise route around which I wanted the car to travel—and agonizing those last seconds before the curtain went up in front of five thousand pairs of eyes.

The Holden Monaro with its throaty V-8 engine and locked rear differential was the perfect car for the job, and I'd wedged a coin into the hand brake button with some duct tape so that I could pull it and have it release instantly.

I must have done that sequence hundreds of times, rehearsed it thousands, but I always felt a deep sense of foreboding. My heart would pound, and my fingers would tingle from the adrenaline, because it was a dangerous sequence. I definitely recommend learning with a rubber cone rather than a human.

The controlled donut is all about accuracy.

Stunt Driving

31. Basic Donut

Skidding

32. Donut: The Black Belt Edition

Catch the slide

Give it some gas

Ease off the gas to widen the arc

The curtain flew up, and a dazzling spotlight flooded the Monaro. I popped the clutch, the tires shrieked across the metal floor. I feathered the throttle to moderate the wheelspin and get some drive, then flicked into second gear and skirted the concrete retaining wall.

Chloé's silk white ninja suit was entering my peripheral view to the right as I aimed for a mark that was one car's width to her left, yanked the hand brake, steered right, and swung the Monaro around into its new trajectory.

The hand brake slewed the car around until it reached a yaw angle of around 45 degrees relative to Chloé. Thirty-five miles per hour of forward momentum scrubbed down to about 15 mph of lateral clockwise drift.

As the Monaro rotated, its mouth pointed perilously toward Chloé's single leg while she wowed the crowd with her spectacular swordplay and high kicks, living up to her world record status. Had the car gripped at that moment, it would have lurched forward and knocked her down like a bowling pin. Hence the nerves.

At that point I could think about *catching* the slide with the steering and adding throttle, to create enough wheelspin to stop the car from gripping and continue the slide. But not too much. That was the tricky part. Knowing precisely how much of each to use, and when, takes practice.

The first catch usually involved some sweeping movements with the steering and active use of the throttle until the car *took a set*—when the rear has swung sideways enough that you can put the steering into opposite lock and catch it, then reduce and modulate the throttle to keep the rears spinning. At that point the car would balance, and I could trim its progress with small corrections of steering and minor adjustments to a fairly constant throttle to keep the rear tires smoking.

In order to creep the car's nose closer to Chloe and scare the crowd, I had to make the car follow a tighter arc, which is just the same as making a sharper turn with a supermarket shopping cart. You kick the rear out wider so the nose stays put.

To ease the tail out wider, I increased the throttle to spin the rears faster and reduce their grip. At first, this made the car want to spin, so I simultaneously added a little more opposite lock to control the additional yaw before ultimately reducing to minimal counter-steering.

Skidding

The result was a tighter, if busier, circle around Chloé and an unblinking fascination with the distance between my bumper and her kneecap. Too much throttle at this point and the car would spin, but too little and it would grip and move forward. Ouch.

If that wasn't enough to think about, the grip level never stays constant in a live arena, so the rear would snap across dollops of water deposited by leaky radiators. I could cope with that; but when my talent ran dry, I had a backup plan: widening my arc.

To push the car away from Chloé, I let the Monaro drift wide. By steering left into the slide and easing off some throttle, it restored a little grip to the rears, reducing the yaw angle, and the car obeyed the direction of the wheel. Once I moved out to the left, I increased the power again to spin up the rears and restore the drift.

Step 1. Walk it. Walk the route sideways to develop your visual reference on the center mark, and rehearse the relationship between your position and the center mark. That distance and your rate of yaw dictate the handling.

Step 2. The throw. As soon as you turn right, the rear will rotate, and you allow this until the car reaches a 45-degree angle (give or take, depending on the model, subject to terms and conditions) and takes a set.

Step 3. The catch. Once the car reaches 45 degrees, you have to catch it. This is the transition from steering right to create the initial slide, to steering left to maintain a steady ship. The hard part is that the rear floats around pretty fast, and the temptation is to overcorrect with steering or spin out. The trick is to back off the throttle the moment you reach 45 so that the rears grip for just a moment as you throw in the opposite lock. Then it's back on with the throttle to maintain the wheelspin, and let the car settle onto a knife-edge. Keep your eye on the center mark to measure the angle.

Step 4. The set. When you get into the sweet spot, balance the slide with small corrections of opposite lock and throttle. Your aim is to hold your yaw steady and reduce your inputs to the bare minimum. Let the car do the work.

"Let the car settle onto a knife-edge."

Arc. On a wider arc you travel faster, and life is actually a little easier, because you have more time to adjust what the car is doing. The higher speed increases your lateral momentum, making it easier to hang the rear out there. If your speed drops on a wide arc, the car will grip, so you need to increase the throttle or turn more tightly. On a tighter arc, the car responds more quickly, and your inputs need to be crisp.

Steering. Steering is not an infinite resource; if you keep winding the car into a skid, it will eventually thud into the bump stops as the steering reaches the point where it can turn no more, proving troublesome when an extra claw of steering is the only thing keeping you from rotating into the boonies. Pro drifters fit exceptionally wide-angle steering to make the job easier and hold their cars super sideways, but you still need to live within your means.

Brake. In the drift universe the brake restricts forward momentum, enabling you to spin up the rear tires even more and slow the car in general. Yes, this involves left-foot braking. With your right foot busily making music, you creep your left foot onto the brake pedal. This mostly binds the front tires and transfers weight their way, which allows you to accelerate harder to really light up the rears, increase yaw, and all that good stuff.

DRIFTING

If you have watched *Top Gear* then you will have seen endless footage of priceless supercars being subjected to a royal pounding—smoke billowing from the wheel arches as burning rubber churns at the asphalt to a cacophony of screeching tires and dubbed music. The car yaws perilously sideways but maintains a surprisingly predictable course through the curve, assuming the nut behind the wheel doesn't run out of talent.

The phenomenon of "drifting" has been the stuff of Hollywood legend ever since Steve McQueen climbed aboard a Ford Mustang in *Bullitt* and proceeded to paint rubber across the cityscape of San Francisco.

If you mastered the donut, then you're ready to drift, because you've just been doing it. The easiest way to get started is to link two donuts together to form a figure 8, but before we get into that, here's some background.

33. Drifting

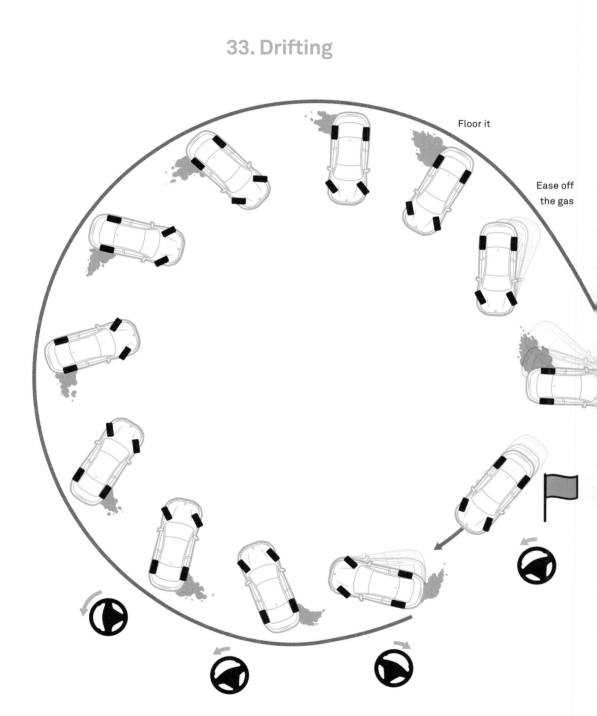

Floor it

Ease off
the gas

Back on
the gas

Drifting as a technique developed in rallying during the 1960s after some Scandinavian drivers drank a lot of vodka in the Jacuzzi. They spoke in short sentences or not at all, and shared their frustration with traditional methods of tackling curves that were painfully inadequate on snow and ice. Their epiphany appeared at the bottom of a shot glass: *"Vee do it sidevays!"*

The conventional style of navigating a curve as quickly as possible had always been to brake in a straight line, get off the brakes, and steer in the direction of the turn. The trouble with ice was that the tires couldn't offer enough traction to overcome the car's forward momentum. The fronts just washed out at low speed, and you missed the curve. There lay the secret.

The Vikings worked out a way to make momentum work for them, and it was as easy, in theory, as swinging an ax. They arrived at a left-hander with the car skidding and pointing in the opposite direction to the curve, the prompt for most people to abandon ship. Then they steered hard left, effectively overcorrecting the slide (remember page 213 on car control, the Tank Slapper), and the car's tail swished across to the other side with enough lateral momentum to propel the whole ordeal around the curve. With the centrifugal forces that previously worked against them during the entry phase averted, temporarily, the car entered the curve at higher speed. Now the problem was keeping it there.

The head of the swinging ax was loose, to say the least. To keep it from falling off and embedding itself deep inside a Swedish pine, the Vikings had to counter the force running down the length of the car's body. The answer to that lay beneath their right foot, and by nailing the throttle to the rug it produced enough driving force to counter and control the pull of gravity. It also accelerated them out of the curve faster than the conventional cornering method.

Tommi Mäkinen, an early pioneer of the "Scandinavian flick" (see following), explained that perfecting this took "at least two years, and many, many cars."

By skidding sideways under braking in the opposite direction to the curve, the tires dig into the surface and slow the car more effectively until you reach the turning point; then you swing it toward the curve and use the pendulum effect to catapult you around. Assuming that your face isn't already embedded in a mountain, the car points toward the curve, enabling early acceleration.

This style of driving would dominate world rally competition for years to come. In Japan it developed a cult status, as the heroes hammering the treacherous mountain pass at Touge (*toe-geh*) began tuning their cars to exaggerate the sideways style way beyond anything performance-related. It was all about style.

GETTING STARTED

Here are the various techniques for initiating a drift. Each scenario creates an abrupt loss of traction to the rears, and you have to be incredibly fast with the steering to control it. So fast, in fact, that there are times when it's better to let go of the steering to allow it to spin through your fingers and catch it again when you have the correct steering angle.

HAND BRAKE

As you approach the curve, pull the hand brake to lock the rears, steer toward the curve, and throw the car into a drift. Once it's sliding, you fling the wheel over and drive the car on the throttle.

HOT TIPS   ▸ As soon as you're controlling proceedings with steering and wheelspin, the hand brake returns as a control feature for advanced drifting. When you want to cut power but retain your angle of yaw, you apply the clutch and pull the hand brake in the curve. This allows the driven wheels to stop turning, and the car will drift around a tighter arc. Then you reapply the power to maintain speed and momentum through the curve.

CLUTCH

You may remember my emphasis on smooth clutching to avoid upsetting the car. Well, being a meathead is a bonus for drifting. There are two ways to use it.

As you approach the curve, you drop a gear and instead of rev matching or gently releasing the clutch pedal, you deliberately allow the revs to drop, and pop the clutch just as you steer in. The sudden take-up of engine braking puts enough shock through the rear axle to break traction and pitch the car sideways as you steer. This technique can be unreliable, and you lose speed.

Stunt Driving

The *clutch-kick* is the best way to get the show on the road. Rather than letting engine braking do the work, you clutch in and accelerate to boost engine revs. With your foot hard on the gas, you steer in, pop the clutch, and the sudden acceleration creates enough wheelspin to send you sideways.

The clutch-kick is used multiple times throughout the turn to maintain wheelspin and yaw angle. You keep the throttle pinned and rapidly kick the clutch in and out as many times as you need to trim the drift.

SCANDINAVIAN FLICK

If it's got an engine, it can drift. Everything in the book up to this point has been about managing weight transfer to produce maximum stability and grip. Now the objective is to disturb the weight so that it overcomes rear traction, and the "flick" is the primary tool in the drift box of tricks.

You approach the curve with slightly too much speed for a conventional entry, breathe on the brake to shift weight off the rears onto the front tires, and then initiate a pendulum turn. That is, you steer toward the outside of the curve and then rapidly twitch it the other way. The rampant weight transfer causes the rear to skid, and then you stamp on the gas to hold it sideways.

LINKING THE CHAIN—FIGURE 8

So you're sideways . . . now what?

Once you've initiated the drift, your attention needs to be drawn to your trajectory. This is very much a seat-of-the-pants vibe and tied to the same technique you deployed in the donut to control your arc.

Having made it through one curve without biting the dust, the next goal is to link two curves together. It requires the most careful execution, and this is where the figure 8 comes in.

The figure 8 is really a pair of opposing donuts with a switchback in the middle. It's the best way to develop a feel, at comparatively low speed, for how the car will cope with a sudden switch of direction while sliding.

The figure 8 is really a pair of opposing donuts with a switchback in the middle.

We call this switch the *transition turn*, and it is the hardest part to control, as well as the most satisfying.

As you circle the first donut in a clockwise direction, you select a pivot point around which to switch directions and point yourself toward a new arc that takes you counterclockwise around the second donut.

You widen your arc out of the initial donut, and on approaching that pivot point you create a moment of grip in the rears by overcorrecting the slide with additional counter-steering (assuming you have any left!) and by releasing some throttle.

The car obeys the steering, and suddenly the tail swishes across the other way. All the counter-steering has to be passed into the opposite direction in order to catch this new slide and balance your new trajectory.

STYLE

Pro drifters are judged by their angle of attack, speed, and the aggression of their transition from one direction to the other as they link two curves. Ideally, you anticipate the turn so that you have enough space and time to really whip the rear across, jump back on the gas, and be lined up nicely for the next curve.

With the engine hammering off the rev limiter and your fists banging the wheel into the bump stops, you couldn't be any more sideways if you tried. You release some gas, and the tail twitches across faster than an Exocet missile.

You spin the wheel like an LP record to catch the opposing slide. It naturally finds its home for the new angle, and you vaporize the scene with smoke as you carve away into the horizon.

This is really making fun of an ordeal that catches so many people out on the road: the tank slapper. And if you can learn to handle this, there's really not much left to teach you.

I guess the only part I left out about drifting is the tandem drift: two cars battling door-handle-to-door-handle to see which can hold it the most sideways for the longest and at the highest speed. It's a messy business, and if you spin, you lose; so maybe it's not the best way to end the book. But then again . . .

EPILOGUE: DRIFTING THROUGH LONDON

Piccadilly Circus, Saturday, an hour before midnight . . .

Tucked inside a bald cap, Vin Diesel's leather jacket, and his Dodge Charger, my own mother wouldn't recognize me. Alongside, in a modified Jensen Interceptor, British rally champ Mark Higgins was doubling the lead lady, Letty—though with ears like wing nuts and a long black wig he looked a whole lot more like Ozzy Osbourne.

We were about to drift the V-8s around the circus at up to 70 mph for *Fast & Furious 6*. And we had three minutes to do it in.

Unlike the lines of girls wearing miniskirts at the peak of an arctic winter, we wouldn't be warming our cockles at the neon-lit bars of China White's. We would be manhandling a pair of recalcitrant beasts around the circus, danger close, and with a Nissan 370Z camera car tracking from just a few feet ahead.

With muscles like mine, it's rare to draw comparisons with Vin Diesel, but this was no ordinary occasion. Having spent two hours at the mercy of the girls in the makeup bus, the hairs on my head had been individually waterboarded and locked securely inside a latex bald cap. I spent the time contemplating the best way to pull this gag off without reshaping a famous monument.

Our boss, stunt coordinator Andy Gill, set out his stall of toy cars beside the memorial fountain underneath the vigilant effigy of Anteros. Gill was my hero growing up because he was the stuntman driving KITT, the Pontiac in Knight Rider. He and his brother Jack jumped, flipped, smashed, and blasted KITT across America for four years of what David Hasselhoff called "nonstop, rock 'n' roll, balls out fun." You wouldn't believe a softly spoken gent from Georgia enjoyed such a violent pastime, but Andy has forgotten more about car stunts than I'll ever know.

A few scratches of chalk later and the pavement at Andy's feet was ready to simulate the action with his Matchbox collection. The two "hero" cars would drive up Piccadilly toward the roundabout, make a sharp left toward Regent Street, then switch right to slide onto Coventry Street, finally making another right down Haymarket. "Sideways all the way, obviously. I want you guys touching door handles. Reckon you can do that?"

Clearly a rhetorical question. We moved off to the cars. My ride was a lowered 1970 Dodge Daytona, so lowered that the front tires caught inside the wheel arches when you turned them. With a 5.4-liter Chevy V-8 under the hood, horsepower was not a problem, and the stripped-out chassis that resembled Frankenstein's monster from the interior made a good power-to-weight ratio.

The similarity between my machine and Mark's ended with the engine. The Jensen would sit down hard on its rear tires whenever Mark planted his right foot, causing it to grip more and more the harder he gassed it sideways. Meanwhile the "Bird," as the Dodge was known, kicked like a mule and spun its wheels if you so much as coughed near the throttle. Getting the two cars to match their speeds and rate of slide, which is essential for a tandem drift, would be no mean feat.

When the car travels sideways, its footprint naturally covers a wider area, and thanks to Google maps our area was half the size we were expecting.

Westminster Council had stuck a bus lane on the roundabout, and, to add insult to injury, the pedestrian curb from Shaftesbury Avenue had been extended by about 8 feet. That left a gap on the road of 22 feet, about a foot longer than the Bird in full drift.

Closing one of London's busiest intersections is rare, so we attracted quite a crowd. As is the norm for filming in London, we had a three-minute filming window and then had to release the traffic onto the streets until we were ready to go again. That meant delivering pinpoint accuracy for each of the exclusive takes.

I lined up alongside Mark to his left, and we took turns in warming up the rear differentials to prepare them for the onslaught. The pair of bellowing V-8s drowned out the crew's radio chatter and silenced the crowd. With the tires, engines, and gears in tune, we waited for the countdown. Gill called it, and the Nissan camera car took the lead as we rolled along the 30-yard, pulse-hardening run toward the square.

In an ideal world we might have kick-started our drift by flipping the clutch and flooring it. However, this being an American production, we were provided with automatics.

I reached the roundabout first, turned left, and yanked on my soggy hand brake for all it was worth. The Bird's tail sailed out in front of Mark's Jensen as he simultaneously wrangled his ride. Never mind the priceless masonry we might reshape, our only focus was the fire-juggling act of keeping these two broncos close but not touching.

When a car slides into oversteer the slip angle in the front tires reduces to zero for a moment, so the wheel goes light for a fraction of a second. Then the steering torque returns as the car yaws the other way and pulls at the fronts again. As the Bird slewed sideways and the windshield flooded with four stories of illuminated advertising billboards, I felt the pull returning—so I let go of the steering wheel.

The front tires effectively stayed pointed where I wanted to go, and the car just rotated around them. Letting go of the wheel allowed it to spin efficiently through my hands. The trick was not letting it spin too far—a skill developed after several weeks of rehearsals on the airfield—and knowing precisely when the rear tires had taken their "set."

With the steering hard over to the right and my foot on the gas keeping the wheels spinning, the Bird was happy to crab through the curve with Mark close alongside. I even had time to notice the jolly expression on Pete White's face through my side window as he drove past in a double-decker bus. "You stick to those little cars, Benjy; leave the big rigs to the real men," he had said before climbing aboard. I never said a word. He's a front-row forward and part-time horse dentist with access to tranquilizers; it's best just to keep smiling.

With the Bird and the Jensen parallel drifting, we were off to a good start.

Since the Jensen was picking up speed at an alarming rate, it was time to flick my old gal into the opposite direction and face it toward the right-hander for Coventry Street. This transition tango slide from drifting one way into another is the traditional occasion for a pileup.

Unfortunately, with the Bird I had no further steering to effect the switch because I was already grinding the wheel arch, so I backed off the gas to let the rears grip a little and kept the steering turned right.

The Bird's tail lurched across to the left and spewed a handsome volume of rubber dust in my face by way of protest. Mark shot up my right side just as the camera car slowed in front of us to get a close-up. We ran to within inches of the camera lens, and with both of us juggling the steering like hot potatoes we somehow

Our only focus was the fire-juggling act of keeping these two broncos close but not touching.

made it through the pedestrian crossing without hitting anything. The first shot of the night was in the can, and to the outside world we almost looked like we knew exactly what we were doing.

Cameras relocated to more perilous positions on the pavement, closer to our line of travel, and Pete's bus was brought in later so that he would appear on our front bumpers during our transition turn.

On the next take we swung through the blur of bright advertising, engines screaming and tires burning, switched direction, and our tails flew toward the crowd. I spun the wheel and lost sight of Mark as he dug in behind. I took a deep breath as the long tail floated oh-so-close to the pedestrian barriers and slammed home third gear for the finale.

Our speeds rose to 70 mph. The suspension tramped and bounced all over the bumpy street. The Bird's steering jammed into the wheel arch and for a moment it looked like the Angus Steakhouse on the corner of Haymarket might be receiving a drive-in. I clawed it back and we shoved our rides into Haymarket corner with Greg Powell's words ringing in our ears: "Don't smash the producer's supercar," which was parked for beauty directly in our line of fire. We skimmed past, and they moved it after that.

By the end of the night we had filmed every conceivable angle of that part of the chase, and everything had run like clockwork. The crew vanished into the night just as silently and effectively as they had arrived, and the city carried on regardless, the way that it always has.

I circled the Bird out of Smithfield Lane and back to its bed for the night in a derelict parking lot, still humming with activity as camera mounts were pulled off their special rigs and the grips swore merrily into the night. I gave it a final stroke of the gas to seven grand, killed the motor, and it shuddered to a still silence.

Life back on terra firma felt considerably slower, but I was grateful to leave the vibrator behind me and climb aboard a modern car. As the door closed on shoot day ninety-six, it dawned on me that I had just completed probably one of the coolest driving capers of my career.

I rolled out and took a leisurely drive home through what felt like a parallel universe. Brake lights flickering and signals winking, signs flashing, and people making their way through the kaleidoscopic canvas of London life. This was no time to rush. This was time to enjoy.

We ran to within inches of the camera lens.

I had just completed probably one of the coolest driving capers of my career.

ACKNOWLEDGMENTS

Jon Butler, for breathing life into this project, applying your invaluable expertise and for your painstaking edit. Few vegetarians, if any, would so willingly endure a charred meat-feast pizza whilst reconstructing a book with a fine-tooth comb and ten million post-it notes.

Courtney Drew and the team of experts at Chronicle Books who left no stone unturned in our quest to speak plainly! Thank you for all your hard work.

Mark Lucas, thank you for your inspirational guidance and for sharing my belief in the merits of driving on eggshells. The loyalty and friendship of the whole team at LAW, especially Alice and Julian, has become an extraordinary pillar of support for which I'm eternally grateful.

Michelin, for providing technical information about their tires as well as keeping me on the black stuff this season. Thanks also to the FIA Foundation for their research and campaigning for driver safety, and to the team at a2om international for their pioneering work on hazard perception.

Ryan and Andy at Here Design, Julie Martin, and James Provost for applying your conscientious craft to my ramblings.

Dusty, Fergus, Laura, and the fearless warriors at Team Macmillan for their ingenuity in bringing this book to market.

EON Productions, for kindly allowing me to share a few trade secrets.

The Metropolitan Police Driving School at Hendon, for sharing your impeccable roadcraft with me and generally keeping us safe at night.

My wife Georgie . . . thank you for putting up with endless demonstrations of driving theory, for your proofreading and forbearance, and for generally being such a lovely legnend.

BIBLIOGRAPHY

I couldn't have written this book without the accumulated wisdom of generations of driving experts and the talented competitors who shaped my knowledge during many a duel. I also found the following titles particularly enlightening:

The Technique of Motor Racing, Piero Taruffi

Steering-Wheel Papers, The Earl of Cottenham

Drive to Win, Carroll Smith

Tune to Win, Carroll Smith

Jackie Stewart's Principles of Performance Driving, Sir Jackie Stewart

Formula 1: The Art and Technicalities of Grand Prix Driving, Niki Lauda

Porsche High Performance Driving Handbook, Vic Elford

Sports Car and Competition Driving, Paul Frère

Roadcraft: the Police Driver's Handbook

The Highway Code

SOURCE MATERIAL

The Department for Transport; accident data kindly provided by Charles More of Actuarial Consultants; driver behavior research kindly provided by Dr. Lisa Dorn of Cranfield University.

INDEX